Drill and Revie...
Study Guide

for use with

Macroeconomics

Third Edition

David C. Colander
Middlebury College

Prepared by
David C. Colander
Middlebury College

Jenifer C. Gamber
Eastern Economic Journal

Irwin McGraw-Hill

Boston, Massachusetts   Burr Ridge, Illinois   Dubuque, Iowa
Madison, Wisconsin   New York, New York   San Francisco, California   St. Louis, Missouri

Irwin/McGraw-Hill

*A Division of The **McGraw·Hill** Companies*

Drill and Review Study Guide for use with
MACROECONOMICS

Copyright ©1998 by MaxiPress. All rights reserved.
Previous edition 1995 by MaxiPress.
Printed in the United States of America.

1 2 3 4 5 6 7 8 9 0 MP/MP 9 0 9 8 7

ISBN 0-256-17267-6

http://www.mhhe.com

Contents

Preface to Students

We wrote this study guide to help you do well in your economics courses. Even using a great book like the Colander textbook, we know that studying is not all fun. The reality is: most studying is hard work and a study guide won't change that. Your text and lectures will give you the foundation for doing well. So the first advice we will give you is:

1. Read the textbook.
2. Attend class.

We cannot emphasize that enough. Working through the study guide will not replace the text or lectures; this study guide is designed to help you retain the knowledge from the text and classroom by practicing the tools of economics. It is not an alternative to the book and class; it is **in addition to them**.

Having said that, we should point out that buying this guide isn't enough. You have to *use* it. Really, if it sits on your desk, or even under your pillow, it won't do you any good. Osmosis only works with plants. This study guide should be well worn by the end of the semester — dog-eared pages, scribble beneath questions, some pages even torn out. It should look used.

WHAT CAN YOU EXPECT FROM THIS BOOK?

This is a *drill and review* study guide, which means that it concentrates on the terminology and models in your text. It does not expand upon the material in the textbook; it reinforces it. It primarily serves to give you a good foundation to understanding principles of economics. Your professor has chosen this study guide for you, suggesting that your economics exams are going to focus on this kind of foundational understanding. You should be sure of this: if your professor is going to give you mainly essay exams, or complex questions about applying the foundations (like the more difficult end-of-chapter questions in your textbook) this study guide will not be enough to ace that exam.

This study guide is designed to prepare you for straightforward multiple choice, short-answer, and short-problem exams. The structure of this study guide reflects that focus. The main parts are short-answer, matching definitions to their terms, problems, and multiple choice questions.

Still, your exam questions may differ from the questions in this book — especially the multiple choice questions. We made these questions up, and compared to those of many professors; they tend to be on the hard side. They focus far less on facts and recall and more on analysis and understanding of the economic models in the text. To get an idea of what your exams will be like, ask your professor to take a look at these questions and tell the class whether they are representative of the type of questions that will be on the exam. And if they will differ, how.

HOW SHOULD YOU USE THIS STUDY GUIDE?

This book works best if you have attended class and read the book. Ideally, you were awake during class and took notes, you have read the textbook chapters more than once, and have worked through some of the questions at the end of the chapter. (So, we're optimists.)

Just in case the material in the book isn't fresh in your mind, before turning to this study guide it is a good idea to refresh your memory about the material in the text. To do so:

1. Read through the margin comments in the text; they highlight the main concepts in each chapter.

2. Turn to the last few pages of the chapter and reread the chapter summary.

3. Look through the key terms, making sure they are familiar. (O.K., we're not only optimists, we're wild optimists.)

Even if you do not do the above, working though the questions in the study guide will help to tell you whether you really do know the material in the textbook chapters.

STRUCTURE OF THE STUDY GUIDE

This study guide has two main components: (1) a chapter-by-chapter drill and review and (2) three pretests based upon groups of chapters.

Chapter-by-chapter drill and review
Each chapter has seven elements:

1. A chapter at a glance: A brief exposition and discussion of the learning objectives for the chapter.
2. Short-answer questions keyed to the learning objectives.
3. A word scramble.
4. A test of matching the terms to their definitions.
5. Problems and exercises.
6. Multiple choice questions.
7. Answers to all questions.

Each chapter presents the sections in the order that we believe they can be most beneficial to you. Here is how we suggest you use them:

Learning Objectives: These should jog your memory about the text and lecture. If you don't remember ever seeing the material before, you should go back and re-read the textbook chapter. The numbers in parentheses following each learning objective refer to the page in the text that covers that objective. Remember, reading a chapter when you are thinking about a fantasy date is almost the same as not having read the chapter at all.

Short-Answer Questions: The short-answer questions will tell you if you are familiar with the learning objectives. Try to answer each within the space below each question. Don't just read the questions and assume you can write an answer. Actually writing an answer will reveal your weaknesses. If you can answer them all perfectly, great. But, quite honestly, we don't expect you to be able to answer them all perfectly. We only expect you to be able to sketch out an answer.

Let's give you an example of what we mean. The first short-answer question for Chapter 1 is, "What are the five important dimensions economic learning?" The answer is "economic reasoning, economic terminology, economic insights, economic institutions, and economic policy options." There are many ways of dividing up what you learn, so if you don't get this list perfect, it is not a big problem in our view. If your exam is a multiple choice exam, the possible answers will jog your memory.

Of course, some other questions are important to know. For example, if there is a question about the economic decision rule and you don't remember that it excludes past costs and benefits, you need more studying. So the rule is: Know the central ideas of the chapter; be less concerned about the specific presentation of those central ideas.

After you have sketched out all your answers, check them with those at the end of the chapter and review those that you didn't get right. Each question is based upon a specific learning objective in the text. For those you didn't get right, you may want to return to the textbook to review the material covering that learning objective.

Word Scrambles: This is meant as a diversion for you. We have chosen what we believe are three key terms from each chapter and mixed up the letters. If you like word scrambles, do it; if you don't, just look up the terms in the answers to see if your three key terms in that chapter matched our three key terms.

Match the Terms and Concepts to Their Definitions: Since the definitions are listed, you should get most of these right. The best way to match these is to read the definition first, and then find the term on the left that it defines. If you are not sure of the matching term, circle that definition and move on to the next one. At the end return to the remaining definitions and look at the remaining terms to complete the matches. After completing this part, check your answers with those in the back of the chapter and figure our what percent you got right. If that percent is below the grade you want to get on your exam, try to see why you missed the ones you did and review those terms and concepts in the textbook.

Problems and Exercises: Now it's time to take on any problems in the chapter. These problems are more difficult than the short-answer questions. These problems focus on numerical and graphical aspects of the chapter.

Working through problems is perhaps one of the best ways to practice your understanding of economic principles. Even if you are expecting a multiple choice exam, working through these problems will give you a good handle on using the concepts in each chapter.

If you expect a multiple choice exam with no problems, you can work through these fairly quickly, making sure you understand the concepts being tested. If you will have a test with problems and exercises, make sure you can answer each of these questions accurately.

Work out the answers to all the problems in the space provided before checking them against the answers in the back of the chapter. Where our answers differ from yours, check to find out why. The answers refer to specific pages in the textbook so you can review the text again too.

Most of the problems are objective and have only one answer. A few are interpretative and have many answers. We recognize that some questions can be answered in different ways than we did. If you cannot reconcile your answer with ours, check with your professor. Once you are at this stage — worrying about different interpretations — you're ahead of most students and, most likely, prepared for the exam.

Multiple Choice Questions: The last exercise in each chapter is the multiple choice test. We leave it for last because it serves to test the breadth of your knowledge of the text material. Multiple choice questions are not the final arbiters of your understanding. They are, instead, a way of determining whether you have read the book and generally understood the material.

Take this test after having worked through the other questions. Give the answer that most closely corresponds to the answer presented in your text. If you can answer these questions you should be ready for the multiple choice part of your exam.

Work through all the questions in the test before grading yourself. Looking up the answer before you try to answer the questions is a poor way to study. For a multiple choice exam, the percent you answer correctly will be a good predictor of how well you will do on the test.

You can foul up on multiple choice questions in two ways—you can know too little and you can know too much. The answer to knowing too little is obvious: Study more—that is, read the chapters more carefully (and maybe more often). The answer to knowing too much is more complicated. Our suggestions for students who know too much is not to ask themselves "What is the answer?" but instead to ask "What is the answer the person writing the question wants?" Since, with these multiple choice questions, the writer of the question is the textbook author, ask yourself: "What answer would the textbook author want me to give?" Answering the questions in this way will stop you from going too deeply into them and trying to see nuances that aren't supposed to be there.

For the most part questions in this study guide are meant to be straightforward. There may be deeper levels at which other answers could be relevant, but searching for those deeper answers will generally get you in trouble and not be worth the cost.

If you are having difficulty answering a multiple choice question, make your best guess. Once you are familiar with the material, even if you don't know the answer to a question you can generally make a reasonable guess. What point do you think the writer of the question wanted to make with the question? Figuring out that point and then thinking of incorrect answers may be a way for you to eliminate wrong answers and then choose among the remaining options.

Notice that the answers at the end of the chapter are not just the lettered answers. We have provided an explanation for each answer — why the right one is right and why some of the other choices are wrong. If you miss a question, read that rationale carefully. If you are not convinced, or do not follow the reasoning, go to the page in the text referred to in the answer and reread the material. If you are still not convinced, see the caveat on the next page.

Questions on Appendices: In the chapters we have included a number of questions on the text appendices. To separate these qustions from the others, the letter A precedes the question number. They are for students who have been assigned the appendices. If you have not been assigned them (and you have not read them on your own out of your great interest in economics) you can skip these.

Answers to All Questions: The answers to all questions, including rationales for those answers, appear at the end of each chapter. They begin on a new page so that you can tear out the answers and more easily check your answers against ours. We cannot emphasize enough that the best way to study is to answer the questions yourself first, and then check out our answers. Just looking at the questions and our answers may tell you what the answers are but will not give you the chance to see where your knowledge of the material is weak.

Pretests

Most class exams cover more than one chapter. To prepare you for such an exam, we provide multiple choice pretests for groups of chapters.

In these pretests each chapter will not be represented equally. Some chapters cover more important concepts and will be tested more heavily. This is most likely the approach your professor will take when designing your classroom test.

We suggest taking these under test conditions. Specifically,

Use a set time period to complete the exam.
Sit at a hard chair at a desk with good lighting.

For these exams, answer each question fully, and complete the entire exam before grading yourself. These pretests consist of 25-50 multiple choice questions from the selected group of chapters. These questions are identical to earlier questions so if you have done the work, you should do well on these.

Each answer will tell you the chapter on which the question is based, so if you did not cover one of the chapters in the text for your class, don't worry if you get that question wrong. If you get a number of questions wrong from the chapters your class has covered, worry.

There is another way to use these pretests which we hesitate to mention, but we're realists so we will. That way is to forget doing the chapter-by-chapter work and simply take the pretests. Go back and review the material you get wrong.

However you use the pretests, if it turns out that you consistently miss questions from the same chapter, return to your notes from the lecture and reread your textbook chapters.

A FINAL WORD OF ADVICE

That's about it. If you use it, this study guide can help you do better on the exam by giving you the opportunity to use the terms and models of economics. However, we reiterate one last time: The best way to do well in a class is to attend every class and read every chapter in the text as well as work through the chapters in this study guide. Start early and work consistently. Do not do all your studying the night before the exam.

A CAVEAT

There is always a chance that there's a correct answer other than the one the book tells you is the correct answer, or even that the answer the book gives is wrong.

We've tried hard to avoid those instances, but we're all human, and make mistakes. If you find a mistake, check the rationale at the end of the chapter justifying the chosen answer, and see if that convinces you. If the rationale does not match the answer given in this book, assume the error is typographical. If that is not the case, and you still think another answer is the correct one, write up an alternative rationale and e-mail Professor Colander the question and the alternative rationale. Professor Colander's e-mail is:

colander@middlebury.edu.

When he gets it he will either send you a note thanking you immensely for finding an example of incorrect reasoning, or explain why we disagree with you. If you're the first one to have pointed out an error he will also send you a copy of a case book in economics—just what you always wanted, right?

David Colander
Jenifer Gamber

Acknowledgements

We want to thank a number of students who worked through the study guide. Umar Serajuddin was helpful in choosing and revising second edition questions and suggesting new ones. We hope that the year he spent on the textbook and this study guide before going on to graduate school at the University of Maryland proved helpful. Senake Gajameragedara provided invaluable help making sure all the answers are correct. Helen Reiff provided her sharp eye in proofreading. Tom Thompson helped with encouragement and general guidance. We would also like to thank our families for giving us the support we needed to get this study guide done.

Dedicated to

Emily and William

Zach and Kasey

Chapter 1: Economics and Economic Reasoning

Chapter at a glance

1. Three central coordination problems any economic system must solve are: (6)

   1) What to produce.
   2) How to produce it.
   3) For whom to produce it.

   Most economic coordination problems involve perceived scarcity.

2. Five important dimensions of economics are: (7)

   1) Economic reasoning *Is really benefit/cost analysis. If the benefits of something outweigh its costs, then do it. If not, don't.*

   2) Economic terminology *Need to know what the terms and concepts mean. Learn them as you go!*

   3) Economic insights *General statements about what causes what—how an economy works (sometimes called economic theories, laws, models, or principles).*

   4) Economic institutions *Need to learn the structure or make-up of businesses, government and society and how they interact.*

   5) Economic policy options *There is more than one way to achieve an end or goal. Need to be aware of the different options and try to choose the "best."*

3. If the relevant benefits of doing something exceed the relevant costs, do it. If the relevant costs of doing something exceed the relevant benefits, don't do it. (9)

   Really need to think in terms of the marginal, or "extra" benefits (MB) and marginal, or "extra" costs (MC) of a course of action.

   Rational decision-making:
   If MB>MC =>Do more of it because "it's worth it."
   If MB<MC =>Do less of it because "it's not worth it."

   NOTE: The symbol "=>" means "implies" or "logically follows."

4. Opportunity cost is the basis of cost/benefit economic reasoning; it is the benefit foregone, or the cost of the next-best alternative to the activity you've chosen. In economic reasoning, that cost is less than the benefit of what you've chosen. (11)

   Opportunity cost => "What must be given up in order to get something else." Opportunity costs are often "hidden." Need to take into consideration all costs.

5. Economic reality is controlled by three invisible forces: (12)

   What happens in a society can be seen as the reaction and interaction of these 3 forces.

   1) The invisible hand (economic forces);
   The market forces of demand, supply, and prices, etc.

   2) The invisible handshake (social and historical forces);
   The impact of generally accepted social morals and customs.

   3) The invisible foot (political and legal forces).
   Political and legal forces affect decisions too.

6. Microeconomics considers economic reasoning from the viewpoint of individuals and builds up; macroeconomics considers economic reasoning from the aggregate and builds down. (17)
   Microeconomics (micro) => concerned with some particular segment of the economy.
   Macroeconomics (macro) => concerned with the entire economy.

7a. Positive economics is the study of what is, and how the economy works. (19)
   Deals with "what is" (objective analysis).

7b. Normative economics is the study of what the goals of the economy should be. (19)
   Deals with "what ought to be" (subjective analysis).

7c. The _art of economics_ is the application of the knowledge learned in positive economics to the achievement of the goals determined in normative economics. (19)

The art of economics is sometimes referred to as "policy economics."

"Good" policy tries to be objective. Tries to weigh all the benefits and costs associated with all policy options and chooses that option in which the benefits outweigh the costs to the greatest degree.

See also, Appendix A: "Economics in Perspective"
See also, Appendix B: "Graphish: The Language of Graphs"

In Appendix B, remember:
2 types of relationships:

1) Direct (Positive) Relationship: expressed as an upward sloping curve.

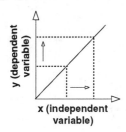

Note: as x increases, y increases; as x decreases, y decreases.

2) Inverse (Negative) Relationship: expressed as a downward sloping curve.

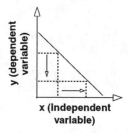

Note: as x increases, y decreases; as x decreases, y increases.

Short-answer questions

1. What are the five dimensions of economic learning? (LO2)

2. What are the three central problems that every economy must solve? (LO1)

3. What is scarcity? Why is defining economics in terms of scarcity problematic? (LO1)

4. State the economic decision rule. (LO3)

5. Define opportunity cost. (LO4)

6. Explain the importance of opportunity cost to economic reasoning. (LO4)

7. Define the three invisible forces that operate in the real world. (LO5)

8. How does microeconomics differ from macroeconomics? Give an example of a macroeconomic issue and a microeconomic issue. (LO6)

9. Define positive economics, normative economics, and the art of economics. How do they relate to one another? (LO7)

Word Scramble

1. _____ 2._____ _____ 3._____ _____
   e i c m m c o i n r o s c o   p y t i r o n o p t u   s c o t   g m r a i l n a   c t o s

Match the Terms and Concepts to Their Definitions

___ 1. art of economics
___ 2. economic decision rule
___ 3. economic forces
___ 4. economic reasoning
___ 5. economic theory
___ 6. economics
___ 7. economy
___ 8. invisible foot
___ 9. invisible hand theory
___ 10. invisible handshake
___ 11. macroeconomics
___ 12. marginal benefit
___ 13. microeconomics
___ 14. opportunity cost
___ 15. positive economics
___ 16. scarcity

a. Additional benefit above what you've already derived.
b. Generalizations about the working of an abstract economy.
c. If benefits exceed costs, do it. If costs exceed benefits, don't.
d. Making decisions on the basis of costs and benefits.
e. The study of individual choice, and how that choice is influenced by economic forces.
f. The forces of scarcity.
g. The benefit forgone, or the cost, of the best alternative to the activity you've chosen.
h. The study of what is, and how the economy works.
i. The insight that a market economy will allocate resources efficiently.
j. Social and historical forces that play a role in deciding whether to let market forces operate.
k. The institutional structure through which individuals in a society coordinate their diverse wants or desires.
l. The study of inflation, unemployment, business cycles, and growth primarily from the whole to the parts, focusing on aggregate relationships and supplementing the analysis with microeconomic insights.
m. The study of how human beings coordinate their wants.
n. Goods available are too few to satisfy individuals' wants.
o. Political and legal forces that play a role in deciding whether to let market forces operate.
p. The application of the knowledge learned in positive economics to the achievement of the goals determined in normative economics.

Problems and Exercises

1. State what happens to scarcity for each good in the following situations:

   a. New storage technology allows college dining services to keep peaches from rotting for a longer time. (Good: peaches).

   b. More students desire to live in single-sex dormitories. No new single-sex dormitories are established. (Good: single-sex dormitory rooms).

2. State as best you can:

   a. The opportunity cost of going out on a date tonight with the date you made last Wednesday.

   b. The opportunity cost of breaking the date for tonight you made last Wednesday.

c.   The opportunity cost of working through this study guide.

d.   The opportunity cost of buying this study guide.

3.   Assume you have purchased a $15,000 car. The salesperson has offered you a maintenance contract covering all major repairs for the next 3 years, with some exclusions, for $750.

a.   What is the opportunity cost of purchasing that maintenance contract?

b.   What information would you need to make a decision based on the economic decision rule?

c.   Based upon that information how would you make your decision?

4.   State for each of the following whether it is an example of an invisible foot, invisible hand, or invisible handshake at work:

a.   Warm weather arrives and more people take Sunday afternoon drives. As a result, the price of gasoline rises.

b.   In some states, liquor cannot be sold before noon on Sunday.

c.   Minors cannot purchase cigarettes.

d.   Many parents will send money to their children in college without the expectation of being repaid.

Multiple Choice Questions

1. Economic reasoning
   a. provides a framework with which to approach questions.
   b. provides correct answers to just about every question.
   c. is only used by economists.
   d. should only be applied to economic business matters.

2. Scarcity could be reduced if
   a. individuals work less and want fewer consumption goods.
   b. individuals work more and want fewer consumption goods.
   c. world population grows and world production remains the same.
   d. innovation comes to a halt.

3. In the textbook, the author focuses on coordination rather than scarcity as the central point of the definition of economics because
   a. economics is not really about scarcity.
   b. scarcity involves coercion, and the author doesn't like coercion.
   c. the author wants to emphasize that the quantity of goods and services depends upon human action and the ability to coordinate that human action.
   d. the concept "scarcity" does not fit within the institutional structure of the economy.

4. In the U.S. economy, who is in charge of organizing and coordinating overall economic activities?
   a. Government.
   b. Corporations.
   c. No one.
   d. Consumers.

5. In the United States more fish is consumed on Friday than on any other day. This is due to the fact that
   a. fishing boats tend to come in on Thursday.
   b. the price of fish is lower on Thursday evenings.
   c. fish would spoil over the weekend.
   d. the Catholic religious tradition limited eating meat on Fridays until recently.

6. You bought stock A for $10 and stock B for $50. The price of each is currently $20. Assuming no tax issues, which should you sell if you need money?
   a. Stock A.
   b. Stock B.
   c. It doesn't matter which.
   d. You should sell an equal amount of both.

7. In deciding whether to go to lectures in the middle of the semester, you should
   a. include tuition as part of the cost of that decision.
   b. not include tuition as part of the cost of that decision.
   c. include a portion of tuition as part of the cost of that decision.
   d. only include tuition if you paid it rather than your parents.

8. In making economic decisions you should consider
   a. marginal costs and marginal benefits.
   b. marginal costs and average benefits.
   c. average costs and average benefits.
   d. total costs and total benefits, including past costs and benefits.

9. In arriving at a decision, a good economist would say that
    a. one should consider only total costs and total benefits.
    b. one should consider only marginal costs and marginal benefits.
    c. after one has considered marginal costs and benefits, one should integrate the social and moral implications and reconsider those costs and benefits.
    d. after considering the marginal costs and benefits, one should make the decision on social and moral grounds.

10. In making decisions economists use only
    a. monetary costs.
    b. opportunity costs.
    c. benefit costs.
    d. dollar costs.

11. The opportunity cost of reading Chapter 1 of the text
    a. is about 1/20 of the price you paid for the book because the chapter is about one twentieth of the price of the book.
    b. zero since you have already paid for the book
    c. has nothing to do with the price you paid for the book.
    d. is 1/20 the price of the book plus 1/20 the price of the tuition.

12. Rationing devices that our society uses include
    a. the invisible hand only.
    b. the invisible hand and invisible handshake only.
    c. the invisible hand and invisible foot only.
    d. the invisible hand, the invisible foot, and the invisible handshake.

13. If at Female College there are significantly more females than males (and there are not a significant number of gays)
    a. economic forces will be pushing for females to pay on dates.
    b. economic forces will be pushing for males to pay on dates.
    c. economic forces will be pushing for neither to pay.
    d. economic forces are irrelevant to this issue. Everyone knows that the males always should pay.

14. Individuals are prohibited from practicing medicine without a license. This is an example of
    a. the invisible hand.
    b. the invisible handshake.
    c. the invisible foot.
    d. the invisible brain.

15. A recent development is that birth mothers are being given more control over specifying the socioeconomic background and other characteristics of the family she is giving her baby to. This is an example of _____ in action.
    a. the invisible hand.
    b. the invisible handshake.
    c. the invisible foot.
    d. the invisible brain.

16. In studying economics,
    a. one should develop a micro foundation first.
    b. one should develop a macro foundation first.
    c. one should study the totality and develop simultaneously a micro and macro foundation.
    d. one should develop a metro foundation for micro and macro.

17. Which of the following is an example of a macroeconomic topic?
    a. The effect of a frost on the Florida orange crop.
    b. Wages of cross-country truckers.
    c. How the unemployment and inflation rates are related.
    d. How income is distributed in the United States.

18. The statement, "The distribution of income should be left to the market," is
    a. a positive statement.
    b. a normative statement.
    c. an art-of-economics statement
    d. an objective statement.

19. "Given certain conditions, the market achieves efficient results" is an example of a
    a. positive statement.
    b. normative statement.
    c. art-of-economics statement.
    d. subjective statement.

A1. Economics that focuses on formal interrelationships is called
    a. Walrasian economics.
    b. Marshallian economics.
    c. Smithian economics.
    d. good economics.

A2. Marshallian economics differs from Walrasian economics in that
    a. it is more concerned with income distribution.
    b. it has more heart.
    c. it takes institutions and political and social dimensions more
       into account.
    d. it focuses more on supply and demand.

B1. In the graph on the right the point A represents
    a. a price of 1 and a quantity of 2.
    b. a price of 2 and a quantity of 2.
    c. a price of 2 and a quantity of 1.
    d. a price of 1 and a quantity of 1.

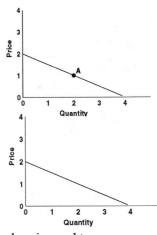

B2. The slope of the line in the graph to the right is
    a. 1/2.
    b. 2.
    c. minus 1/2.
    d. minus 2.

B3. At the maximum and minimum points of the nonlinear curve, the value of the slope is equal to
    a. 1.
    b. zero.
    c. minus 1.
    d. indeterminate.

B4. Which of the four lines in the accompanying graph at the right has the larger slope?
    a. A.
    b. B.
    c. C.
    d. A and C.

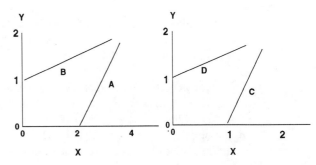

Answers

Short-answer questions

1. Five important dimensions of economic learning are: economic reasoning, economic terminology, economic insights, economic institutions, and economic policy options. (7)

2. The three central problems that every economy must solve are (1) what to produce, (2) how to produce it, and (3) for whom to produce it. (6)

3. Scarcity occurs when there are not enough goods available to satisfy individuals' desires. Defining economics in terms of scarcity is problematic for two reasons. First, scarcity is a perceived concept. If individuals could be encouraged to work more and want less, scarcity could be reduced or even eliminated. Second, the quantity of usable resources depends upon technology and human action. Defining economics in terms of scarcity suggests that eliminating scarcity would eliminate economics. Even if scarcity did not exist, society would still face a coordination problem. The coordination definition of economics includes scarcity but is a much more inclusive definition. (6)

4. If the relevant benefits of doing something exceed the relevant costs, do it. If the relevant costs of doing something exceed the relevant benefits, don't do it. (9)

5. Opportunity cost is the benefit forgone, or the cost, of the best alternative to the activity you have chosen. (11)

6. Opportunity cost is the basis of cost/benefit economic reasoning. In economic reasoning, opportunity cost is less than the benefit of what you have chosen. (11)

7. The three invisible forces are the invisible hand, the invisible handshake, and the invisible foot. The invisible hand is the price mechanism, the rise and fall of prices that guides our actions in a market. The invisible handshake is social and historical forces that play a role in deciding whether to let market forces operate. The invisible foot is political and legal forces that play a role in deciding whether to let market forces operate. (12)

8. Microeconomic theory considers economic reasoning from the viewpoint of individuals and builds up while macroeconomics considers economic reasoning from the aggregate and builds down. Microeconomics studies things like household buying decisions. Macroeconomics studies things like the unemployment rate. (16-17)

9. Positive economics is the study of what is and how the economy works. Normative economics is the study of what the goals of the economy should be. The art of economics is the application of the knowledge learned in positive economics to the achievement of the goals one has determined in normative economics. (19)

Word Scramble   1. microeconomics   2. opportunity cost   3. marginal cost.

Match the Terms and Concepts to Their Definitions
1-p; 2-c; 3-f; 4-d; 5-b; 6-m; 7-k; 8-o; 9-i; 10-j; 11-l; 12-a; 13-e; 14-g; 15-h; 16-n.

Problems and Exercises

1. a. Scarcity will fall because fewer peaches will rot. (12)
    b. Scarcity of single-sex dorm rooms will rise since the number of students desiring single-sex dorm rooms has risen, but the number available has not. (12)

2. a. The opportunity cost of going out on a date tonight that I made last Wednesday is the benefit forgone of the best alternative. If my best alternative was to study for an economics exam, it would be the increase in my exam grade that I would have gotten had I studied. Many answers are possible. (11-12)
    b. The opportunity cost of breaking the date for tonight that I made last Wednesday is the benefit forgone of going out on that date. It would be all the fun I would have had on that date. Other answers are possible. (11-12)

   c. The opportunity cost of working through this study guide is the benefit forgone of the next-best alternative to studying. It could be the increase in the grade I would have received by studying for another exam, or the money I could have earned if I were working at the library. Many answers are possible. (11-12)

   d. The opportunity cost of buying this study guide is the benefit forgone of spending that money on the next-best alternative. Perhaps it is the enjoyment forgone of eating two pizzas. Other answers are possible. (11-12)

3. a. The opportunity cost of purchasing the maintenance contract is the benefit I could receive by spending that $750 on something else like a moon roof. (11-12)

   b. I would need to know the benefit of the maintenance contract to assess whether the cost of $750 is worth-while. (11-12)

   c. For me the benefit of the maintenance contract is the expected cost of future repairs that would be covered and the peace of mind of knowing that future repairs are covered by the contract. The cost is the opportunity cost of using the $750 in another way. If the benefit exceeds the cost, do it. If the cost exceeds the benefit, do not do it. (11-12)

4. a. This is an example of the invisible hand. (12)

   b. This is an example of the invisible foot. Some states have laws, called blue laws, against selling liquor on Sundays altogether or selling it before noon. (12)

   c. This is an example of the invisible foot. This is a federal law. (12-14)

   d. This is an example of a social force, the invisible handshake. (12-14)

Multiple Choice Questions

1. a. As discussed on page 8, the textbook author clearly believes that economic reasoning applies to just about everything. This eliminates c and d. He also carefully points out that it is not the only reasoning that can be used; hence b does not fit. So the correct answer must be a.

2. b. On page 6 of the textbook, the author states that the problem of scarcity could be reduced if individuals worked more and wanted less. Scarcity results when more people want more of something than is currently available.

3. c. On page 8 of the book the author emphasizes the human action reason for focusing on coordination. He explicitly points out that scarcity is important, but that the concept, coordination, is broader.

4. c. As discussed on page 8, the invisible hand of the market coordinates the activities and is a composite of many individuals rather than just any one individual. If you were tempted to say b, corporations, your instincts are right, but the "overall" eliminated that as even a possible answer.

5. d. This is an example of cultural norms affecting demand, as is discussed on page 8. The other answers might have some validity but they are far less significant than d.

6. c. As is discussed on pages 9 and 10 of the book, in making economic decisions you consider that only costs from this point on are relevant; historical costs have no relevance. Since the prices of the stocks are currently the same, it doesn't matter which you sell.

7. b. As discussed on page 9, in economic decisions, you only look at costs from this point on; sunk costs are sunk costs, so tuition can be forgotten. In economic decisions, forward looking marginal costs and marginal benefits are focused on.

8. a. The economic decision rule is "If benefits exceed costs, do it." As is discussed on pages 9 and 10 of the text, however, the relevant benefits and relevant costs to be considered are marginal (additional) costs and marginal benefits. The answer d is definitely ruled out by the qualifying phrase referring to past benefits and costs. Thus, only a is correct.

9. c. As the textbook points out on pages 9 and 10, economists use a framework of costs and benefits initially, but then later they add the social and moral implications to their conclusions. Adding these can change the estimates of costs and benefits, and in doing so can change the result of economic analysis, so there is an integration between the two. (This was a hard question which required careful reading of the text to answer correctly.)

10. b.   As discussed on pages 10 and 11 of the text opportunity costs include measures of nonmonetary costs. The other answers either do not include all the costs that an economist would consider, or are simply two words put together. The opportunity costs include the benefit forgone by undertaking an activity.

11. c.   As discussed on pages 10-12 the correct answer is that it has nothing to do with the price you paid since that is already paid, so a and d are wrong. The opportunity cost is not zero, however, since there are costs of reading the book. The primary opportunity cost of reading the book is the value of the time you're spending on it which is determined by what you could be doing with that time otherwise.

12. d.   As discussed on pages 12 and 13 of the text, all of these are rationing devices. The invisible hand works through the market and thus is focused on in economics. However the others also play a role in determining what people want, either through legal means or through social control.

13. a.   As discussed on pages 12 and 13 of the text, if there are significantly more of one gender than another, dates with that group must be rationed out among the other group. Economic forces will be pushing for the group in excess supply (in this case women) to pay. Economic forces may be pushing in that direction even though historical forces may push us in the opposite direction. Thus, even if males pay because of social forces, economic forces will be pushing for females to pay.

14. c.   As discussed on page 12-14 of the text, legal forces are called the invisible foot.

15. a.   As discussed on page 13 of the text, even though the invisible hand is not allowed to operate directly in the adoption market, it operates indirectly. It gives more power to the supplier of something that's in short supply, so when there is excess supply we are likely to see rules changed to reflect more the desires of that supplier. That's what's happening here.

16. c.   As discussed on page 17, neither micro nor macro is prior; one needs both a micro foundation for macro and a macro foundation for micro. Thus, the best answer is c. The d answer, metro foundation, is meaningless. What is a metro foundation? We don't know. (Actually, if it had said "metafoundation" it might have been justifiable as an answer, but it did not.) Be careful when you see something totally unfamiliar such as the d answer here. It's often thrown in there to make sure you really know what you are talking about. Alternatively, it might be that the individual making out these questions had to think of four alternatives and sometimes there are only three likely ones.

17. c.   As discussed on pages 16 and 17, Macroeconomics is concerned with inflation, unemployment, business cycles and growth. Microeconomics is the study of individuals. The distribution of income is a micro topic because it is concerned with the distribution of income among individuals.

18. b.   As discussed on page 19, this could be either a normative or an art-of-economics statement, depending on whether there is an implicit "given the way the real-world economy operates to best achieve the growth rate you desire." Since these qualifiers are not there, "normative" is the preferable answer.

19. a.   As discussed on page 19 this is a positive statement. It is a statement about *what is*, not about what should be.

A1. a.   As discussed in Appendix A, page 23, Walrasian economics focuses on formal relationships.

A2. c.   This is a hard question because each of the four answers is in some sense true. However, the focus of the discussion in Appendix A, page 23, is on Marshallian economics considering the social and political dimensions more so than Walrasian economics. Thus, c is the best answer.

B1. a.   As discussed in Appendix B, page 23 and 24, a point represents the corresponding numbers on the horizontal and vertical number lines.

B2. c.   As discussed on page 26 of Appendix B, the slope of a line is defined as rise over run. Since the rise is -2 and the run is 4, the slope of the above line is minus 1/2.

B3. b.   As discussed on page 27 of Appendix B, at the maximum and minimum points of the curve the slope is zero.

B4. c.   As discussed in Appendix B, page 26, the slope is defined as rise over run. Line C has the largest rise for a given run so c is the answer. Even though, visually, line A seems to have the same slope as line C it has a different coordinate system. Line A has a slope of 1 whereas line B has a slope of 2. Always be careful about checking coordinate systems when visually interpreting a graph. (See pages 28-29).

Chapter 2:
The Economic Organization of Society

Chapter at a glance

1a. <u>Capitalism</u> is an economic system based on private property and the market. It gives private property rights to individuals, and relies on market forces to coordinate economic activity. (32)
Capitalism ("market-oriented economy") is characterized by:
(I) mainly private ownership of resources
(II) market system solves the What? How? and For whom? problems.

1b. <u>Socialism</u> is, in theory, an economic system that tries to organize society in the same way as most families are organized—all people should contribute what they can, and get what they need. (33-34)
Socialism ("government-controlled economy") is characterized by:
(I) government control over resources
(II) government solves the What? How? and For whom? problems.

✔ *All real-world economies have elements of both capitalism and socialism.*

2. Exhibit 1 in the textbook shows capitalism's and Soviet-style socialism's solutions to the three central planning problems. (35)

Capitalism's solutions to the central economic problems:
1. What to produce: what businesses believe people want, and is profitable.
2. How to produce: businesses decide how to produce efficiently, guided by their desire to make a profit.
3. For whom to produce: distribution according to individuals' ability and/or inherited wealth.

Soviet-style socialism's solutions to the three problems:
1. What to produce: what central planners believe is socially beneficial.
2. How to produce: central planners decide, based on what they think is good for the country.
3. For whom to produce: central planners distribute goods based on what they determine are individuals' needs.

3. Markets coordinate economic activity by using the price mechansim to direct individuals' self-interest into society's interest. (37)
Unbridled, pure or laissez-faire capitalism led to many abuses. This created support for at least some socialism.

✔ *We now have "Welfare Capitalism"—a mix of capitalism and socialism.*

4. Remember this graph:

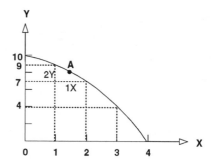

Production Possibilities Curve
Shows the trade-off (or opportunity cost) between two things.
The slope tells you the opportunity cost of good X in terms of good Y. In this particular graph you have to give up 2 Y to get 1 X when you're around point A. (40)

13

5 . The principal of increasing marginal opportunity cost states that opportunity costs increase the more you concentrate on the activity. In order to get more of something, one must give up ever-increasing quantities of something else. (41)

Production Possibility Curve

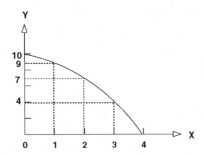

Production Possibility Table

		Opportunity cost of X	
X	Y	(amount of Y which must be foregone)	
0	10		
		>1	
1	9		
		>2	Note: As you get more of X
2	7		
		>3	you have to give up larger
3	4		
		>4	amounts of Y.
4	0		

6. When individuals trade, using their comparative advantages, their combined production possibility curve shifts out. (43)

Specialization and trade along the lines of comparative advantage is mutually beneficial to all involved.

Markets and trading make people better off.

7. Because decisions are contextual, what the prodution possibility curve for a particular decision looks like depends upon the existing insitutions, and the analysis can be applied only in that institutional and historical context. (46)

The production possibility curve is an engine of analysis to make contextual choices, not a definitive tool to decide what one should do in all cases.

See also, Appendix A: "The History of Economic Systems."

Short-answer questions

1. What is capitalism? (LO1)

2. What is socialism? (LO1)

3. How does a capitalist economy solve the three central economic problems? (LO2)

4. How does a Soviet-style socialist economy solve the three central economic problems? (LO2)

5. How can markets coordinate economic decisions without the active involvement of government? (LO3)

6. Design a grade production possibility curve and show how it demonstrates the concept of opportunity cost. (LO4)

7. State the principle of increasing marginal opportunity cost. (LO5)

8. What would the production possibility curve look like if opportunity cost were constant? (LO5)

9. Explain what happens to the production possibility curve with trade and why trade makes individuals better off. (LO6)

10. Why is the production possibility curve more useful in discussing small changes than it is when discussing changes in entire economic systems? (LO7)

A1. Why did feudalism evolve into mercantilism?

A2. Why did mercantilism evolve into capitalism?

A3. Explain what is meant by the statement that capitalism has evolved into welfare capitalism.

Word Scramble

1. _____   2._____   3._____
      a c i i l m o s s   a a c i i l p s s t t   n f c c e y f i i e

Match the Terms and Concepts to Their Definitions

___ 1. comparative advantage

___ 2. economic system

___ 3. feudalism

___ 4. NIMBY

___ 5. Industrial Revolution

___ 6. principle of increasing marginal opportunity cost

___ 7. productive efficiency

___ 8. production possibility curve

___ 9. private property rights

___ 10. socialism

___ 11. Soviet-style socialism

___ 12. welfare capitalism

a. Control of an asset or a right given to an individual or a firm.

b. Period when technology and machines rapidly modernized industrial production and mass produced goods replaced handmade goods.

c. Economic system in which the market operates but government regulates markets significantly.

d. Economic system that tries to organize society in the same way that families do — people contribute what they can and get what they need.

e. Economic system that uses central planning and government ownership of the means of production to answer the questions what to produce, how to produce it, and for whom to produce it.

f. Represents <u>N</u>ot <u>I</u>n <u>M</u>y <u>B</u>ack <u>Y</u>ard; a phrase used by people who may approve of a project, but don't want it to be near them.

g. Political system divided into small communities in which a few powerful people protect those who are loyal to them.

h. The set of economic institutions that determine a country's important economic decisions.

i. The advantage that attaches to a resource when that resource is better suited to the production of one good than to the production of another good.

j. In order to get more of something, one must give up ever-increasing quantities of something else.

k. A curve measuring the maximum combination of outputs that can be obtained from a given number of inputs.

l. Getting as much output for as few inputs as possible.

Problems and Exercises

1. Suppose a restaurant has the following production possibility table:

Labor devoted to pizza in % of total	Output of pizza in pies per week	Labor devoted to spaghetti in % of total	Output of spaghetti in bowls per week
100	50	0	0
80	40	20	10
60	30	40	17
40	20	60	22
20	10	80	25
0	0	100	27

a. Plot the restaurant's production possibility curve.

b. What happens to the marginal opportunity cost as the output of bowls of spaghetti increases?

c. What would happen to the production possibility curve if the restaurant found a way to toss and cook pizzas faster?

d. What would happen to the production possibility curve if the restaurant bought new stoves and ovens that cooked both pizzas and spaghetti faster?

2. Suppose Ecoland has the following production possibilities table:

% resources devoted to production of guns	Number of guns	% resources devoted to production of butter	Pounds of butter
100	50	0	0
80	40	20	5
60	30	40	10
40	20	60	15
20	10	80	20
0	0	100	25

a. Plot the production possibility curve for the production of guns and butter. Put guns on the horizontal axis.

b. What is the per unit opportunity cost of increasing the production of guns from 20 to 30? From 40 to 50?

c. What happens to the opportunity cost of producing guns as the production of guns increases?

d. What is the per unit opportunity cost of increasing the production of butter from 10 to 15? From 20 to 25?

e. What happens to the opportunity cost of producing butter as the production of butter increases?

f. Given this production possibility curve, is producing 26 guns and 13 pounds of butter possible?

g. Is producing 34 guns and 7 pounds of butter possible? Is it efficient?

3. Show, given the following production possibility tables and using production possibility curves, that the United States and Japan would be better off specializing in the production of either food or machinery and then trading rather than producing both food and machinery themselves and not trading.

United States Production per year		Japan Production per year	
Tons of food	Thousands of units of machinery	Tons of food	Thousands of units of machinery
10	0	12.2	0
8	5	10	1
6	10	7.5	2
4	15	5	3
2	20	2.5	4
0	25	0	5

4. Assume that France can produce wine at 25 francs per bottle and can produce butter at 5 francs per pound. Assume that Italy can produce wine at 16,000 lire per bottle and butter at 10,000 lire per pound.

a. In terms of pounds of butter, what is the opportunity cost of producing wine in each country?

b. Who has the comparative advantage in producing butter?

c. Which country should most likely specialize in wine and which should specialized in butter?

Multiple Choice Questions

1. An economic system works via
   a. the invisible hand.
   b. the invisible hand and the invisible foot.
   c. the invisible hand and the invisible handshake.
   d. the invisible hand and the invisible foot and the invisible handshake.

2. For a market to exist, you have to have
   a. public property rights.
   b. private property rights.
   c. a combination of public and private property rights.
   d. coordination rights.

3. In a pure capitalist society, the concept of fairness embodied is
   a. to each according to their needs; from each according to their ability.
   b. to each according to their ability; from each according to their needs.
   c. them that works, gets; them that don't, starve.
   d. everyone gets enough, but those who work harder get more.

4. In theory
   a. socialism is an economic system that tries to organize society in the same ways as most families organize, striving to see that individuals get what they need.
   b. socialism is an economic system based on central planning and government ownership of the means of production.
   c. socialism is an economic system based on private property rights.
   d. socialism is an economic system based on markets.

5. Soviet-style socialism is
   a. an economic system that tries to organize society in the same ways as most families organize, striving to see that individuals get what they need.
   b. an economic system based on central planning and government ownership of the means of production.
   c. an economic system based on private property rights.
   d. an economic system based on markets.

6. In capitalism, the "what to produce" decision is made by
   a. what people want.
   b. what firms believe people want and will make a profit for the firms.
   c. what government believes people want and will make a profit for the government.
   d. what central planners believe is socially beneficial.

7. In Soviet-style socialism, the "what to produce" decision is made by
   a. what people want.
   b. what firms believe people want and will make a profit for firms.
   c. what government believes people want and will make a profit for government.
   d. what central planners want or what they believe is socially beneficial.

8. The U.S. economy today can best be described as
   a. socialist.
   b. pure capitalist.
   c. welfare capitalist.
   d. state socialist.

9. If the opportunity cost of good X in terms of good Y is 2Y, so you'll have to give up 2Y to get one X, the production possibility curve would look like
    a. a.
    b. b.
    c. c.
    d. d.

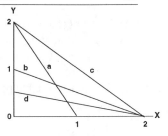

10. If the opportunity cost of good X in terms of good Y is 2Y, so you'll have to give up 2Y to get one X, the production possibility curve would look like
    a. a.
    b. b.
    c. c.
    d. d.

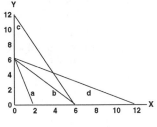

11. If the opportunity cost of good X in terms of good Y is 2Y, so you'll have to give up 2Y to get one X, the production possibility curve would look like
    a. a.
    b. b.
    c. c.
    d. a, b, and c

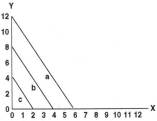

12. If the opportunity cost is constant for all combinations, the production possibility frontier will look like
    a. a.
    b. b.
    c. c.
    d. d.

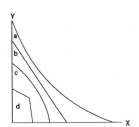

13. If the principle of increasing marginal opportunity cost applies at all points, the production possibility curve looks like
    a. a.
    b. b.
    c. c.
    d. d.

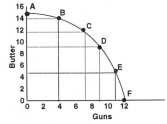

14. Given the accompanying production possibility curve, when you're moving from point C to B the opportunity cost of butter in terms of guns is
    a. 1/3.
    b. 1.
    c. 2.
    d. 3/2.

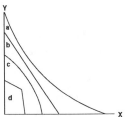

15. In the graph to the right, in the range of points between A and B there is
    a. a high opportunity cost of guns in terms of butter.
    b. a low opportunity cost of guns in terms of butter.
    c. no opportunity cost of guns in terms of butter.
    d. a high monetary cost of guns in terms of butter.

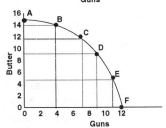

16. In the accompanying production possibility diagram, point A would be
    a. an efficient point.
    b. a super-efficient point.
    c. an inefficient point.
    d. a non-attainable point.

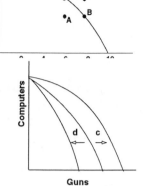

17. A law about the growth of efficiency of computers states that computer chip technology doubles the efficiency of computers each year. If that holds true, which of the four arrows would demonstrate the appropriate shifting of the production possibility curve?
    a. a.
    b. b.
    c. c.
    d. d.

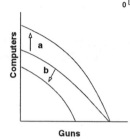

18. Say that methods of production are tied to particular income distributions, so that choosing one method will help some people but hurt others. Say also that method A produces significantly more total output than method B. In this case
    a. method A is more efficient than method B.
    b. method B is more efficient than method A.
    c. if method A produces more and gives more to the poor people, method A is more efficient.
    d. one can't say whether A or B is more efficient.

19. If the United States and Japan have production possibility curves as shown in the diagram on the right, at what point would they most be after trade?
    a. A
    b. B
    c. C
    d. D

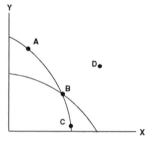

A1. In feudalism the most important invisible force was
    a. the invisible hand.
    b. the invisible handshake.
    c. the invisible foot.
    d. the invisible brain.

A2. When there is not a lot of significant technological change
    a. feudalism is highly inefficient.
    b. feudalism is reasonably efficient.
    c. technological change has no relation to whether feudalism would be efficient or not.
    d. feudalism is inefficient, no matter what.

A3. In mercantilism, the guiding invisible force is
    a. the invisible hand.
    b. the invisible foot.
    c. the invisible handshake.
    d. the invisible brain.

A4. Mercantilism evolved into capitalism because
    a. government investments did not pan out.
    b. the Industrial Revolution undermined the craft guilds' mercantilist method of production.
    c. the guilds wanted more freedom.
    d. serfs wanted more freedom.

A5. Marx saw significant tension between
   a. rich capitalists and poor capitalists.
   b. capitalists and government.
   c. capitalists and the proletariat.
   d. government and the proletariat.

A6. Asian economies tend to be
   a. more feudalistic than the U.S. economy.
   b. more capitalistic than the U.S. economy.
   c. more socialistic than the U.S. economy.
   d. more mercantilist than the U.S. economy.

A7. State socialism is an economic system in which
   a. business sees to it that people work for their own good until they can be relied upon to do that on their own.
   b. business sees to it that people work for the common good until they can be relied upon to do that on their own.
   c. government sees to it that people work for their own good until they can be relied upon to do so on their own.
   d. government sees to it that people work for the common good until they can be relied upon to do so on their own.

Answers

Short-answer questions

1. Capitalism is an economic system based on private property and the market. It gives private property rights to individuals, and relies on market forces to coordinate economic activity. (32)

2. Socialism is an economic system that tries to organize society in the same way as do most families — all people should contribute what they can, and get what they need. (33)

3. A capitalist economy solves the problem what to produce: what businesses believe people want and think they can make a profit supplying. It solves the problem how to produce: businesses decide how to produce efficiently, guided by their desire to make a profit. It solves the problem for whom to produce: distribution according to individuals' ability and/or inherited wealth. (35)

4. A Soviet-style socialist economy solves the problem what to produce: what central planners believe is socially beneficial. It solves the problem how to produce: central planners decide, based, one hopes, on what they think is good for the country. It solves the problem for whom to produce: central planners distribute goods based on what they determine are individuals' needs. (35)

5. The invisible hand — the price mechanism — guides the actions of suppliers and consumers to the general good. That is, competition directs individuals pursuing profit to do what society needs to have done. Markets coordinate economic decisions by turning self-interest into social good. (37)

6. The production possibility curve shows the highest combination of grades you can get with 20 hours of studying economics and English. The grade received in economics in on the vertical axis and the grade received in English is on the horizontal axis. The graph tells us the opportunity cost of spending any combination of hours on economics and English. For example, the opportunity cost of increasing your grade in economics by 6 points is decreasing your English grade by 4 points. (38-39)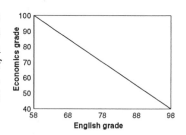

7. The principle of increasing marginal opportunity cost states that in order to get more of something, one must give up ever-increasing quantities of something else. (41)

8. Such a production possibility curve would be a straight line connecting the maximum number of units that could be produced of each product if all inputs were devoted to one or the other good. (40)

9. By comparing individual production possibility curves, one can determine those activities in which each has a comparative advantage. By concentrating on those activities for which one has a comparative advantage and trading those goods for goods for which others have a comparative advantage, individuals can end up with a combination of goods not attainable without trade. The production possibility curve shifts out with trade. (41-43)

10. The production possibility curve is best used given an existing economic system because an economic system determines relationships that affect costs in everyday decisions and in production. The example in the text of how changing from socialism to capitalism would affect the production possibility curve is a good example of how the production possibility curve can mask the probability that beneficial result of major structural changes may take many years. (45-46)

A1. Feudalism evolved into mercantilism as the development of money allowed trade to grow, undermining the traditional base of feudalism. Politics rather than social forces came to control the central economic decisions. (53-54)

A2. Mercantilism evolved into capitalism because the Industrial Revolution shifted the economic power base away from craftsmen toward industrialists and toward an understanding that markets could coordinate the economy without the active involvement of the government. (54-55)

A3. Capitalism has evolved into welfare capitalism. That is, the human abuses marked by early capitalist developments led to a criticism of the market economic system. Political forces have changed government's role in the market, making government a key player in determining distribution and in making the what, how, and for whom decisions. This characterizes the U.S. economy today. (55-57)

Word Scramble   1. socialism   2. capitalists   3. efficiency

Match the Terms and Concepts with Their Definitions
1-i; 2-h; 3-g; 4-f; 5-b; 6-j; 7-l; 8-k; 9-a; 10-d; 11-e; 12-c.

Problems and Exercises

1. a. The restaurant's production possibility curve is shown to the right. (39)
    b. The number of pizza pies that must be given up to make an additional bowl of spaghetti increases as the number of bowls of spaghetti produced increases. (40)

    c. If the restaurant found a way to toss and cook pizzas faster, the production possibility curve would rotate out along the pizza axis as shown on the right. (43)

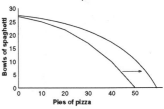

    d. The production possibility curve would shift out to the right as shown in the figure on the right. (43)

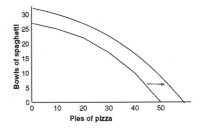

2. a. The production possibility curve is a straight line as shown on the right. (39-40)
    b. The opportunity cost of increasing the production of guns from 20 to 30 is 0.5 pounds of butter per gun. The opportunity cost of increasing the production of guns from 40 to 50 is also 0.5 pounds of butter per gun. (40-41)

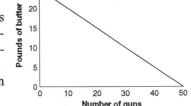

    c. The opportunity cost of producing guns stays the same as the production of guns increases. (41-42)
    d. The opportunity cost of increasing the production of butter from 10 to 15 is 2 guns per pound of butter. The opportunity cost of increasing the production of butter from 20 to 25 is 2 guns per pound of butter. (41-42)
    e. The opportunity cost of producing butter stays the same as the production of butter increases. (41-42)
    f. Producing 26 guns and 13 pounds of butter is not attainable given this production possibility curve. We can produce 20 guns and 15 pounds of butter. To produce six more guns, Ecoland must give up 3 pounds of butter. Ecoland can produce only 26 guns and 12 pounds of butter. (41-42)
    g. Ecoland can produce 34 guns and 7 pounds of butter. To see this, begin at 30 guns and 10 pounds of butter. To produce 4 more guns, 2 pounds of butter must be given up. Ecoland can produce 34 guns and 8 pounds of butter, which is more than 34 guns and 7 pounds of butter. This is an inefficient point of production. (41-42)

3. The production possibility of producing food and machinery for both Japan and the United States is shown in the graph on the right. The combined production possibility curve with trade is also shown. Clearly, trade shifts the production possibility curve out, showing that the two countries are better off with trade. The United States has a comparative advantage in the production of machinery. It must give up only 0.2 tons of food for each additional thousand units of machinery produced. Japan must give up 2.5 tons of food for each additional thousand units of machinery produced. A specific example is if Japan produced 12.5 tons of food and no machines while the United States produced 0 tons of

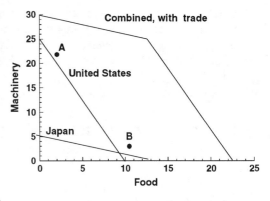

food and 15 thousand units of machinery, Japan could offer the United States 2 tons of food for 3 thousand units of machinery. The United States would be at point A and Japan would be at point B. Each would be able to attain a level of production not attainable before. (41-42)

4. a. In France, the opportunity cost of producing wine is 5 pounds of butter. In Italy, the opportunity cost of producing wine is 1.6 pounds of butter. Calculate this by finding how much butter must be forgone for each bottle of wine in each country. (41-42)

   b. France has the comparative advantage in producing butter because it can produce butter for a lower opportunity cost. (41-42)

   c. Italy should specialize in producing wine and France should specialize in producing butter assuming one can produce only wine and the other must produce only butter. This is concluded from the principle of comparative advantage. (41-42)

Multiple Choice

1. d   As discussed on page 31, an economic system works via the interaction of all three invisible forces.

2. b   As discussed on page 32, markets require private property rights because these give people the framework within which they can trade from one to another and markets rely on trading. Markets also require government, but government and public property rights are not the same thing, which rules out a and c. And d is a throwaway answer.

3. c   As discussed on page 33, c represents the concept of fairness in a pure capitalist economy. In a welfare capitalist economy d would be a possible answer. We should also point out that c leaves out issues of inheritance and luck, which complicate the ethics of capitalism, but c is nevertheless by far the best answer.

4. a   As discussed on page 33, a is the correct answer. If the question had said "Soviet-style socialism," b would have been an acceptable answer, but Soviet-style socialism was a response to real-world implementation problems, not part of the theory of socialism.

5. b   As discussed on page 34, b is the correct answer. If the question had said simply "socialism." a would have been an acceptable answer, but given that it said Soviet-style socialism, b is the preferable answer.

6. b   As discussed in Exhibit 1, page 35, the correct answer is b.

7. d   As discussed Exhibit 1, page 35, the correct answer is d. We should point out that this is *ideally*; in practice, central planners may not be concerned with society. Thus c is a possible answer, but the term "profit" makes it unacceptable. Planners would not get profit—they might get rich, but it wouldn't be through profits.

8. c   See pages 37 and 38 of the text.

9. a   As discussed on page 39, the production possibility curve tells how much of one good you must give up to get more of the other good; here you must give up 2Y to get one X, making a the correct answer.

10. c   As discussed on page 39, the production possibility curve tells how much of one good you must give up to get more of another good. Opportunity costs is a ratio; it determines the slope, not the position, of the ppc curve. Thus, the correct answer is c because the 12 to 6 trade-off reduces to a 2 to 1 trade-off.

11. d   As discussed on page 39, the production possibility curve tells how much of one good you must give up to get more of the other good. Opportunity costs is a ratio; it determines the slope, not the position, of the ppc curve. Since all have the same correct slope, all three are correct, so d is the right answer.

12. b   As discussed on pages 39 and 40 of the book, if the opportunity costs are constant, the ppc is a straight line, so b must be the answer.

13. c   As discussed on pages 40 and 41 of the book, with increasing marginal opportunity costs, as you produce more and more of a good, you will have to give up more and more of the other good to do so. This means that the slope of the ppc must be bowed outward, so c is the correct answer. (See Exhibit 3, page 40 for an in-depth discussion.)

14. d   As discussed on page 40, the slope of the ppc measures the trade-off of one good for the other. Since moving from point c to b means giving up 3 guns for 2 pounds of butter, the correct answer is 3/2 or d.

15. b   As discussed on page 41, the flatter the slope, the higher the opportunity cost of the good measured on the vertical axis; alternatively, the flatter the slope the lower the opportunity cost of that good measured on the horizontal axis. In the AB range the slope is flat so guns have a low opportunity cost in terms of butter; one need give up only one pound of butter to get four guns.

16. c   As discussed on page 44 (See Exhibit 5), point A is an inefficient point.

17. a   As discussed on page 44 (See Exhibit 5), technological change that improves the efficiency of producing a good shifts the ppc out in that good, but not in the other good. So a is the correct answer.

18. d   The answer is "You can't say," as discussed on page 43. The term "efficiency" involves *achieving a goal as cheaply as possible.* Without specifying one's goal one cannot say what method is more efficient. The concept efficiency generally presumes that the goal includes preferring more to less, so if any method is more productive, it will be method A. But because there are distributional effects that involve making additional judgments, the correct answer is d. Some students may have been tempted to choose c because their goals involve more equity, but that is their particular judgment, and not all people may agree. Thus c would be incorrect, leaving d as the correct answer.

19. d   As discussed in Exhibit 4 on page 42, with trade, both countries can attain a point outside each production possibility curve. The only point not already attainable is D.

A1. b   As discussed on page 53, in feudalism tradition reigned.

A2. b   As discussed on page 53, as long as society doesn't change too much, tradition operates reasonably well. Hence b is the best answer.

A3. b   As discussed on page 53, in mercantilism government directed the economy.

A4. b   See page 54.

A5. c   See page 55. To the degree that government was controlled by capitalists, d would be a correct answer, but it is not as good an answer as c, which represents the primary conflict. Remember, you are choosing the answer that best reflects the discussion in the text.

A6. d   See page 57, where it is stated that Asian economies have many similarities to mercantilism.

A7. d   See pages 56 and 57.

Chapter 3:
Supply and Demand

Chapter at a glance

1. The <u>law of demand</u> states that the quantity of a good demanded is <u>inversely related</u> to the good's price. When price goes up, quantity demanded goes down. When price goes down, quantity demanded goes up. (60)

✔ *Law of Demand (Inverse Relationship):*
    arrows move in $\uparrow P \Rightarrow \downarrow Q_d$
    opposite directions $\downarrow P \Rightarrow \uparrow Q_d$

    Law of Demand expressed as a <u>downward-sloping curve</u>:

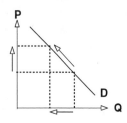

2a. The law of demand is based upon opportunity cost and individuals' ability to substitute. If the relative price of a good rises, the opportunity cost of purchasing that good will also rise and demanders will substitute for it a good with a lower opportunity cost. (61)
    As the P of beef $\uparrow$ s, we buy more chicken.

2b. The law of supply, like the law of demand, is based on opportunity cost and the individual firm's ability to substitute. Suppliers will substitute toward goods for which they receive higher relative prices. (68)
    If the P of wheat $\uparrow$ s, farmers grow more wheat and less corn.

3. Changes in quantity demanded are shown by movements along a demand curve. Shifts in demand are shown by a shift of the entire demand curve. (62-63) *(Note: "Δ" means "change.")*
    Don't get this confused on the exam!
    ΔQ_d is caused <u>only</u> by a Δ in the P of the good itself.

✔ $\Delta P \Rightarrow \Delta Q_d \Rightarrow$ *movement along a given D curve*

    $\uparrow P \Rightarrow \downarrow Q_d$: *movement along a curve (e.g. from point A to point B).*

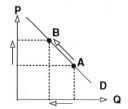

    ΔD is caused only by Δs in the shift factors of D(<u>not</u> a Δ in the P of the good itself!)

✔ <u>Δ in shift factors of D $\Rightarrow$ ΔD $\Rightarrow$ shift of a D curve</u>

✔ *Know what can cause an increase and decrease in demand:*
    $\uparrow D \Rightarrow$ <u>Rightward Shift</u> $\downarrow D \Rightarrow$ <u>Leftward Shift</u>

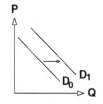 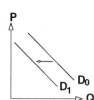

4. To derive a demand curve from a demand table you plot each point on the demand table on a graph and connect the points. (64)

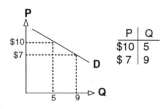

P	Q
$10	5
$ 7	9

5. The <u>law of supply</u> states that the quantity supplied of a good is <u>directly related</u> to the goods' price. When price goes up, quantity supplied goes up. When price goes down, quantity supplied goes down. (68)

✔ *Law of Supply (Direct Relationship):*
    arrows move in $\uparrow P \Rightarrow \uparrow Q_s$
    same direction $\downarrow P \Rightarrow \downarrow Q_s$

Law of Supply expressed as an <u>*upward-sloping curve*</u>:

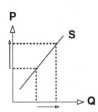

6. Just as with demand, it is important to distinguish between a shift in supply (a shift of the entire supply curve) and a movement along a supply curve (a change in the quantity supplied due to a change in price). (69-70)

    Don't get this confused on the exam!
    ΔQ_s *is caused* <u>*only*</u> *by a* Δ *in the P of the good itself.*

✔ $\Delta P \Rightarrow \Delta Q_s \Rightarrow$ *movement along a given S curve.*

    $\uparrow P \Rightarrow \uparrow Q_s$: *movement along a curve (e.g. from point A to point B).*

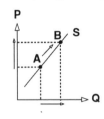

    ΔS *is caused only by* Δ*s in the shift factors of S (*<u>*not*</u> *a* Δ *in the P of the good itself!)*
✔ <u>Δ *in shift factors of S* $\Rightarrow$ ΔS $\Rightarrow$ *shift of a S curve*</u>

✔*Know what can cause an increase and decrease in supply:*
$\uparrow S \Rightarrow$ <u>*Rightward Shift*</u> $\downarrow S \Rightarrow$ <u>*Leftward Shift*</u>

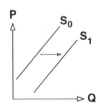 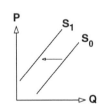

7. To derive a supply curve from a supply table, you plot each point on the supply table on a graph and connect the points. (70-72)

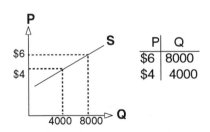

P	Q
$6	8000
$4	4000

8. The three dynamic laws of supply and demand are:
1. If quantity demanded is greater than quantity supplied, prices tend to rise; when quantity supplied is greater than quantity demanded, prices tend to fall. (72-73)
2. The larger the difference between quantity demanded and quantity supplied, the greater the pressure for prices to rise (if there is excess demand) or fall (if there is excess supply). (73)
3. When quantity demanded equals quantity supplied, prices have no tendency to change. (73-74)

✔ <u>*Know this!*</u>
1. If $Q_d > Q_s \Rightarrow$ Shortage $\Rightarrow$ P will $\uparrow$.
2. If $Q_s > Q_d \Rightarrow$ Surplus $\Rightarrow$ P will $\downarrow$.
3. If $Q_s = Q_d \Rightarrow$ Equilibrium $\Rightarrow$ no tendency for P to change (because there is neither a surplus nor a shortage).

Shortage	Surplus	Equilibrium
$(Q_d > Q_s)$	$(Q_s > Q_d)$	$(Q_s = Q_d)$
P is below equilibrium	P is above equilibrium	

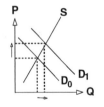 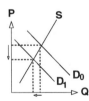

ALSO NOTE:

$\uparrow D \Rightarrow \uparrow P; \uparrow Q$ $\downarrow D \Rightarrow \downarrow P; \downarrow Q$

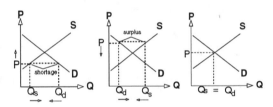

$\uparrow S \Rightarrow \downarrow P; \uparrow Q$ $\downarrow S \Rightarrow \uparrow P; \downarrow Q$

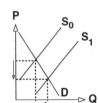 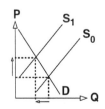

See also, "Appendix A: Algebraic Representation of Demand, Supply, and Equilibrium."

Short-answer questions

1. What is the law of demand? (LO1)

2. What does the law of supply say would most individuals do if their wage increased? Relate your answer to opportunity cost and substitution. (LO2)

3. Suppose the price of Red Hot Chili Pepper CDs rose 2% and the average price of all other goods rose 10%. What does the law of demand say would happen to the quantity of Red Hot Chili Pepper CDs demanded? (LO2)

4. Demonstrate graphically a shift in demand. (LO3)

5. Demonstrate graphically a movement along a demand curve. (LO3)

6. Draw a demand curve from the following demand table. (LO4)

    Demand Table

Q	P
50	1
40	2
30	3
20	4

7. State the law of supply. (LO5)

8. Demonstrate graphically the effect on the supply of Red Hot Chili Pepper CDs of a new technology that reduces the cost of producing Red Hot Chili Pepper CDs. (LO6)

9. Demonstrate graphically the effect of a rise in the price of Red Hot Chili Pepper CDs on supply. (LO6)

10. Draw a supply curve from the following supply table. (LO7)

    Supply Table

Q	P
20	1
30	2
40	3
50	4

11. State the first dynamic law of supply and demand and demonstrate it graphically. (LO8)

12. State the second dynamic law of supply and demand and demonstrate it graphically. (LO8)

13. Given the graph on the right, at what price is there no pressure on price to change? Why? (LO8)

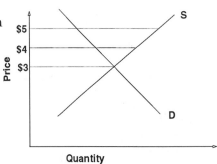

Word Scramble

1. _____   2._____   3._____ _____
     b e i i i l m q r u u   l p p s u y   a e e i l r t v   c e i p r

Match the Terms and Concepts to Their Definitions

___ 1.   demand curve

___ 2.   equilibrium price

___ 3.   excess supply

___ 4.   factors of production

___ 5.   first dynamic law of supply and demand

___ 6.   law of demand

___ 7.   law of supply

___ 8.   market demand curve

___ 9.   movement along a supply curve

___ 10. quantity demanded

___ 11. relative price

___ 12. second dynamic law of supply and demand

___ 13. shift factor of demand

___ 14. shift in supply

___ 15. third dynamic law of supply and demand

a.   A specific amount that will be demanded per unit of time at a specific price. Refers to a point on a demand curve.

b.   Curve that tells how much of a good will be bought at various prices.

c.   If how much of a good is supplied is affected by a shift factor, there is said to be a shift in supply. Graphically, a shift in supply will cause the entire supply curve to shift.

d.   In a market, the larger the difference between quantity supplied and quantity demanded, the greater the pressure on prices to rise (if there is excess demand) or fall (if there is excess supply).

e.   Method of representing a change in the quantity supplied. Graphically, a change in quantity supplied will cause a movement along the supply curve.

f.   More of a good will be demanded the lower its price, other things constant. Also can be stated as: Less of a good will be demanded the higher its price, other things constant.

g.   More of a good will be supplied the higher its price, other things constant. Also can be stated as: Less of a good will be supplied the lower its price, other things constant.

h.   Price of a good compared to the price of some other good.

i.   Quantity supplied is greater than quantity demanded.

j.   Resources, or inputs, necessary to produce goods.

k.   Something, other than the good's price, that affects how much of the good is demanded.

l.   The price toward which the invisible hand (economic forces) drives the market.

m.   The horizontal sum of all individual demand curves.

n.   When quantity demanded is greater than quantity supplied, prices tend to rise; when quantity supplied is greater than quantity demanded, prices tend to fall.

o.   When quantity supplied equals quantity demanded, prices have no tendency to change.

Problems and Exercises

1.   Draw two linear curves on the same graph from the following table, one relating P with Q_1 and the other relating P with Q_2.

P	Q_1	Q_2
25	50	110
30	60	100
35	70	90
40	80	80
45	90	70

a.   Label the curve that is most likely a demand curve. Explain your choice.

b. Label the curve that is most likely a supply curve. Explain your choice.

c. What is equilibrium price and quantity? Choose points above and below that price and explain why each is not the equilibrium price.

2. You are given the following individual demand tables for compact discs.

Price	Juan	Philippe	Ramone
$7	3	20	50
$10	2	10	40
$13	1	7	32
$16	0	5	26
$19	0	3	20
$22	0	0	14

a. Determine the market demand table.

b. Graph the individual and market demand curves.

c. If the current market price is $13, what is the total market demand? What happens to total market demand if price rises to $19 a disc?

d. Say that a new popular Vanilla Ice compact disc hits the market which increases demand for compact discs by 25%. Show with a demand table what happens to the individual and market demand curves. Demonstrate graphically what happens to market demand.

3. Draw a hypothetical demand and supply curve for cyber cafes — coffee houses with computers hooked up to the Internet with access to daily newspapers (among other things) at each table. Show how the equilibrium price and quantity is affected by the following:

   a. A technological breakthrough lowers the cost of computers.

   b. Consumers' income rises.

   c. A per-hour fee is charged to coffee houses to use the Internet.

   d. The price of newspapers in print rises.

   e. Possible suppliers expect Cyber cafes to become more popular.

4. The invention of a self-milking cow machine allows cows to milk themselves. Not only does this reduce the need for higher-cost human assistance in milking, but it also allows the cow to milk herself three times a day instead of two, leading to both a healthier cow and increased milk production.

   a. Show the effect of this innovation on the equilibrium quantity and price of milk.

   b. Show the likely effect on equilibrium price and quantity of apple juice (a substitute for milk).

A1. The supply and demand equation for strawberries is given by

$Q_s = -10 + 5P$
$Q_d = 20 - 5P$

where P is price in dollars per quart, Q_s is millions of quarts of strawberries supplied, and Q_d is millions of quarts of strawberries demanded.

    a.   What is the equilibrium market price and quantity for strawberries in the market?

    b.   Suppose a new preservative is introduced that prevents more strawberries from rotting on their way from the farm to the store. As a result supply of strawberries increases by 20 million quarts. What effect does this have on market price and quantity sold?

    c.   Suppose it has been found that the spray used on cherry trees has ill effects on those who eat the cherries. As a result, the demand for strawberries increases by 10 million quarts. What effect does this have on market price for strawberries and quantity of strawberries sold?

A2. In Bangladesh, it is common for ear cleaners (individuals who clean other people's ears) to offer their services to passers-by along the road. The supply and demand equations for ear cleaners can be expressed as

$Q_s = -20 + 8P$
$Q_d = 40 - 12P$,

where P is price in takas (currency in Bangladesh) and quantity is interpreted as thousands of ear cleaners.

    a.   What is the equilibrium market price and quantity of ear cleaners?

    b.   Suppose the incomes of consumers in Bangladesh rise and the demand for ear cleaners to clean ears increases by 20 thousand. What is the resulting equilibrium price and quantity of ear cleaners?

    c.   Suppose the Health Department of Bangladesh relaxes a previous regulation that only high quality cotton can be used for ear cleaning. Many ear cleaners switch to less-expensive lower-quality cotton and the supply of ear clearners increases by 10 thousand at each price. What is the new equilibrium price and quantity of ear cleaners?

Multiple Choice Questions

1. The law of demand states
   a. more of a good will be demanded the lower its price, other things constant.
   b. more of a good will be demanded the higher its price, other things constant.
   c. people always want more.
   d. you can't always get what you want at the price you want.

2. If the weather gets very hot, what will likely happen?
   a. The supply of air conditioners will increase.
   b. Quantity demanded of air conditioners will increase.
   c. Demand for air conditioners will increase.
   d. The quality demanded of air conditioners will increase.

3. If the price of air conditioners falls, there will be
   a. an increase in demand for air conditioners.
   b. an increase in the quantity demanded of air conditioners.
   c. an increase in the quality demanded of air conditioners.
   d. a shift in the demand for air conditioners.

4. In partial equilibrium analysis one assumes
   a. other things constant and forgets them.
   b. other things are not constant.
   c. other things are constant but one brings them back into the analysis later when one applies it.
   d. other things are not constant, and one partially fits them into the analysis.

5. The demand curve has just shifted in. Which of the following would not be an explanation?
   a. The price of some other good has risen.
   b. The price of some other good has fallen.
   c. The price of this good has fallen.
   d. Society's income has fallen.

6. In Brazil in the 1980s the price of pencils doubled in a year, but simultaneously so did the price of almost every good. In applying the law of demand, one would expect
   a. the quantity demanded of pencils to increase.
   b. the quantity demanded of pencils to decrease.
   c. the quantity demanded of pencils to remain constant.
   d. the demand for pencils to increase.

7. Using the standard axes, the demand curve associated with the following demand table is

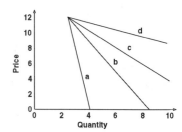

	Demand Table	
	p	q
a. a	7	5
b. b	9	4
c. c	11	3
d. d		

8. There are many more substitutes for good A than for good B.
   a. The demand curve for good A will likely be flatter.
   b. The demand curve for good B will likely be flatter.
   c. You can't say anything about the likely relative flatness of the demand curves.
   d. The demand curve for good B will likely shift out further.

9. To derive a market demand curve from two individual demand curves
   a. one adds the two demand curves horizontally.
   b. one adds the two demand curves vertically.
   c. one subtracts one demand curve from the other demand curve.
   d. one adds the demand curves both horizontally and vertically.

10. The market demand curve will always
    a. be flatter than the individual demand curves that make it up.
    b. be steeper than the individual demand curves that make it up.
    c. have the same slope as the individual demand curves that make it up.
    d. be unrelated to the individual demand curves and slope.

11. The movement in the graph at the right from point A to point B represents
    a. an increase in demand.
    b. an increase in the quantity demanded.
    c. an increase in the quantity supplied.
    d. an increase in supply.

12. The law of supply states that
    a. more of a good will be supplied the higher its price, other things constant.
    b. less of a good will be supplied the higher its price, other things constant.
    c. more of a good will be supplied the higher its price, other things changing proportionately.
    d. less of a good will be supplied the higher its price, other things changing proportionately.

13. In the graph on the right, the arrow refers to
    a. a shift in demand.
    b. a shift in supply.
    c. a change in the quantity demanded.
    d. a change in the quantity supplied.

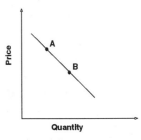

14. The market supply curve for the following two individual supply curves
    S_1 and S_2 would be
    a. S_3.
    b. S_4.
    c. S_5.
    d. S_6.

15. If there is an improvement in technology one would expect
    a. a movement along the supply curve.
    b. a shift upward of the supply curve.
    c. a shift downward of the supply curve.
    d. a movement down along the supply curve.

16. You're the supplier of a good and suddenly a number of your long-lost friends call you. Your good is most likely
    a. in excess supply.
    b. in excess demand.
    c. in equilibrium.
    d. in both excess supply and demand.

17. At which point will you expect the stronger downward pressure on prices?
    a. a.
    b. b.
    c. c.
    d. d.

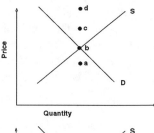

18. If the invisible handshake and invisible foot are strong in the following diagram
    a. you expect the equilibrium price to be at A.
    b. you expect the equilibrium price to be at B.
    c. you expect the equilibrium price to be at C.
    d. it is difficult to know where to expect the equilibrium price to be unless one knows more about these other invisible forces.

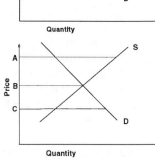

19. If the demand for a good increases you will expect
    a. price to fall and quantity to rise.
    b. price to rise and quantity to rise.
    c. price to fall and quantity to fall.
    d. price to rise and quantity to fall.

20. If there is a flood, what will likely happen to the price of bottled water?
    a. It will rise.
    b. It will fall.
    c. It will remain the same.
    d. It will fall to zero.

A1. The supply and demand equations for Nantucket Nectar's Kiwi-berry juice are given by
    $Q_s = -4 + 5P$ and $Q_d = 18 - 6P$ respectively, where price is dollars per quart and quantity is thousands of quarts. The equilibrium market price and quantity is
    a. P = $2, Q = 6 thousand quarts.
    b. P = $3, Q = 6 thousand quarts.
    c. P = $14, Q = 66 thousand quarts.
    d. P = $22, Q = 106 thousand quarts.

A2. The supply and demand equations for sidewalk snow removal in a small town in Montana are given by $Q_s = -50 + 5P$ and $Q_d = 100 - 5P$ respectively, where price is in dollars per removal and quantity is numbers of removals per week. It snows so much that demand for sidewalk snow removals increases by 30 per week. The equilibrium market price and quantity is
    a. P = $15, Q = 6 sidewalk snow removals.
    b. P = $15, Q = 6 sidewalk snow removals.
    c. P = $18, Q = 66 sidewalk snow removals.
    d. P = $18, Q = 40 sidewalk snow removals.

A3. The supply and demand equations for sidewalk snow removal in a small town in Montana are given by $Q_s = -50 + 5P$ and $Q_d = 100 - 5P$ respectively, where price is in dollars per removal and quantity is numbers of removals per week. (Same equations as for A2.) Suppose snowfall is so light demand for sidewalk snow removals decreases by 10 per week. The equilibrium market price and quantity is
    a. P = $18, Q = 40 sidewalk snow removals.
    b. P = $16, Q = 30 sidewalk snow removals.
    c. P = $14, Q = 20 sidewalk snow removals.
    d. P = $8, Q = 10 sidewalk snow removals.

A4. The supply and demand equations for beef in England are given by $Q_s = -18 + 7P$ and $Q_d = 72 - 8P$ respectively, where price is in £ per pound and quantity is millions of pounds of beef per year. Mad cow disease reduces the supply of beef by 15 million pounds per year. What is the new equilibrium price and quantity of beef?

   a. P = £5/lb, Q = 32 million pounds of beef per year.
   b. P = £6/lb, Q = 24 million pounds of beef per year.
   c. P = £7/lb, Q = 16 million pounds of beef per year.
   d. P = £7/lb, Q = 31 million pounds of beef per year.

A5. The supply and demand equations for beef in England are given by $Q_s = -18 + 7P$ and $Q_d = 72 - 8P$ respectively, where price is in £ per pound and quantity is millions of pounds of beef per year. (Same equations as in A4.) Mad cow disease reduces the supply of beef by 15 million pounds per year and subsequent fear by consumers reduces demand by 30 million pounds per year. What is the new equilibrium price and quantity of beef?

   a. P = £3/lb, Q = 18 million pounds of beef per year.
   b. P = £5/lb, Q = 2 million pounds of beef per year.
   c. P = £7/lb, Q = 46 million pounds of beef per year.
   d. P = £9/lb, Q = 30 million pounds of beef per year.

Answers

Short-Answer Questions

1. The law of demand states that the quantity of a good demanded is inversely related to the good's price. When price goes up, quantity demanded goes down. (60)

2. The law of supply states that as the price of supplying a good rises, the quantity supplied will rise. According to this law, most individuals would choose to supply more labor if their wage increased. By working more hours, individuals forgo the benefit of leisure, so as wages increase, the opportunity cost of not working increases and individuals will substitute work for leisure. (68)

3. Since the money price of all goods has risen 10% and the money price of Red Hot Chili Pepper CDs has risen 2%, the relative price of Red Hot Chili Pepper CDs has fallen 8%. The law of demand states that as the relative price of a good falls, the quantity demanded rises. Remember, it is the good's relative price, not its money price, that the law of demand refers to. The opportunity cost of buying a CD has fallen (because its relative price has fallen) and individuals will substitute away from all other goods toward Red Hot Chili Pepper CDs. (60-61)

4. A shift in demand is shown by a shift of the entire demand curve resulting from a change in a shift factor of demand as shown in the graph on the right. (63)

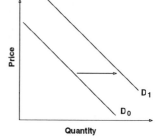

5. A movement along a demand curve is a change in quantity demanded resulting from a change in price as is shown in the graph on the right as a movement from Q_0 to Q_1. (63)

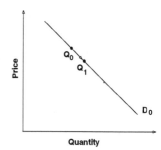

6. To derive a demand curve from a demand table, you plot each point on the demand table on a graph and connect the points. This is shown on the graph on the right. (64)

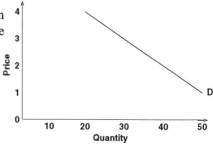

7. The law of supply states that the quantity of a good supplied is directly related to the good's price. When price goes up, quantity supplied goes up. (68)

8. A new technology that reduces the cost of producing Red Hot Chili Pepper CDs will shift the entire supply curve to the right from S_0 to S_1, as shown in the graph on the right. (69-70)

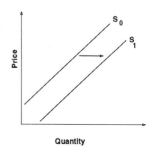

9. A rise in the price of Red Hot Chili Pepper CDs from P_0 to P_1 results in a movement along a supply curve to the right; quantity of Red Hot Chili Pepper CDs supplied will rise from Q_0 to Q_1 as shown in the graph on the right. (69)

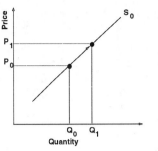

10. To derive a supply curve from a supply table, you plot each point on the supply table on a graph and connect the points. This is shown on the graph on the right. (70)

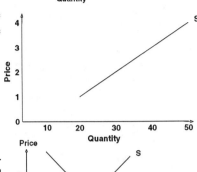

11. The first dynamic law of supply and demand states that (a) when quantity demanded is greater than quantity supplied, prices tend to rise and (b) when quantity supplied is greater than quantity demanded, prices tend to fall. Each case is demonstrated in the graph on the right. Price tends away from P_1 and P_2 and toward P_0. (72-73)

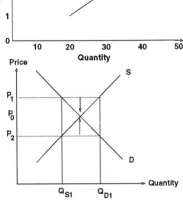

12. The second dynamic law of supply and demand states that in a market, the larger the difference between quantity supplied and quantity demanded, the greater the pressure on prices to rise (if there is excess demand) or fall (if there is excess supply). This demonstrated in the graph on the right. At P_2, the pressure for prices to fall toward P^* is greater than the pressure at P_1 because excess supply is greater at P_2 compared to excess supply at P_1. (73)

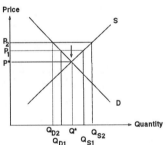

13. Assuming only market forces are operating, at price $3 there is no pressure for prices to change because quantity demanded equals quantity supplied. At $4 and $5, quantity supplied exceeds quantity demanded and there is excess supply; prices will tend to fall. The third dynamic law of supply and demand states that when quantity supplied equals quantity demanded, prices have no tendency to change. (73)

Word Scramble   1. equilibrium   2. supply   3. relative price

Match the Terms and Concepts to Their Definitions
1-b; 2-l; 3-i; 4-j; 5-n; 6-f; 7-g; 8-m; 9-e; 10-a; 11-h; 12-d; 13-k; 14-c; 15-o.

Problems and Exercises

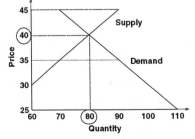

1. The linear curves are shown on the right. (60-69)
   a. As shown in the graph, the downward sloping curve is a demand curve. We deduce this from the law of demand: more of a good will be demanded the lower its price. (60-69)
   b. As shown in the graph, the upward sloping curve is a supply curve. We deduce this from the law of supply: more of a good will be supplied the higher its price. (60-69)
   c. The equilibrium price and quantity are where the demand and supply curves intersect. This is at $P = \$40$, $Q = 80$. At a price above $40, such as $45, quantity supplied exceeds quantity demanded and there is pressure for price to fall. At a price below $40, such as $35, quantity demanded exceeds quantity supplied and there is pressure for price to rise. (60-69)

2. a. The market demand table is the summation of individual quantities demanded at each price as follows (64-65):

Price	Market quantity demanded
$7	73
10	52
13	40
16	31
19	23
22	14

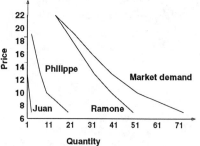

b. The individual and market demand curves are shown to the right of the demand table. (64-65)

c. At $13 a disc, total market demand is 40 discs. Total market demand falls to 23 when the price of discs rises to $19 per disc. (64-65)

d. Quantity demanded at each price rises by 25% for each individual and for the market as a whole. The new demand table is shown below. Graphically, both the individual and market demand curves shift to the right. The graph on the right shows the rightward shift in market demand. (64-65)

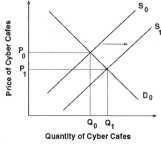

Price	Juan	Philippe	Ramone	Market
$7	3.75	25	62.50	91.25
$10	2.50	12.5	50	65
$13	1.25	8.75	40	50
$16	0	6.25	32.5	38.75
$19	0	3.75	25	28.75
$21	0	0	17.5	17.5

3. A hypothetical market for cyber cafes is drawn on the right. (76-77)

a. A technological breakthrough that lowers the cost of computers will shift the supply of cyber cafes to the right as shown. Equilibrium price will fall. Equilibrium quantity will rise. (76-77)

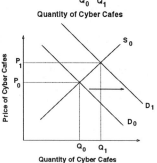

b. A rise in consumers' income will shift the demand for cyber cafes to the right as shown in the graph to the right. Equilibrium price will rise. Equilibrium quantity will rise. (76-77)

c. If a fee is charged to coffee houses to use the Internet, the supply of cyber cafes will shift to the left as shown. Equilibrium price will rise. Equilibrium quantity will fall. (76-77)

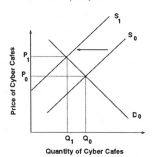

d. If the price of newspapers in print rises, the demand for cyber cafes will shift to the right as shown. Equilibrium price will rise. Equilibrium quantity will rise. (76-77)

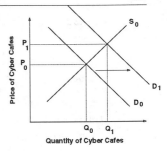

e. If possible suppliers expect cyber cafes to become more popular, the supply of cyber cafes will shift to the right as shown. Equilibrium price will fall. Equilibrium quantity will rise. (76-77)

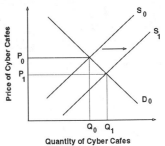

4. a. This innovation will shift the supply curve to the right. Equilibrium price will fall. Equilibrium quantity will rise. (76-77)

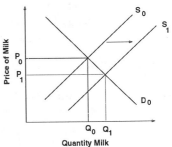

b. The market demand and supply for apple juice is shown on the right. As a result of the fall in milk prices, the demand for apple juice shifts to the left. Equilibrium price will fall. Equilibrium quantity will fall. (76-77)

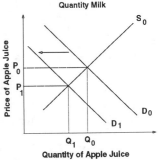

A1. a. Equating Q_s to Q_d and then solving for equilibrium price gives us $3 per quart. Substituting $3 into either the demand or supply equation, we find that equilibrium quantity is 5 million quarts. (81-83)

b. Since supply increases by 20 million quarts, the new supply equation is $Q_s = 10 + 5P$. Equating this with the demand equation, we find the new equilibrium price to be $1 per quart. Substituting into either the new supply equation or the demand equation we find that equilibrium quantity is 15 million quarts. (81-83)

c. With demand increasing, the new demand equation is $Q_d = 30 - 5P$. Setting Q_s equal to Q_d and solving for price we find equilibrium price to be $4 per quart. Substituting this into either the new demand or supply equation we find equilibrium quantity to be 10 million quarts. (81-83)

A2. a. Setting the demand and supply equations equal to one another, we find equilibrium price of 3 takas per ear cleaner. Substituting 3 takas into either the demand or supply equation we find equilibrium quantity to be 4 thousand ear cleaners. (81-83)

b. With increased demand for ear cleaners, the new demand equation becomes $Q_d = 60 - 12P$. Setting supply equal to demand, we find that the new equilibrium price is 4 takas per ear cleaner. Substituting 4 takas into either the demand or supply equation, we find equilibrium quantity to be 12 thousand ear cleaners. (81-83)

c. As supply rises by 10 thousand ear cleaners, the new supply equation becomes $Q_s = -10 + 8P$. Setting this new supply equation equal to the demand equation, we find equilibrium price to be 2.5 takas. Substituting 2.5 takas into either the demand or supply equation, we find equilibrium quantity to be 10 thousand ear cleaners. (81-83)

Multiple Choice

1. a   As discussed on page 60, the correct answer is a. A possible answer is d, which is a restatement of the law of demand, but since the actual law was among the choices, and is more precise, a is the correct answer.

2. c   As discussed on pages 62 and 63, it is important to distinguish between a change in the quantity demanded and a change in demand. Weather is a shift factor of demand, so demand, not quantity demanded, will increase. Supply will not increase; the quantity supplied will, however. Who knows what will happen to the quality demanded?—We don't.

3. b   As discussed on pages 62 and 63, when the price falls there is a movement along the demand curve which is expressed by saying the quantity demanded increased.

4. c   As discussed on page 62, in partial equilibrium analysis one assumes other things constant but keeps these other things in the back of one's mind and adds them back later.

5. c   The price of this good is the only one of the four that would cause a movement along a demand curve. The others are all shift factors. Some of you may have thought that 'a' was a possible answer since, generally, a rise in the price of another good shifts the demand curve for a good out, not in. That's true generally, but there are cases where goods are complements and the rise in the price of another good will shift the demand for this good in. Since c is clearly a correct answer, you didn't have to know this information to answer the question. We suggest the following rule: if one answer fits choose it; worry about fine distinctions later and only if you have time. If you can' t figure out whether one answer might be right, choose the one you are sure is right. See page 63.

6. c   As is discussed on page 60, it is important to remember that partial equilibrium supply/demand analysis refers to relative price. This question focuses on one dimension of that relative price issue. Since all prices went up in the same proportion, the relative price of pencils has not changed. Therefore, the law of demand would predict no change in the quantity demanded of pencils.

7. b   This demand curve is the only demand curve that goes through all the points in the table. See page 64.

8. a   This is a hard question at this point in the course because it is not explicitly discussed in the text. However, the basic ideas are found from pages 60 to 63 of the text, and if you understand the idea behind the law of demand, you will be able to deduce that the more substitutes, the flatter the demand curve, assuming roughly the same quantities are demanded and they are drawn on the same axes. The reason is that an equal rise in price will cause individuals to switch to other goods more, the more substitutes there are.

9. a   As discussed in the text on pages 64 and 65 (Exhibit 4), market demand curves are determined by adding individuals' demand curves horizontally.

10. a   Since the market demand curve is arrived at by adding the individual demand curves horizontally, it will always be flatter. See page 65.

11. b   The curve slopes downward, so we can surmise that it is a demand curve; and the two points are on the demand curve, so the movement represents an increase in the quantity demanded, not an increase in demand. A shift in demand would be a shift of the entire curve. (See Exhibit 2, page 63 of the text.)

12. a   As discussed on page 68, the law of supply is stated in a. The others either have the movement in the wrong direction or are not holding all other things constant.

13. b   It is a shift in supply because the curve is upward sloping; and it's a shift of the entire curve, so it is not a movement along. See page 69.

14. c   The market supply curve is determined by the horizontal addition of individual supply curves. See pages 70-72.

15. c   As discussed on page 70, technology is a shift factor of supply so it must be a shift of the supply curve. Since it is an improvement, it must be a shift downward—at each quantity the price will be lower.

16. b   When there is excess demand, demanders start searching for new suppliers, as discussed on page 73.

17. d   This is an example of the second dynamic law of supply and demand: the greater the difference between quantity supplied and quantity demanded, the greater the pressure for the prices to rise or fall. See pages 73-74.

18. d   There is no way of choosing among a, b, and c without knowing the relative strengths and direction of these other forces. The other forces are likely to move the equilibrium price away from B, but they might be working against each other, leaving equilibrium price unchanged. So the best answer is d. See pages 71-74.

19. b   Since this statement says demand increases, it is the demand curve shifting. Assuming an upward sloping supply curve, that means that quantity will rise and price will rise. See page 77.

20. a   A flood will likely bring about a significant increase in the demand for bottled water since a flood makes most other water undrinkable. Assuming an upward sloping supply curve, this will cause the price of bottled water to rise. See pages 76-77.

A1. a.   Setting the supply and demand equations equal to one another we find equilibrium price and quantity to be option a. (81)

A2. d.   The new demand equation is $Q_d = 130 - 5P$. Setting this equal to the supply equation and solving for equilibrium P and Q gives you option d. (81-83)

A3. c.   The new demand equation is $Q_d = 90 - 5P$. Setting this equal to the supply equation and solving for equilibrium P and Q gives you option c. (81-83)

A4. c.   The new supply equation is $Q_s = -33 + 7P$. Setting this equal to the supply equation and solving for equilibrium P and Q gives you option c. (81-83)

A5. b.   The new demand and supply equation are $Q_d = 42 - 8P$ and $Q_s = -33 + 7P$ respectively. Setting this equal to the supply equation and solving for equilibrium P and Q gives you option b. (81-83)

Chapter 4: Using Supply and Demand

Chapter at a glance

1. Price ceilings cause shortages; price floors cause surpluses. (86, 91)

   A price ceiling is a legal price set by government below equilibrium. A price floor is a legal price set by government above equilibrium.

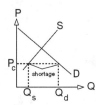 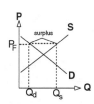

   Price Ceiling   **Price Floor**

2. Supply and demand can shed light on a variety of real-world events. (86-89)

   Supply and demand analysis is not just an academic exercise! Businesspeople, policy makers, and others find it extremely useful. You can too. See "Problems and Applications" and "Brain Teasers" for this and the last chapter.

3. As long as one remembers what prices and quantities go on each axis, exchange rate determination can be described by supply and demand graphs. (90-91)

   Most countries' currencies are traded in foreign exchange markets. The interaction of demand and supply determines the currency's value (price)–just as if does for any other good.

4. Taxes and tariffs raise price and reduce quantity. Quotas are a numerical limit on the number imported. (95-97)

   A tariff is an excise tax on an imported good. Any excise tax imposed on suppliers shifts the supply curve up by the amount of the tax. Rarely is the tax __entirely__ passed on to consumers in the form of a higher price. Although a quota can have the same effect as a tariff, suppliers prefer quotas becuase the suppliers get the revenues.

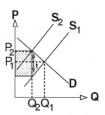

   With tax t, price rises to P_2 and the government collects revenue shown by the shaded region. A quota Q_2 has the same effect on price and quantity. The difference is in who gets the revenue.

5. When analyzing the aggregate, small effects that can be put aside in micro can add up, and hence cannot be forgotten. (97-98)

   The fallacy of composition is the false assumption that what is true for a part will also be true for the whole. This means that what is true in microeconomics, may not be true in macroeconomics.

6. When there is an interdependence between supply and demand, a movement along one curve can cause a shift of the other curve. Thus, supply and demand analysis used alone is not enough to determine where the equilibrium will be. (99-100)

   When the "other things are constant" assumption is not realistic, then feedback effects can become relevant. The degree of interdependence differs among various sets of issues. That is why there is a separate micro and macro analysis–microeconomics and macroeconomics.

   See also, Appendix A: "Algebraic Representation of Interferences with Demand and Supply."

Short-answer questions

1. What is a price ceiling? Demonstrate graphically the effect of a price ceiling on a market. (LO1)

2. What is a price floor? Demonstrate graphically the effect of a price floor on a market. (LO1)

3. Demonstrate graphically what happens to the equilibrium price and quantity of m&ms if they suddenly become more popular. (LO2)

4. Demonstrate graphically what happens to the equilibrium price and quantity of oranges if a frost destroys 50 percent of the orange crop. (LO2)

5. Demonstrate graphically what happens in the following situation: Income in the U.S. rose in the 1990s and more and more people began to buy luxury items such as caviar. However, about that same time, the dissolution of the Soviet Union threw suppliers of caviar from the Caspian Sea into a mire of bureaucracy, reducing their ability to export caviar. Market: Caviar sold in the United States. (LO2)

6. Draw the supply and demand for U.S. dollars, remembering to label the axes. Explain what creates the demand and supply for U.S. dollars. (LO3)

7. Demonstrate graphically how the government maintains a fixed exchange rate when demand for its currency rises. (LO3)

8. Why are rent controls likely to worsen an existing shortage of housing? (LO1)

9. Demonstrate graphically what happens to equilibrium price and quantity when a tariff is imposed on imports. (LO4)

10. What is the difference between partial equilibrium and general equilibrium analysis? (LO5)

11. How is the fallacy of composition related to why economists separate micro from macro economics? (LO5)

12. What happens to equilibrium price and quantity when supply and demand are interdependent? (LO6)

Word Scramble

1. _____ _____   2._____   3._____ __ _____

    creip   gcielni   prietondieca   yalfcla   fo   npscimtiooo

Match the Terms and Concepts to Their Definitions

___ 1. price ceiling

___ 2. price floor

___ 3. depreciation

___ 4. nonconvertible currency

___ 5. fixed exchange rate

___ 6. rent control

___ 7. excise tax

___ 8. tariff

___ 9. quota

___ 10. partial equilibrium analysis

___ 11. fallacy of composition

a. A fall in the exchange rate.
b. Analysis that is partial or incomplete and holds other things equal.
c. Tax that is levied on a specific good.
d. The false assumption that what is true for a part will also be true for the whole.
e. A government-imposed limit on how high a price can be charged.
f. A quantitative restriction on the amount that one country can export to another.
g. Price ceiling on rents set by government.
h. A government-imposed limit on how low a price can be charged.
i. The rate at which a currency can be exchanged is set by the government.
j. A currency that cannot be freely exchanged except at the government set rate.
k. Excise tax on an imported good.

Problems and Exercises

1. The following table depicts the market supply and demand for milk in the United States.

Price in dollars per gallon	Quantity of gallons supplied in 1,000 of gallons	Quantity of gallons demanded in 1,000 of gallons
$1.50	600	800
$1.75	620	720
$2.00	640	640
$2.25	660	560
$2.50	680	480

a. Graph the market supply and demand for milk.

b. What is the equilibrium market price and quantity in the market?

c.   Show the effect of a government imposed price floor of $2.25 on the market price, quantity supplied, and quantity demanded.

d.   Show the effect of a government imposed price ceiling of $2.25 on the market price, quantity supplied, and quantity demanded.

e.   Show the effect of a government imposed price ceiling of $1.75 on the market price, quantity supplied, and quantity demanded.

f.   Show the effect of a government subsidy of $0.50 per gallon on the market demand and market supply table. What happens to the equilibrium price and quantity for milk? (You do not need to give specific values).

2.   What would happen to equilibrium price and quantity in the previous problem if the government imposes a $1 per gallon tax on the sellers and as a result supply decreases by 100 thousand gallons? What price would the sellers receive?

3.   Graphically show market demand and supply curves with government-set prices that best described the market for the majority of consumer goods in Soviet-style socialist economies.

4. Suppose 1994 Phoenix Suns games with 200,000 tickets sell out in preseason at a price of $30. Some people did not get tickets. Also assume that tickets are scalped during the season. ("Scalping" is the name given to the buying of tickets at a low price and reselling them at a high price.)

   a. Demonstrate this situation at preseason with supply and demand curves.

   b. Demonstrate the effect of an unbeaten Suns record on the supply and demand for scalped tickets mid-season. What happens to equilibrium price?

5. The invention of a self-milking cow machine allows cows to milk themselves. Not only does this reduce the need for higher-cost human assistance in milking, but it also allows the cow to milk herself three times a day instead of two, leading to both a healthier cow and increased milk production.

   a. Show the effect of this innovation on the equilibrium quantity and price of milk.

   b. Suppose farmers have decried the effects of this new technology on price and have lobbied the government to set the price floor for milk at the price before the invention. Show the result for equilibrium price, quantity supplied, and quantity demanded in the market.

6. Describe what likely happens to market price and quantity for the particular goods in each of the following cases:

   a. A technological breakthrough lowers the costs of producing tractors in India while there is an increase in incomes of all citizens in India. Market: tractors.

   b. The United States imposes a ban on the sales of oil companies that do business with Libya and Iran. At the same time, very surprisingly, a large reserve of drillable oil is discovered in Barrington, Rhode Island. Market: Oil.

   c.   In the summer of 1996, many people watched the Atlanta Summer Olympics on NBC instead of going to the movies. At the same time, thinking that summer time is the peak season for movies, Hollywood released a record number of movies. Market: movie tickets.

   d.   After a promotional visit by Michael Jordan to France, a craze for Nike Air shoes develops, while a worker strike in Nike's manufacturing plants in Honduras decreases the production of these shoes. Market: Nike shoes.

   e.   Due to restored political and economic stability, demand for tourism and foreign investment in South Africa increases. At the same time, an increased number of South Africans want to hold their own currency. Market: SA rand. (The rand is the South African currency.)

7.   The supply and demand for Ireland's currency, the punt, is given by the following diagram. It currently trades at price of P_1.

   a.   If left to the market, would the punt appreciate or depreciate? Would goods imported into Ireland become more or less expensive?

   b.   What does its government need to do to maintain the exchange rate fixed at P_1?

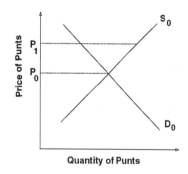

8.   Buchananland wants to restrict its number of auto imports from Zachstan. It is trying to decide whether it should impose a tariff or set quotas on Zachstani cars. With the help of a diagram, explain why auto makers in Zachstan have hired a lobbyist to persuade the government of Buchananland to set quotas instead of imposing tariffs.

A1. The supply and demand equations for roses are given by $Q_s = -10 + 3P$ and $Q_d = 20 - 2P$ respectively, where P is dollars per dozen roses and Q is dozens of roses in hundred thousands.

    a.   What is the equilibrium market price and quantity of roses sold?

    b.   Suppose the government decides to make it more affordable for individuals to be able to give roses to their significant others, and sets a price ceiling for roses at $4 a dozen. What is the likely result?

    c.   It is highly likely that because of the resulting distortion in the market due to the price ceiling at $4, a number of highly dedicated, and perhaps desperate, individuals will resort to buying roses for their significant others in the black market. What will the black market price for roses likely be?

    d.   Suppose the government decides to tax the suppliers of roses $1 per dozen roses sold. What is the equilibrium price and quantity in the market? How much do buyers pay for each rose they buy for their significant others? How much do suppliers receive for each rose they sell?

    e.   Suppose the government decides instead to impose a $1 tax on buyers for each dozen roses purchased. (Government has determined buying roses for love to be a demerit good.) What is the equilibrium price and quantity in the market? How much do the buyers pay, and the sellers receive?

Multiple Choice Questions

1. If there is an effective price ceiling
    a. the quantity demanded exceeds the quantity supplied.
    b. the quantity supplied exceeds the quantity demanded.
    c. the demand exceeds supply.
    d. the supply exceeds demand.

2. If a price ceiling is instituted that is above the equilibrium price, then
    a. the quantity demanded exceeds the quantity supplied.
    b. the quantity supplied exceeds the quantity demanded.
    c. the quantity supplied equals the quantity demanded.
    d. the demand exceeds the supply.

3. If the government institutes a price floor at P_0 in the accompanying diagram, which of the following represents the likely quantity supplied?
    a. Q_0.
    b. Q_1.
    c. Q_2.
    d. Q_3.

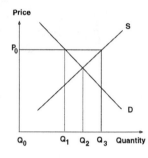

4. If the government institutes a price floor at P_0 in the accompanying diagram, which of the following points represents the likely quantity supplied?
    a. Q_0.
    b. Q_1.
    c. Q_2.
    d. Q_3.

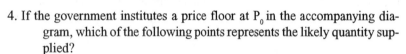

5. The equilibrium price in a market is given in the graph on the right. Is this economy most likely
    a. a socialist economy?
    b. a capitalist economy?
    c. a Soviet-style socialist economy?
    d. a welfare capitalist economy?

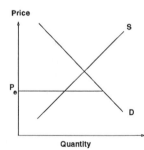

6. If the government set rent controls at P_c the black market rental price of housing will be
    a. P_c.
    b. P_e.
    c. P_m.
    d. at or between P_c and P_m.

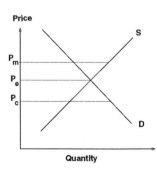

7. What will likely happen to the price and quantity of Gillette's Advanced Performance shaving cream as demand for it increases?
    a. The price will rise, and as a result, quantity will fall.
    b. Both price and quantity will rise.
    c. The price will fall, and quantity will rise.
    d. The price will fall, what happens to quantity is not clear.

8. Assume that the cost of shipping automobiles from the U.S. to Japan decreases. What will likely happen to the equilibrium price and quantity of cars made in the U.S. and sold in Japan?
    a. The price will rise, and quantity will fall.
    b. Both price and quantity will rise.
    c. The price will fall, and quantity will rise.
    d. The price will fall, what happens to quantity is not clear.

9. What will likely happen to equilibrium price and quantity of paper if school enrollment increases while a tornado destroys the largest paper mill in Tanzania?
    a. The price will increase, and so will quantity.
    b. The price will increase, and quantity will decrease.
    c. The price will decrease, but what happens to quantity is not clear.
    d. The price will increase, but what happens to quantity is not clear.

10. What will likely happen to the price and quantity of light bulbs as the costs of manufacturing them increases, while cheap alternative solar bulbs invented by University of Colorado student Paolo Raden are introduced into the market?
    a. The price will decrease, but what happens to quantity is not clear.
    b. What happens to price isn't clear, but quantity will increase
    c. What happens to price isn't clear, but quantity will decrease.
    d. It is not clear what happens to either price or quantity.

11. What will likely happen to price and quantity of roses in Babylon if the major purchasers of roses, women, decide that men (for whom women buy the roses) are too unreasonable to deal with, while the men, in frustration, destroy many commercial rose gardens?
    a. The price will decrease, but what happens to quantity is not clear.
    b. What happens to price isn't clear, but quantity will increase
    c. What happens to price isn't clear, but quantity will decrease.
    d. It is not clear what happens to either price or quantity.

12. What will likely happen to the price and quantity of cricket bats in Trinidad as interest in cricket dwindles following the dismal performance of the national cricket team, while at the same time taxes are repealed on producing cricket bats?
    a. The price will decrease, but what happens to quantity is not clear.
    b. The price will decrease, and quantity will increase.
    c. The price will increase, but what happens to quantity is not clear.
    d. It is not clear what happens to either price or quantity.

13. What will likely happen to the price of Venezuelan currency (Bolivars) in terms of dollars if demand for its exports falls while its nationals want to get their money out of Venezuela due to economic instability?
    a. It will fall.
    b. It will basically remain the same.
    c. It will rise.
    d. It is difficult to say.

14. In the foreign exchange market for Mexican pesos and U.S. dollars, the demand for the peso reflects
    a. The demand by Mexican citizens for U.S. goods.
    b. The demand by U.S. citizens for Mexican goods.
    c. The supply by Mexican citizens of Mexican goods.
    d. The demand by Mexican citizens for Mexican goods.

15. If a currency has appreciated in value, you know that
    a. It will take more of the currency that has appreciated to buy other currencies.
    b. It will take less of the currency that has appreciated to buy other currencies.
    c. Foreign goods will cost more to import.
    d. Domestic goods will cost less to foreigners.

16. What will likely happen to the value of the Malaysian ringgit in terms of dollars as more foreigners want to invest in Malaysia, and at the same time Mahathir Perot, a wealthy Malaysian businessman, decides to sell his huge holdings of Malaysian ringgit?
    a. It will fall.
    b. It will remain the same.
    c. It will rise.
    d. It is difficult to say.

17. A fixed exchange rate involves a currency
    a. that cannot be freely exchanged except at the government set rate.
    b. that can be exchanged freely.
    c. where the rate at which a currency can be exchanged is set by government.
    d. where the rate which is maintained by the invisible handshake.

18. Under a fixed exchange rate, if there is excess demand for its currency, the government
    a. must reduce the supply of its currency.
    b. must increase the supply of its currency.
    c. must increase the demand for its currency.
    d. must let the invisible hand operate.

19. Given the supply and demand curves on the right, to impose the equivalent of a quota of 5,000 computers, the amount of tariff that has to be imposed on each computer is
    a. below $2,000.
    b. $2,000.
    c. $2,500.
    d. above $2,500.

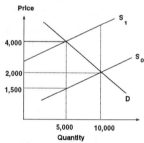

20. For governments
    a. tariffs are profitable compared to quotas because tariffs can help them collect revenues.
    b. quotas are profitable compared to tariffs because quotas can help them collect revenues.
    c. neither quotas nor tariffs can help collect revenues.
    d. both quotas and tariffs are sources of revenues.

21. The fallacy of composition is
    a. the false assumption that what is false for a part will also be false for the whole.
    b. the false assumption that what is true for a part will also be true for the whole.
    c. the false assumption that what is false for a whole will also be false for the part.
    d. the false assumption that what is true for a whole will also be true for the part.

22. Partial equilibrium analysis is most likely applicable without modification for interdependencies to
    a. the egg market.
    b. the aggregate labor market.
    c. the aggregate goods market.
    d. the savings/investment market.

A1. The supply and demand equations for umbrellas in Holland are $Q_s = -30 + 10P$ and $Q_d = 95 - 15P$ respectively, where P is the guilder price of umbrellas and Q is thousands of umbrellas per week. The Dutch government sets a price ceiling for umbrellas at 4 guilder per umbrella. What will likely happen in the market for umbrellas?
    a. Quantity supplied will exceed quantity demanded by 10 umbrellas per week.
    b. Quantity supplied will exceed quantity demanded by 25 umbrellas per week.
    c. Quantity demanded will exceed quantity supplied by 15 umbrellas per week.
    d. Quantity demanded will exceed quantity supplied by 25 umbrellas per week.

A2. The supply and demand equations for umbrellas in Holland are $Q_s = -30 + 10P$ and $Q_d = 95 - 15P$ respectively, where P is the guilder price of umbrellas and Q is thousands of umbrellas per week. (The same as in A1.) What will likely happen if the floor is set at 4 guilder?
    a. Quantity supplied will exceed quantity demanded by 10 umbrellas per week.
    b. Quantity supplied will exceed quantity demanded by 25 umbrellas per week.
    c. Quantity demanded will exceed quantity supplied by 15 umbrellas per week.
    d. Quantity demanded will equal quantity supplied.

A3. The supply and demand equations for Arizona Ice Tea in Arizona is given by $Q_s = -10 + 6P$ and $Q_d = 40 - 8P$; P is price of each bottle in dollars; and quantity is in hundreds of thousands of bottles per month. Suppose the state government imposes a $1 per bottle tax on the suppliers. The market price the suppliers receive and the equilibrium quantity in the market are
    a. $3 per bottle and 8 hundred thousand bottles per month.
    b. $3 per bottle and 16 hundred thousand bottles per month.
    c. $4 per bottle and 8 hundred thousand bottles per month.
    d. $4 per bottle and 16 hundred thousand bottles per month.

A4. The supply and demand equations for Arizona Ice Tea in Arizona is given by $Q_s = -10 + 6P$ and $Q_d = 40 - 8P$; P is price of each bottle in dollars, quantity in hundreds of thousands of bottles per month. (The same as in A4.) Suppose the state government imposes a $1 per bottle tax on the demanders. The likely price the suppliers receive and the equilibrium quantity after the tax is imposed are
    a. $3 per bottle and 8 hundred thousand.
    b. $44/14 per bottle and 208/14 hundred thousand.
    c. $4 per bottle and 8 hundred thousand.
    d. $58/14 per bottle and 208/14 hundred thousand.

Answers

Short-Answer Questions

1. A price ceiling is a government imposed limit on how high a price can be charged. An effective price ceiling below market equilibrium price will cause $Q_D > Q_S$ as shown in the graph on the right. (86)

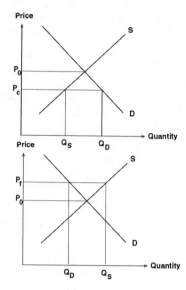

2. A price floor is a government imposed limit on how low a price can be charged. An effective price floor above market equilibrium price will cause $Q_S > Q_D$ as shown in the graph on the right. (91)

3. Increasing popularity of m&ms means that at every price, more m&ms are demanded. The demand curve shifts out to D_1, and both equilibrium price and quantity rise to P_1 and Q_1 respectively. (86-90)

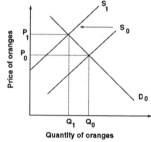

4. A frost damaging oranges means that at every price, suppliers are willing to supply fewer oranges. The supply curve shifts to the left to S_1, and equilibrium price rises to P_1, and quantity falls to Q_1. (86-90)

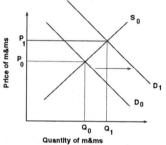

5. The demand curve for Russian caviar shifts out; the supply shifts in; the price rises substantially. What happens to quantity depends upon the relative sizes of the shifts. (86-90)

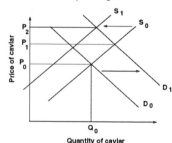

6. The demand and supply for U.S. dollars is shown in the graph on the right. The y-axis is labelled "price of U.S. dollars in foreign currency per U.S. dollar" and the x-axis is labelled "quantity of U.S. dollars." The demand for U.S. dollars is created by the demand by foreigners for U.S. goods and assets. The supply of U.S. dollars is created by the demand by U.S. citizens for foreign goods and assets. (86-91)

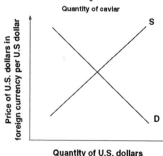

7. With a fixed exchange rate, the government adjusts its demand or supply for its currency to offset any change in private or international demand or supply for the currency so that it can maintain the exchange rate fixed. Supposing the demand for currency shifts out to D_1, to keep the exchange rate constant, the government must increase the supply of currency to S_1. (90-91)

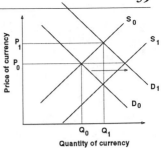

8. Rent controls are price ceilings and result in shortages in rental housing. As time passes and as the population rises, and the demand for rental housing also rises, other ventures become more lucrative relative to renting out housing. Owners have less incentive to repair existing buildings, let alone build new ones, further reducing the supply of rental housing. The housing shortage increases. (92-94)

9. As a tariff of t is imposed, the supply curve shifts leftward to S_1 by the amount of the tariff. The equilibrium price goes up and quantity goes down. (95)

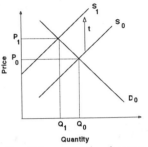

10. Partial equilibrium is the analysis that is partial or incomplete because it holds other things equal, whereas general equilibrium is the analysis that considers all changes. (97)

11. Fallacy of composition is the false assumption that what is true for a part will also be true for the whole. In micro, economists isolate an individual person's or firm's behavior and consider its effects, while the many side effects are kept in the background. In macro, those side effects become too large and can no longer be held constant. These side effects are what account for the interdependence of supply and demand. Macro, thus, is not simply a summation of all micro results; it would be a fallacy of composition to take the sum of each individual's (micro) actions and say that it is the aggregate (macro) result. (97-98)

12. When supply and demand are interdependent, a movement along one curve can cause a shift in the other curve. Equilibrium price and quantity change as there is movement toward equilibrium. (98-100)

Word Scramble   1. price ceiling   2. depreciation   3. fallacy of composition

Match the Terms and Concepts with Their Definitions
1-e; 2-h; 3-a; 4-j; 5-i; 6-g; 7-c; 8-k; 9-f; 10-b; 11-d.

Problems and Exercises

1. a. The market supply and demand for milk is graphed on the right.
   b. The equilibrium market price is $2 and equilibrium quantity in the market is 640 thousand gallons of milk. This is point A on the graph on the right. (84-86)

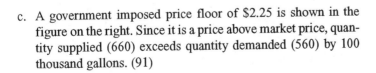

   c. A government imposed price floor of $2.25 is shown in the figure on the right. Since it is a price above market price, quantity supplied (660) exceeds quantity demanded (560) by 100 thousand gallons. (91)

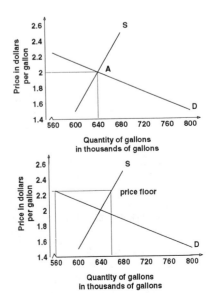

d. A government imposed price ceiling of $2.25 will have no effect on the market price of $2 per gallon since it is a ceiling above equilibrium price. Equilibrium quantity in the market remains at 640 thousand gallons. This is shown on the right. (84-86)

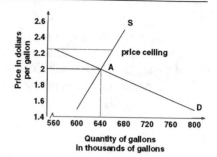

e. A government imposed price ceiling of $1.75 is below market price. Quantity supplied (620 thousand gallons) will be less than quantity demanded (720 thousand gallons) by 100 thousand gallons as shown on the right. (85-86)

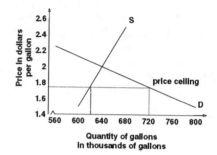

f. A government subsidy of $0.50 per gallon will change the market supply and demand table as follows:

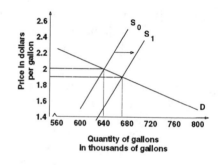

Price in dollars per gallon	Quantity of gallons supplied in 1,000 of gallons	Quantity of gallons demanded in 1,000 of gallons
$1.50	640	800
$1.75	660	720
$2.00	680	640
$2.25	700	560
$2.50	720	480

The supply curve shifts to the right as shown in the figure on the right side of the demand table. Equilibrium price will be lower than $2 and equilibrium quantity will be higher than 640 thousand gallons, though from the table it is not clear where precisely they will be. (95-96)

2. Because of the tax, the quantity supplied for every price level will decline. The supply and demand table will change as follows:

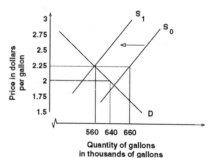

Price in dollars per gallon	Quantity of gallons supplied in 1,000 of gallons	Quantity of gallons demanded in 1,000 of gallons
$1.50	500	800
$1.75	520	720
$2.00	540	640
$2.25	560	560
$2.50	580	480

The market equilibrium price would be $2.25 and quantity would be 560 thousand gallons.   Since the sellers will have to pay $1 tax on every gallon they sell, they will receive $1.25 per gallon milk. (95-96)

3. In Soviet-style socialist countries, prices of most consumer goods tended to be set below market equilibrium prices. The result was a shortage of goods. As shown on the graph to the right, at the price ceiling P_c, quantity demanded exceeds quantity supplied. (85-86)

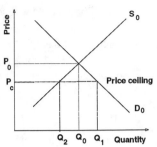

4. a. This situation is shown on the right. Supply is perfectly elastic at $30 until the maximum number of tickets, at which point it becomes perfectly inelastic. After 200,000 tickets are sold, no tickets are available at any price from the ticket booth. The demand curve can be any number of places on this graph, but it must intersect the supply curve at or to the right of 200,000 tickets. (88-89)

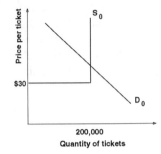

   b. After preseason tickets are sold, the supply curve for tickets is now upward sloping (until the 200,000 level) because some current ticket holders are willing to sell their tickets (scalping). An unbeaten Suns record shifts the demand for Suns tickets to the right, increasing the scalping price of tickets. This is shown on the right. (88-89)

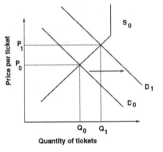

5. a. This innovation will shift the supply curve to the right. Equilibrium price will fall. Equilibrium quantity will rise. (88-89)

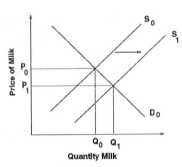

   b. A price floor for milk at the price before the invention is shown on the right as $P_f = P_0$. Quantity supplied, Q_1, exceeds quantity demanded, Q_0. (91-92)

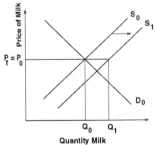

6. a. The supply curve will shift out from S_0 to S_1 as the new technology makes it cheaper to produce tractors. Increased incomes will shift the demand for tractors out from D_0 to D_1. Equilibrium price may go up, remain the same, or go down, depending on the relative shifts in the two curves. Equilibrium quantity, however, will definitely increase. (88-89)

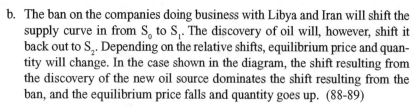

b. The ban on the companies doing business with Libya and Iran will shift the supply curve in from S_0 to S_1. The discovery of oil will, however, shift it back out to S_2. Depending on the relative shifts, equilibrium price and quantity will change. In the case shown in the diagram, the shift resulting from the discovery of the new oil source dominates the shift resulting from the ban, and the equilibrium price falls and quantity goes up. (88-89)

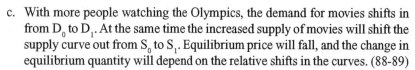

c. With more people watching the Olympics, the demand for movies shifts in from D_0 to D_1. At the same time the increased supply of movies will shift the supply curve out from S_0 to S_1. Equilibrium price will fall, and the change in equilibrium quantity will depend on the relative shifts in the curves. (88-89)

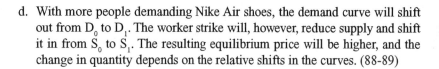

d. With more people demanding Nike Air shoes, the demand curve will shift out from D_0 to D_1. The worker strike will, however, reduce supply and shift it in from S_0 to S_1. The resulting equilibrium price will be higher, and the change in quantity depends on the relative shifts in the curves. (88-89)

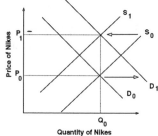

e. With increased demand for tourism and foreign investment in South Africa, the demand for its currency will increase, shifting the demand curve out from D_0 to D_1. At the same time, because more South Africans want to hold their own currency, the supply curve will shift in. The exchange rate will appreciate. The quantity traded will go up or down depending on the relative shifts in the supply and demand curves. (88-89)

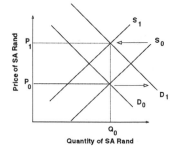

7. a. If left to the market, the punt would depreciate. That is, it would take fewer amounts of a foreign currency to purchase the same number of punts. Since the punts would purchase fewer amounts of a foreign currency, imports would cost more. (90)

b. To maintain the exchange rate at P_1 dollars, which is above the equilibrium price, and therefore at a level where quantity supplied exceeds quantity demanded, the government of Ireland will have to buy Q_1-Q_2 of its own currency. As it will do so, the demand for its currency will shift out from D_0 to D_1. (91-93)

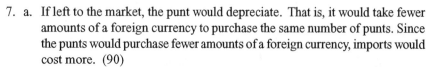
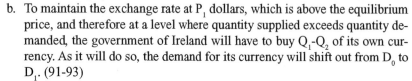

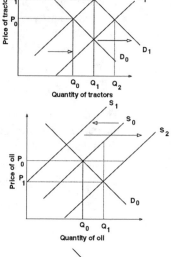
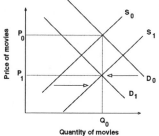
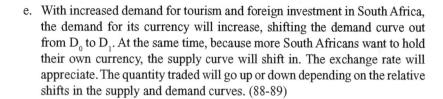
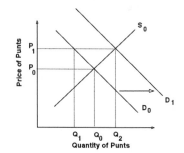

8. The supply and demand equilibrium are at price P_e and quality Q_e. If quotas for Zachstani cars are set at Q_2, the price received for each car sold is P_2, which is well above P_t, the price they would normally sell for at that quantity. A tariff of t would have to be imposed to reduce imports to Q_2 reflected by the supply curve shifting in to S_1. In both cases, consumers pay Zachstan producers P_2 for each car. In the case of the quota, Zachstan producers keep P_2 for each car. In the case of the tariff, Zachstan producers must give up t for each car sold. Profits are higher with the quota. For this reason they have the lobbyist lobbying for quotas. (95-97)

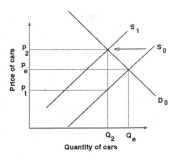

A1.a. Equating Q_s and Q_d, then solving gives equilibrium price \$6 and quantity 8 hundred thousand dozen. (103)

  b. If price ceiling is set at \$4, $Q_s = 2$, and $Q_d = 12$; resulting shortage is 10 hundred thousand dozen. (103)

  c. This is a bit tricky. Since price ceiling is at \$4, only 2 hundred thousand dozen roses will be supplied in the market. To find the black market price you have to see what the demand price of roses will be if quantity is 2 hundred thousand dozen. Solving for $Q = 2$ in the demand equation gives demand price at \$9. The black market price will be somewhere between \$4 and \$9. (103)

  d. If a \$1 tax is imposed on suppliers, the new supply equation will be $Q_s = -10 + 3(P-1) = -13 + 3P$. Equating this with Q_d gives equilibrium price \$6.40 and quantity 6-4/5 hundred thousand. Buyers pay \$6-3/5 for each rose they buy, and the sellers receive \$1 less than that, or \$5-3/5, for each rose they sell. (103)

  e. As a result of the tax, the new demand equation will be $Q_d = 20 - 2(P+1) = 18 - 2P$. Equating this with Q_s gives equilibrium price \$5.40 and quantity 6-4/5 hundred thousand. Buyers pay \$6.40 $(P + 1)$ for each rose they buy, and the sellers receive \$5.40 for each rose they sell. (103)

Multiple Choice

1. a As discussed on page 86, the correct answer here is the quantity demanded exceeds the quantity supplied. You don't use the terms demand and supply because that usage refers to the entire schedule.

2. c Here the answer is the quantity supplied equals the quantity demanded because the price ceiling is put above the equilibrium price and hence is not effective. It would become effective only if the equilibrium price exceeded that price ceiling. See page 86.

3. d You determine the quantity supplied in an effective price floor by determining where the price floor intersects the supply curve. Effective price floors create excess supply. See page 91.

4. c In this case the price floor is not effective, so the market moves to the equilibrium price and quantity Q_2. See page 91.

5. c In reality, Soviet-style socialist economies had shortages. In the others there is less of a reason to believe that the actual price would deviate from market equilibrium price. See page 34 of Chapter 2 and 92 of this chapter.

6. d See discussion on Exhibit 5 in page 92.

7. b As the demand curve shifts out, equilibrium market price and quantity will rise. See pages 88-89 of textbook for related discussion.

8. c As the supply curve will shift out market price will fall while the quantity will rise. See pages 88-89 of text.

9. d As school enrollment increases, the demand curve for paper will shift out. At the same time the supply curve will shift in because of the tornado. Price will definitely rise while quantity will change depending on the relative shifts in the curves. See pages 88-89 of textbook for related discussion.

10. c   The supply curve for light bulbs will shift in due to increased manufacturing costs, while the demand curve will shift in because of the cheap alternatives available. Price will change depending on the relative shifts of the curves while equilibrium quantity will decrease. See pages 88-89 of the textbook for related discussion.

11. c   As both the demand and the supply curve shift in, equilibrium quantity will fall and price will change depending in the relative shifts of the supply and demand curves. See pages 88-89.

12. a   Demand for cricket bats will fall, shifting the demand curve in, while the tax repeal will shift the supply curve out. Price will fall, and quantity will change depending on the relative shifts of the supply and demand curves. Related issues are discussed in pages 88-89 of the textbook.

13. a   With a fall in demand for Venezuela's exports, the demand curve for its currency will shift in, while the supply curve will shift out with its nationals wanting to get their money out of their country. The net result will be that the exchange rate will fall. See discussion pages 90 and 91 of textbook.

14. b   See page 91.

15. b   See page 91.

16. d   Since both demand and supply are increasing, the answer could be a, b, or c. Which it is depends on the relative shifts in the supply and the demand curves. So, d is the correct answer. See discussion on pages 91 and 92 of the textbook.

17. c   See page 92 of book.

18. b   See page 92 of textbook.

19. c   Per computer a tariff of $2,500 is needed to limit supply to 5,000. See page 95 of textbook.

20. a   See discussion on pages 95-97 of the textbook.

21. b   See page 97 of the textbook.

22. a   The smaller the market the more likely partial equilibrium analysis is applicable without modification. (97)

A1. d   Plugging in $P = 4$ in the supply and demand equations gives $Q_s = 10$, and $Q_d = 35$. So, quantity demanded exceeds quantity supplied by 25, and d is the correct answer. See page 103 of the textbook.

A2. d   Since the price floor is set below the equilibrium market price it has no effect on the market, and quantity supplied will equal quantity demanded. See page 103 of the textbook.

A3. a   A $1 per bottle tax on suppliers makes the supply equation $Q_s = -10 + 6(P-1) = -16 + 6P$. Equating this with the demand equation gives equilibrium $P = \$4$ and $Q = 8$ hundred thousand. The supplier receives $3 ($4 − $1). See page 103 of the textbook.

A4. a   A $1 per bottle tax on demanders makes the demand equation $Q_d = 40 - 8(P+1) = 32 - 8P$. Equating this with the supply equation gives equilibrium $P = \$3$ and $Q = 8$ hundred thousand. The supplier receives $3. See page 103 of the textbook.

Chapter 5: U.S. Economic Institutions

Chapter at a glance

1. Ultimately the U.S. economy's strength is its people and its other resources. (105)

   For a bird's-eye view of the U.S. economy see Exhibit 1 (sometimes called the "circular flow of income model"). Be able to draw and explain it.

   Note, there are 3 basic economic institutions:
   1) Businesses:
   *   a. Supply goods in goods market*
   *   b. Demand factors in factor market*
   *   c. Pay taxes and receive benefits from government*
   2) Households:
   *   a. Supply factors*
   *   b. Demand goods*
   *   c. Pay taxes and receive benefits from government*
   3) Government:
   *   a. Demands goods*
   *   b. Demands factors*
   *   c. Collects taxes and provide services*

2. Although businesses decide what to produce, they are guided by consumer sovereignty. (107)

   Businesses produce what consumers want.

3. The advantages and disadvantages of the three forms of business are shown in Exhibit 4 on page 110. (110)

   ✔ *Know the advantages and disadvantages of the three forms of business:*
   *   1) Sole Proprietorship*
   *   2) Partnership*
   *   3) Corporation*

4. Although, in principle, ultimate power resides with the people and households (consumer sovereignty), in practice the representatives of the people–firms and government–are sometimes removed from the people and, in the short run, are only indirectly monitored by the people. (112)

   Note:
   1) Do we control business and government or do they control us?
   2) The distribution of income (rich vs. poor) determines the "for whom" question. If you're rich you get more.
   3) The invisible handshake affects what business and government do or don't do.

5a. Two general roles of government are: (114)
   1. **As an actor:** Collects taxes and spends money.
   2. **As referee:** Sets the rules governing relations between households and businesses.

5b. Seven specific roles of government are: (116)

   1. Providing a stable structure within which markets can operate.

   What the government rules "ought to be" is debatable.

   2. Promoting workable, effective competition.

   Know the different consequences associated with competition vs. monopoly power.

   3. Correcting for external effects of individuals' decisions.

   ✔ *Know the distinction between <u>positive</u> and <u>negative</u> externalities and how government tries to correct for them.*

   4. Providing public goods that the market doesn't adequately supply.

   Government provides these by collecting taxes from everyone to try to eliminate the free-rider problem

5.   Ensuring economic stability and growth.

Government tries to ensure:
   1. Full employment
   2. Low inflation
   3. Economic growth (which increases the
      standard of living)

6.   Providing acceptably fair distribution of society's production among its individuals.

In order to redistribute money and therefore goods the government uses taxes (and other methods).

✔ *Know the difference between progressive, regressive, and proportional taxes.*

VII. Encouraging merit and discouraging demerit goods or activities.

Should government decide what is "good" or "bad" for us?

Government may:
   1) subsidize merit (socially desirable) goods
   2) tax demerit (socially undesirable) goods

✔ *The first 5 specific roles of government are economic roles which are generally less controversial while the last two are political roles.*

✔ *Government intervenes in the economy in an attempt to correct for "market failures." But just as the market can sometimes provide undesirable results, there is also government failure–government intervention which makes things worse.*

See also, Appendix A: "A Deeper Look at Business."
See also, Appendix B: "Households, Culture, and Ideology."

Short-answer questions

1. What are the three groups that comprise the U.S. economy? (LO1)

2. What is the role of each group in the economy? (LO1)

3. Draw a diagrammatic representation of the U.S. economy using these three groups. Label the market in which businesses and households interact. (LO1)

4. Although businesses decide what to produce, who ultimately makes the decision what to produce? (LO2)

5. What are the three major forms of businesses? (LO3)

6. Your friend wants to buy a coin-operated laundramat. Her brother has offered to be a partner in the operation and put up half the money to buy the business. They have come to you for advice about what form of business to create. Of course you oblige, letting them know the advantages and disadvantages of each. (LO3)

7. Why is much of the economic decision making done by business and government even though households have the ultimate power? (LO4)

8. What are two general roles of government? (LO5)

9. What are seven specific roles of government? (LO5)

10. What potential role does the government have when externalities exist? (LO5)

Word Scramble

1. _____ 2._____ 3._____

     c e i i m n o o p t t   r e n t a l i t e x y   f i o p r t

Match the Terms and Concepts to Their Definitions

____ 1. consumer sovereignty

____ 2. corporation

____ 3. entrepreneurship

____ 4. externality

____ 5. free rider

____ 6. macroeconomic externality

____ 7. merit goods or activities

____ 8. monopoly power

____ 9. partnership

____ 10. progressive tax

____ 11. public goods

____ 12. stock

____ 13. market failure

a. Ability to prevent others from entering a business field, which enables a firm to raise its price.

b. Situation in which the market does not lead to a desired result.

c. Business that is treated like a person, legally owned by its stockholders. Its stockholders are not personally liable for the actions of the corporate "person."

d. Business with two or more owners.

e. Certificate of ownership in a company.

f. Effect of a trade or agreement on third parties that people did not take into account when they entered the trade or agreement.

g. Externality that affects the levels of unemployment, inflation, or growth in the economy as a whole.

h. Goods whose consumption by one individual does not prevent their consumption by other individuals.

i. Person who participates in something for free because others have paid for it.

j. Principle that the consumer's wishes rule what's produced.

k. Tax whose rates increase as a person's income increases.

l. The ability to organize and get something done.

m. Things government believes are good for you, although you may not think so.

Problems and Exercises

1. List the three types of businesses from largest in number to smallest in number.

2. List the three types of businesses from largest in annual receipts to smallest in annual receipts.

3. For each of the following, state for which form or forms of business it is an advantage: Sole proprietorships, partnerships, or corporations:

   a. Minimum bureaucratic hassle.

   b. Ability to share work and risks

   c. Direct control by owner.

   d. Relatively easy to form.

   e. No personal liability.

    f.   Increasing ability to get funds.

4.   For each of the following, state for which form or forms of business it is a disadvantage: Sole proprietorships, partnerships, corporations:

    a.   Unlimited personal liability.

    b.   Possible double taxation of income.

    c.   Limited ability to get funds.

    d.   Legal hassle to organize.

5.   Order the following federal government income from largest to smallest: Social insurance taxes and contributions, excise taxes, individual income taxes, corporate income taxes.

6.   Order the following federal expenditures from largest to smallest: Interest, income security, national defense, health and education.

7.   For each of the following state what economic role government is playing or did play: Providing a stable institutional framework, promoting effective and workable competition, correcting for externalities, providing for public goods, ensuring economic stability and growth.

    a.   The judicial system recognizes the value of contracts of exchange between consumers and businesses.

    b.   A municipality prohibits smoking in malls.

    c.   The antitrust division of the government's Justice Department successfully pursued antitrust violations by AT&T in the 1980s.

    d.   The Federal Reserve (a semiautonomous branch of government) tries to keep the economy from overheating and from going into recession.

    e.   The federal government maintains an army.

8.   State for each of the following tax tables whether the tax is progressive, regressive, or proportional.

a.

Tax rate	Income Level
10%	0-$10,000
10	$10,001-$30,000
10	$30,001-$60,000
10	$60,001 and above

b.

Tax rate	Income Level
35%	0-$10,000
30	$10,001-$30,000
25	$30,001-$60,000
20	$60,001 and above

c.

Tax rate	Income Level
8%	0-$10,000
10	$10,001-$30,000
16	$30,001-$60,000
24	$60,001 and above

Multiple Choice Questions

1. The labor force of the United States is approximately
   - a. 100,000 people.
   - b. 50 million people.
   - c. 130 million people.
   - d. 760 million people.

2. The population in the United States is approximately
   - a. 10 million.
   - b. 50 million.
   - c. 270 million.
   - d. 2 billion.

3. The ability to organize and get something done generally goes under the term
   - a. the corporate approach.
   - b. entrepreneurship.
   - c. economicship.
   - d. consumer sovereignty.

4. By number, the largest percentage of businesses are
   - a. partnerships.
   - b. corporations.
   - c. sole proprietorships.
   - d. nonprofit companies.

5. By receipts, the largest percentage of business is undertaken by
   - a. partnerships.
   - b. corporations.
   - c. sole proprietorships.
   - d. nonprofit companies.

6. Over-the-counter stock
    a. is traded on the New York Stock Exchange counter.
    b. is traded on all exchanges.
    c. is traded in odd lots.
    d. is not traded over a counter.

7. An odd lot refers to
    a. a set of shares in a strange company.
    b. shares not traded on the New York Stock Exchange.
    c. a purchase of fewer than 100 shares of a corporation.
    d. any non-even number of shares traded.

8. When a corporation's stock price goes up
    a. the corporation gets more revenue.
    b. the corporation gets less revenue.
    c. the corporation's revenue does not change.
    d. the yield on that company increases.

9. In reality, businesses are usually controlled by
    a. stockholders.
    b. managers.
    c. government.
    d. consumers.

10. The poverty level for a family of four in the United States is approximately
    a. $6,000 per year.
    b. $16,000 per year.
    c. $30,000 per year.
    d. $50,000 per year.

11. The largest percentage of state and local expenditures is on
    a. education.
    b. health and medical care.
    c. highways.
    d. income security.

12. The largest percentage of federal government expenditures is on
    a. income security.
    b. national defense.
    c. education.
    d. interest.

13. If an effect of a trade or agreement between two people affects some other party, that effect is called
    a. a monopoly.
    b. anti-competition.
    c. an externality.
    d. free ridership.

14. An example of a negative externality is
    a. education.
    b. pollution.
    c. government intervention.
    d. monopoly.

15. If the consumption of a good by one individual does not prevent its consumption by another individual, that good is called
    a. a public good.
    b. a private good.
    c. a macroeconomic good.
    d. a demerit good.

16. If the rates of a tax increase as a person's income increases, the tax is
    a. a progressive tax.
    b. a regressive tax.
    c. a proportional tax.
    d. a merit tax.

17. Economic theory says government should
    a. follow a policy of laissez-faire.
    b. get intricately involved in the economy.
    c. not get involved in the economy.
    d. base government intervention upon the costs and benefits.

A1. In the United States the fastest growing sector has been
    a. the manufacturing sector.
    b. the service sector.
    c. the agricultural sector.
    d. the government sector.

Answers

Short-Answer Questions

1. The three groups that comprise the U.S. economy are households, businesses, and government. (106)

2. Households supply factors of production to businesses; business produces goods and services and sells them to households and government. Government taxes businesses and households, buys goods and services from businesses and labor services from households, and provides goods and services to businesses and households. (106)

3. A diagrammatic representation of the U.S. economy is shown to the right. Households provide factors of production to firms in return to payment in the factor market. Households buy goods and services from businesses in the goods market. The government taxes businesses and households and provides goods and services to each of them. (106)

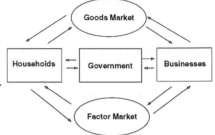

4. Although businesses decide what to produce, they are guided by consumer sovereignty. Businesses want to make a profit, so they will produce what they believe consumers will buy. That is not to say that businesses don't affect the desires of the consumer through advertising. (107)

5. The three major forms of businesses are sole proprietorship, partnership, and corporation. (109)

6. I would advise each of them to think hard about their situation. Each form of business has its disadvantages and advantages. If your friend wants to minimize bureaucratic hassle and be her own boss, the best form of business would be a sole proprietorship. However, she would be personally liable for all losses and might have difficulty obtaining additional funds should that be necessary. If her brother has some skills to offer the new business and is willing to share in the cost of purchasing the company, she might want to form a partnership with him. Beware, though: Both partners are liable for any losses regardless of whose fault it is. I would ask her if she trusts her brother's decision-making abilities.

   As a partnership they still might have problems getting additional funds. What about becoming a corporation? Her liability would be limited to her initial investment, her ability to get funds is greater, and she can shed personal income and gain added expenses to limit taxation. However, a corporation is a legal hassle to organize, may involve possible double taxation of income, and if she plans to hire many employees it involves monitoring problems once she becomes less involved. I would tell her she needs to weigh the costs and benefits of each option and choose the one that is best for her. (110)

7. Much of the economic decision making is done by business and government even though households have the ultimate power because in practice the representatives of the people — firms and government — are sometimes removed from the people. In the short run, government and business are only indirectly monitored by the people. (112)

8. Two general roles of government are referee and actor. (114)

9. Seven specific roles of government are (1) providing a stable structure within which markets can operate; (2) promoting workable, effective competition; (3) correcting for external effects of individuals' decisions; (4) providing public goods that the market does not adequately supply; (5) ensuring economic stability and growth; (6) providing acceptably fair distribution of society's production among its individuals; and (7) encouraging merit goods or activities and discouraging demerit goods or activities. (116)

10. The potential role for government when externalities exist is for government to institute policies that require market participants to take into account the effect of their actions on third parties. Government, however, cannot always institute policies that succeed in doing so without other negative effects. (117)

Word Scramble   1. competition   2. externality   3. profit

Match the Terms and Concepts to Their Definitions

1-j; 2-c; 3-l; 4-f; 5-i; 6-g; 7-m; 8-a; 9-d; 10-k; 11-h; 12-e; 13-b.

Problems and Exercises

1. Sole proprietorships, corporations, partnerships. (109)

2. Corporations, sole proprietorships, and partnerships. (Sole proprietorships and partnerships have equal percentages of annual receipts.) (109)

3. a. Sole proprietorship. No special forms are required to begin one. (110)
   b. Partnership. The owners have one another to work with and the financial risk is shared. (110)
   c. Sole proprietorship. This is a firm of one person who controls the business. (110)
   d. Partnership. This is easy to form relative to the easiest (sole proprietorship) and the hardest (corporation). (110)
   e. Corporation. The individual liability is only to the extent of the individual investment. (110)
   f. Corporation. Corporations are more developed firms and have more access to capital. (110)

4. a. Sole proprietorship and partnership. (110)
   b. Corporation. (110)
   c. Sole proprietorship and partnership. (110)
   d. Corporation. (110)

5. Individual income taxes, social insurance taxes and contributions, corporate income taxes, excise taxes. (110)

6. Income security, national defense, interest, health and education. (115)

7. a. Providing a stable institutional framework. (116)
   b. Correcting for externalities. (117)
   c. Promoting effective and workable competition. (117)
   d. Ensuring economic stability and growth. (118)
   e. Providing for public goods. (117-118)

8. a. Proportional because the rate remains the same regardless of income. (118)
   b. Regressive because the rate declines as income rises. (118)
   c. Progressive because the rate increases as income rises. (118)

Multiple Choice

1. c   See page 113.
2. c   See page 112.
3. b   See page 107, where entrepreneurship is defined.
4. c   See Exhibit 3, page 109.
5. b   See Exhibit 3, page 109.
6. d   See page 111.
7. c   See page 111.
8. c   Corporations get money only from new issues of stock. Their revenue does not change. The yield is the earnings divided by stock price, so that will fall, not increase, with a rise in the stock price. See page 111.
9. b   As discussed on page 112, although in theory stockholders control businesses, in reality generally managers do.
10. b   See page 113.
11. a   See Exhibit 7, page 115.
12. a   See Exhibit 8, page 115.
13. c   See page 117 for a definition of externality.
14. b   See page 117.
15. a   See pages 117-118.
16. a   See page 118.
17. d   As discussed on page 120, economic theory does not prescribe any particular role for government.
A1. b   As discussed on pages 123-124, the answer is the service sector.

Chapter 6:
An Introduction to the World Economy

Chapter at a glance

1. The industrial countries of the world have a large industrial base and a per capita income of about $20,000 a year; the developing countries of the world include low- and median-income economies that have a per capita income of between $300 and $2,000 a year. (131)

    There are also:
    1. high income oil exporting countries
    2. transitional economies
    3. Soviet-style socialist economies

    ✔ *Know the names of where all these countries are.*

2. Some major producing areas for some important raw materials are: (132)
    Aluminum–Guinea, Australia
    Cobalt–Zaire, Zambia, Russia
    Copper–Chile, U.S., Poland
    Iron–Russia, Brazil, Australia
    Zinc–Canada, Australia, Russia

    ✔ *Helps explain strategic roles some countries play in the world economy.*

    ✔ *Geography also helps explain why countries have the comparative advantages they do.*

3. Two ways in which *inter*national trade differs from *intra*national (domestic) trade are: (135)

    1. International trade involves potential barriers to trade; and

    Free and open international trade along the lines of comparative advantage is mutually beneficial to all economies involved.

    2. International trade involves multiple currencies.

    Foreign exchange markets exist to swap currencies.

4. By looking at an exchange rate table, you can determine how much various goods will likely cost in different countries. (135)

    An exchange rate table shows the relative value of other currencies in terms of the dollar and vice versa.

    In addition, note that a change in the exchange rate value of a currency will effect the country's balance of payments accounts. When the balance of payments account is in equilibrium, the quantity of a currency supplied equals the quantity of currency demanded.

5. Two important causes of a trade deficit are: (140)

    1. A country's competitiveness; and

    Reduced competitiveness ↑ *s a trade deficit due to:*
    a) relatively lower productivity
    b) and ↑ *in the value of the country's currency.*

    2. The relative state of a country's economy.

    A stronger economy means higher incomes, therefore more imports and a greater trade deficit.

6. Five important international economic institutions are: (141)
    1. The UN
    2. The WTO
    3. The World Bank
    4. The IMF; and
    5. The EU

    They are designed to enhance negotiations (to avoid trade wars).

    ✔ *Also know about global corporations.*

    ✔ *Think internationally because we live in a global economy.*

    See also, Appendix A: "Our International Competitors."

Short-answer questions

1. What is the per capita income of *the industrial countries of the world* and *the developing countries of the world*? (LO1)

2. Classifying countries by output levels misses some aspects of importance in the world economy. Name one of these. (LO1)

3. Where would you find information about the flows of resources among nations? Why is this information important? (LO2)

4. State two ways international trade differs from domestic trade. (LO3)

5. Based on Exhibit 3 on page 136, calculate the following: (LO4)

    a. How many British pounds would you receive for $100?

    b.   What is the exchange rate for U. S. dollars in German marks?

    c.   If 7.7 Hong Kong dollars equals one U.S. dollar, how many U. S. dollars equal one Hong Kong dollar?

6.   What are two important causes of a trade deficit? How does each affect the trade deficit? (LO5)

7.   What are the World Trade Organization (WTO) and the General Agreement on Trade and Tariffs (GATT)? How do they differ? (LO6)

8.   What are five important international economic institutions? (LO6)

Word Scramble

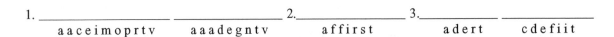

1. _____ _____ 2._____ 3._____ _____
     a a c e i m o p r t v   a a a d e g n t v   a f f i r s t   a d e r t   c d e f i i t

Match the Terms and Concepts to Their Definitions

___ 1. competitiveness

___ 2. foreign exchange market

___ 3. General Agreement on Tariffs and Trade (GATT)

___ 4. global corporations

___ 5. Group of Seven

___ 6. International Monetary Fund (IMF)

___ 7. NAFTA

___ 8. nontariff barriers

___ 9. trade deficit

___ 10. World Bank

___ 11. World Trade Organization

a. A multinational, international financial institution concerned primarily with monetary issues.

b. A country's ability to produce goods and services more cheaply than can other countries.

c. A multinational, international financial institution that works with developing countries to secure low-interest loans.

d. Corporations with substantial operations on both the production and sales sides in more than one country.

e. Group that meets to promote negotiations and coordinate economic relations among countries. The Seven are Japan, Germany, Britain, France, Canada, Italy, and the United States.

f. Indirect regulatory restrictions on exports and imports.

g. A past agreement among subscribing countries on certain limited conditions of international trade.

h. Market in which one country's currency can be exchanged for another country's.

i. The result of a country's imports exceeding its exports.

j. Free trade zone including the United States, Canada and Mexico.

k. An international organization committed to getting countries to agree not to impose new tariffs or other trade restrictions except under certain limited condition.

Problems and Exercises

1. State whether the trade restriction is a quota, tariff, or nontariff barrier.

   a. The U.S. charges Toyota Corporation 10% of the value of each Toyota imported into the United States.

   b. The EU allowed only beef that was not treated with growth-inducing hormones to be traded in EU markets.

   c. To encourage domestic production of automobile parts, Japan limits the importation of automobile parts according to a rigid schedule of numbers.

   d. The United States requires sheet metal used in the production of automobiles to be of a certain compound that is different than the compound used by foreign producers of sheet metal.

2. Assume that Germany can raise pork at a cost of 4 marks per pound and can raise beef at a cost of 8 marks per pound. In the United States, pork can be produced at $2 per pound and beef at $3 per pound.

    a. In terms of pounds of pork, what is the opportunity cost of producing beef in each country?

    b. Who has the comparative advantage in producing pork?

    c. Assume Americans eat 22,500 pounds of beef per year and 16,250 pounds of pork each year. Germans eat 10,000 pounds of beef and 20,000 pounds of pork each year. Which country should specialize in beef and which should specialize in pork?

3. Refer to the following table to answer the questions

Currency	U.S. $ equivalent	Currency per U.S. $
British pounds	_____	0.67
Italian lira	_____	1660.00
Chilean peso	_____	420.00
Swiss franc	0.67	_____
Japanese yen	0.009	_____

    a. Complete the blanks in the table above.

    b. How many Italian lire buys one dollar?

    c. How many Chilean pesos buy one Japanese yen?

d. How many U.S. dollars are needed to buy a British Rolls Royce at a cost of 75,000 pounds?

4. Consider the following Balance of Payments account for the United States in 1960:

		Dollars in millions
	Current Account	
	Exports (goods and services)	19,658
	Imports (goods and services)	-14,758
	Net investment income	3,390
1.	Balance on the current account	_____
	Capital Account	
	Capital inflows	2,294
	Capital outflows	-4,099
2.	Balance on the capital account	_____
3.	Current and capital account balance	_____
4.	Official transactions account	_____
5.	Total	_____

a. Fill in the missing values on the balance of payments account.

b. Is the current account in deficit or surplus? Are Americans buying fewer foreign assets or are foreigners buying more U.S. assets?

c. What is the quantity of U.S. dollars demanded? What is the dollar value of foreign currencies demanded?

d. What is the U.S. doing on the foreign exchange market? How do you know?

5. As Exhibit 4 in Chapter 6 shows, the United States had a merchandise trade balance surplus for most years after World War II until the mid-1970s. Since then the merchandise trade balance has been in deficit. For each of the following events, explain how the event would affect the trade deficit.

    a. Technological innovations in the United States make U.S. firms more competitive.

    b. The exchange value of the dollar falls.

    c. The level of U.S. income rises.

Multiple Choice Questions

1. If you hear the term, "the industrial countries of the world," you will likely think of
    a. the United States, Australia, and the Sudan.
    b. Germany, Russia, and Japan
    c. Germany, Australia, and France.
    d. Saudi Arabia, the United States, and Germany

2. If a country can produce a good at a lower opportunity cost than another country can produce it, we say it has
    a. a comparative advantage in the production of that good.
    b. an export advantage in the production of that good.
    c. an import advantage in the production of that good.
    d. a production advantage in the production of that good.

3. Say the United States can produce widgets at $4 apiece and wadgets at $4 apiece while South Korea can produce widgets at 500 won apiece and wadgets at 200 won apiece.
    a. The United States has a comparative advantage in widgets.
    b. The United States has a comparative advantage in wadgets.
    c. The U.S. cost of widgets is lower.
    d. The U.S. cost of wadgets is lower.

4. If a country imposes numerical limitations on how much of a good can be shipped into that country, the country has imposed
    a. a quota.
    b. a tariff.
    c. a nontariff barrier.
    d. a customs fee.

5. In a foreign exchange market
    a. imports are exchanged for exports.
    b. exports are exchanged for imports.
    c. labor services, exports, imports, and currencies are exchanged.
    d. one currency is exchanged for another.

6. In the mid-1990s the United States
    a. has run rather large trade surpluses.
    b. has run rather large trade deficits.
    c. has run an approximate trade balance.
    d. has fluctuated between trade deficits and trade surpluses.

7. Debtor nations will
    a. run trade deficits.
    b. run trade surpluses.
    c. not necessarily run a trade surplus or a trade deficit.
    d. run foreign exchange sales.

8. Which of the following is NOT an account in the balance of payments accounts?
    a. exchange rate account
    b. current account
    c. capital account
    d. official transactions account

9. If a country is maintaining an exchange rate above its market equilibrium determined by private supply and demand for its currency, then that country's
    a. official transaction account would be in surplus.
    b. official transaction account would be in deficit.
    c. current account would be in surplus.
    d. current account would be in deficit.

10. If the U.S. economy expands relative to other countries' economies, other things constant, the U.S. trade balance will likely
    a. be unaffected.
    b. move toward both deficit and surplus.
    c. move toward surplus.
    d. move toward deficit.

11. When the U.S. dollar fell substantially relative to the yen in the mid-1990s, that fall had a tendency to
    a. both increase and decrease U.S. competitiveness.
    b. increase U.S. competitiveness.
    c. decrease U.S. competitiveness.
    d. have no effect on U.S. competitiveness.

12. Important international institutions include all the following except
    a. NAFTA.
    b. IMF.
    c. WTO.
    d. DU.

13. The Group of Five consists of
    a. Japan, Germany, Britain, France, and the United States.
    b. Japan, Germany, Britain, France, and Italy.
    c. Italy, Japan, Germany, Britain, and the United States.
    d. Canada, Japan, Germany, the United States, and France.

14. If a country is found guilty in the World Court
    a. its leaders will be put in jail.
    b. it will be forced by the UN to pay a fine.
    c. it may or may not comply with the remedy decreed by the Court, depending on whether it chooses to comply or not.
    d. its dues to finance the World Court will be doubled.

15. The general plan of NAFTA is
    a. to raise tariffs on most goods so the tariffs are equal among countries.
    b. to replace tariffs with quotas.
    c. to move towards political integration among Canada, Mexico, and the United States.
    d. to remove tariffs on most goods within 15 years of signing.

16. NAFTA
    a. is scheduled for elimination in the year 2010
    b. involves countries in all hemispheres.
    c. involves countries in the western hemisphere.
    d. is to be combined with the EU within 5 years.

A1. The EU is an economic free trade area
    a. but not a political organization.
    b. and a loose political organization.
    c. and a federation of individual countries.
    d. and a nation-state.

A2. The EU is moving towards the establishment of a single currency, which is to be called
    a. the European dollar.
    b. the Euro.
    c. the European mark.
    d. the European pound.

A3. Members of the European Union include
    a. Germany, France, and Switzerland.
    b. Great Britain, Spain, and Norway.
    c. Greece, Italy, and Switzerland.
    d. Greece, Denmark, and Portugal.

A4. The Japanese economy is sometimes called
    a. a neo-feudalist economy.
    b. a neo-capitalist economy.
    c. a neo-mercantilist economy.
    d. a neo-socialist economy.

A5. MITI refers to
    a. entrepreneurial dreamings, such as those of Walter Mitty.
    b. a Japanese government agency.
    c. a U.S. government agency.
    d. a UN agency.

A6. Some of the reasons for Japan's economic success include all the following except
    a. its population's commitment to hard work.
    b. its high level of saving.
    c. its population's individualism.
    d. its institutional commitment to exports.

Answers

Short-Answer Questions

1. The per capita income of *the industrial countries of the world* is about $20,000 per year. The per capita income of *the developing countries of the world* is between $300 per year and $2,000 per year. (131)

2. Classifying countries by output is one way to group countries. Countries with low output share similar problems with countries that have high per capita income. This classification, however, misses the strategic importance of some countries in the world. For instance, Saudi Arabia has a relatively small output, but its importance lies in its control of a significant portion of the world's oil supply, an important input to production worldwide. Other dimensions missed include cultural and social dimensions. (132-133)

3. You would find information about the flows of resources among nations in the library (for example, in *The Times Atlas of Natural Resources*). This information is important because a country's resources contribute to its strategic importance to the world economy. (133)

4. Two ways international trade differs from domestic trade are (1) international trade involves potential barriers to trade; and (2) international trade involves multiple currencies. (135)

5. a. £59: Look at Exhibit 4 and find British pounds. I find that on Tuesday the equivalent of one U.S. dollar was 0.59 pounds (column 3). Multiply this by 100 to find out how many pounds equal $100. (136)
    b. One would receive 1.56 German marks for one U.S. dollar. This is read right off the table, column 3. (136)
    c. 0.13 U.S. dollars. The reciprocal of the exchange rate from Hong Kong dollars to U.S. dollars is the exchange from U.S. dollars to Hong Kong dollars (1/7.7). (136)

6. Two important causes of a trade deficit are a country's competitiveness and the relative state of a country's economy. A country's competitiveness affects how cheaply a country can sell its goods. The more a country is competitive, the cheaper it can sell its goods and the lower its trade deficit will be. The relative state of a country's economy affects the trade deficit through imports. When U.S. income rises, so do imports, and the trade deficit worsens. The trade deficit also affects U.S. income. An increase in imports means U.S. production falls and U.S. income falls. (140)

7. The WTO is an organization committed to getting countries to agree not to impose new tariffs or other trade restrictions except under certain limited conditions. The GATT was an agreement among many subscribing countries on certain conditions of international trade. An important difference between the two is that the WTO has some enforcement mechanisms while GATT did not. (141)

8. Five important international economic institutions: the UN, GATT, the World Bank, the IMF, and the EU. (141-142)

Word Scramble   1. comparative advantage   2. tariffs   3. trade deficit

Match the Terms and Concepts to Their Definitions
1-b; 2-h; 3-g; 4-d; 5-e; 6-a; 7-j; 8-f; 9-i; 10-c; 11-k.

Problems and Exercises

1. a. Tariff because it is a tax on imports. (135)
    b. Nontariff barrier because this was not a tax or a numerical restriction on imports, but a regulation that had the effect of reducing imports. (135)
    c. Quota because it is a numerical restriction on imports. (135)

d. Nontariff barrier because this is not a tax or a numerical restriction on imports, but it is a regulation that will have the effect of reducing imports. (135)

2. a. In the United States, the opportunity cost of producing one pound of beef is 1.5 pounds of pork. In Germany, the opportunity cost of producing one pound of beef is 2 pounds of pork. Calculate this by determining how much pork can be produced with $1 (or 1 DM in Germany) and how much beef can be produced with $1 (or 1 DM in Germany) and comparing the two. For the United States this is 1/2 pound of pork and 1/3 pound of beef. So, 1/2 pound of pork can be exchanged for 1/3 pound of beef. Or likewise, 1.5 pounds of pork can be exchanged for 1 pound of beef. (133-134)

    b. Germany has the comparative advantage in producing pork because the opportunity cost of producing pork in terms of forgone beef production is lower than it is in the United States. (133-134)

    c. The United States should specialized in beef because it has the comparative advantage in producing beef. Germany should specialize in pork because it has the comparative advantage in producing pork. This is concluded from the principle of comparative advantage. (133-134)

3. a. These blanks are filled in the table below. (135)

	Currency	U.S. $ equivalent	Currency per U.S. $
A	British pounds	1.49	0.67
B	Italian lire	0.0006	1660.00
C	Chilean peso	0.0024	420.00
D	Swiss franc	0.67	1.49
E	Japanese yen	0.009	111.10

    b. 1660 Italian lire buys one dollar. Look at column three, row B, for the exchange of lire per U.S. dollar. (135)

    c. One Japanese yen buys 3.78 Chilean pesos. Calculate this by first finding the yen per dollar (111.1) and Chilean pesos per dollar (420). To find Chilean pesos per Japanese yen, divide the Chilean peso per dollar by yen per dollar. (135)

    d. $111,940.30 are needed to buy a British Rolls Royce at a cost of 75,000 pounds. To calculate this, find the British pound per U.S. dollar (0.67) and divide this into the cost of the Rolls Royce in pounds. (112)

4. a. The missing blanks are filled in below:

    Current Account

	Exports	$19,650
	Imports	-14,758
	Net investment income	3,390
1.	Balance on the current account	8,290
	Capital Account	
	Capital inflows	2,294
	Capital outflows	-4,099
2.	Balance on the capital account	-1,805
3.	Current and capital account balance	6,485
4.	Official transactions account	-6485
5.	Total	0

    b. The current account is in surplus. Since capital inflows are less than capital outflows, the value of foreign assets bought by Americans exceed the value of U.S. assets bought by foreigners.

    c. The quantity of U.S. dollars demanded in 1960 equals imports plus capital outflows, or $18,857 million. The dollar value of foreign currencies demanded is exports plus capital inflows, or $21,944 million.

    d. Since the current and capital account balance is in surplus, the U.S. government must be selling $6,485 million U.S. dollars. We know this because the balance of payments must be zero, implying an official transactions account of $6,485 million, enough to offset the current and capital account surplus. (137-139)

5. a. Technological innovations in the United States making U.S. firms more competitive will tend to reduce the trade deficit. This is because U.S. goods will tend to be cheaper. Americans will substitute domestic goods for imports and foreigners will substitute U.S. exports for other goods. (140-141)

b. A fall in the exchange value of the dollar will tend to reduce the U.S. trade deficit. This is because U.S. goods will be cheaper. (140-141)

c. A rise in the level of U.S. income will tend to increase the U.S. trade deficit. This is because as domestic income increases, the demand for imports rises. (140-141)

Multiple Choice Questions

1. c   All other answers include at least one country that is not an industrial country of the world. See Exhibit 1, pages 130-131.

2. a   See page 133, where comparative advantage is defined. The other choices are simply words thrown together.

3. a   In the United States, producing one more widget costs one wadget; in South Korea producing one more widget costs 2.5 wadgets. So the opportunity cost of widgets is lower in the United States and therefore it has a comparative advantage in widgets. See page 133.

4. a   While it could be argued that quotas are a type of nontariff barrier, that is not the way they are defined in this text, and "quota" is the better answer. See page 135 of the text.

5. d   See page 135.

6. b   See Exhibit 4, page 138.

7. c   One must always distinguish between debt and deficit. A debtor nation may be running a trade surplus. See page 136.

8. a   The balance of payments account is comprised of the current account, the capital account, and the official transactions account. See page 139.

9. a   The government must be buying up the excess supply of its currency that is an inflow of its currency, which shows up as a positive official transactions balance. The country's current account could be in surplus or deficit depending upon what's happening with the capital account. (138-139)

10. d   As the U.S. economy expands, its imports increase, moving the trade balance towards deficit. See page 140.

11. b   As discussed on page 140, a fall in the value of a country's currency increases its competitiveness.

12. d   DU are two letters chosen at random. See pages 133, 141, and 142 for definitions of the others.

13. a   See page 142.

14. c   The World Court has no supra-national enforcement mechanism. See page 142.

15. d   See pages 133-134.

16. c   See pages 133-134.

A1. b   See page 147.

A2. b   See page 147.

A3. d   See Exhibit A1, page 148.

A4. c   See page 149.

A5. b   See page 150.

A6. c   See page 149. Japanese culture emphasizes cooperation far more than individualism.

Pretest I
Chapters 1 - 6

Take this test in test conditions, giving yourself a limited amount of time to complete the questions. Ideally, check with your professor to see how much time he or she allows for an average multiple choice question and multiply this by 25. This is the time limit you should set for yourself for this pretest. If you do not know how much time your teacher would allow, we suggest 1 minute per question, or 25 minutes.

1. Economic reasoning
   a. provides a framework with which to approach questions.
   b. provides correct answers to just about every question.
   c. is only used by economists.
   d. should only be applied to economic business matters.

2. In making economic decisions you should consider
   a. marginal costs and marginal benefits.
   b. marginal costs and average benefits.
   c. average costs and average benefits.
   d. total costs and total benefits, including past costs and benefits.

3. The opportunity cost of reading Chapter 1 of the text
   a. is about 1/20 of the price you paid for the book because the chapter is about one twentieth of the price of the book.
   b. zero since you have already paid for the book
   c. has nothing to do with the price you paid for the book.
   d. is 1/20 the price of the book plus 1/20 the price of the tuition.

4. "Given certain conditions, the market achieves efficient results" is an example of a
   a. positive statement.
   b. normative statement.
   c. art-of-economics statement.
   d. subjective statement.

5. In theory
   a. socialism is an economic system that tries to organize society in the same ways as most families organize, striving to see that individuals get what they need.
   b. socialism is an economic system based on central planning and government ownership of the means of production.
   c. socialism is an economic system based on private property rights.
   d. socialism is an economic system based on markets.

6. If the opportunity cost of good X in terms of good Y is 2Y, so you'll have to give up 2Y to get one X, the production possibility curve would look like
   a. a.
   b. b.
   c. c.
   d. d.

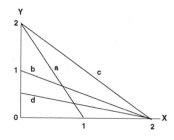

7. In the graph to the right, in the range of points between A and B there is
   a. a high opportunity cost of guns in terms of butter.
   b. a low opportunity cost of guns in terms of butter.
   c. no opportunity cost of guns in terms of butter.
   d. a high monetary cost of guns in terms of butter.

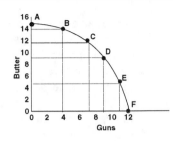

8. A law about the growth of efficiency of computers states
   that computer chip technology doubles the efficiency
   of computers each year. If that holds true, which of the
   four arrows would demonstrate the appropriate shifting of the production possibility curve?
   a. a.
   b. b.
   c. c.
   d. d.

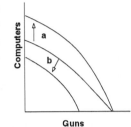
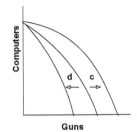

9. In partial equilibrium analysis one assumes
   a. other things constant and forgets them.
   b. other things are not constant.
   c. other things are constant but one brings them back into the analysis later when one applies it.
   d. other things are not constant, and one partially fits them into the analysis.

10. There are many more substitutes for good A than for good B.
    a. The demand curve for good A will likely be flatter.
    b. The demand curve for good B will likely be flatter.
    c. You can't say anything about the likely relative flatness of the demand curves.
    d. The demand curve for good B will likely shift out further.

11. The movement in the graph at the right from point A to point B represents
    a. an increase in demand.
    b. an increase in the quantity demanded.
    c. an increase in the quantity supplied.
    d. an increase in supply.

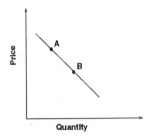

12. If there is an improvement in technology one would expect
    a. a movement along the supply curve.
    b. a shift upward of the supply curve.
    c. a shift downward of the supply curve.
    d. a movement down along the supply curve.

13. At which point will you expect the stronger downward pressure on prices?
    a. a.
    b. b.
    c. c.
    d. d.

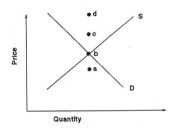

14. If there is an effective price ceiling
    a. the quantity demanded exceeds the quantity supplied.
    b. the quantity supplied exceeds the quantity demanded.
    c. the demand exceeds supply.
    d. the supply exceeds demand.

15. If the government institutes a price floor at P_0 in the accompanying diagram,
    which of the following points represents the likely quantity supplied?
    a. Q_0.
    b. Q_1.
    c. Q_2.
    d. Q_3.

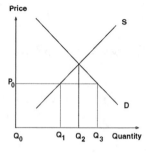

16. What will likely happen to the price and quantity of Gillette's Advanced Performance shaving cream as demand for it increases?
    a. The price will rise, and as a result, quantity will fall.
    b. Both price and quantity will rise.
    c. The price will fall, and quantity will rise.
    d. The price will fall, what happens to quantity is not clear.

17. What will likely happen to the price and quantity of cricket bats in Trinidad as interest in cricket dwindles following the dismal performance of the national cricket team, while at the same time taxes are repealed on producing cricket bats?
    a. The price will decrease, but what happens to quantity is not clear.
    b. The price will decrease, and quantity will increase.
    c. The price will increase, but what happens to quantity is not clear.
    d. It is not clear what happens to either price or quantity.

18. What will likely happen to the value of the Malaysian ringgit in terms of dollars as more foreigners want to invest in Malaysia, and at the same time Mahathir Perot, a wealthy Malaysian businessman, decides to sell his huge holdings of Malaysian ringgit?
    a. It will fall.
    b. It will remain the same.
    c. It will rise.
    d. It is difficult to say.

19. The fallacy of composition is
    a. the false assumption that what is false for a part will also be false for the whole.
    b. the false assumption that what is true for a part will also be true for the whole.
    c. the false assumption that what is false for a whole will also be false for the part.
    d. the false assumption that what is true for a whole will also be true for the part.

20. The ability to organize and get something done generally goes under the term
    a. the corporate approach.
    b. entrepreneurship.
    c. economicship.
    d. consumer sovereignty.

21. In reality, businesses are usually controlled by
    a. stockholders.
    b. managers.
    c. government.
    d. consumers

22. An example of a negative externality is
    a. education.
    b. pollution.
    c. government intervention.
    d. monopoly.

23. If a country can produce a good at a lower opportunity cost than another country can produce it, we say it has
    a. comparative advantage in the production of that good.
    b. an export advantage in the production of that good.
    c. an import advantage in the production of that good.
    d. a production advantage in the production of that good.

24. If a country is maintaining an exchange rate above its market equilibrium determined by private supply and demand for its currency, then that country's
    a. official transaction account would be in surplus.
    b. official transaction account would be in deficit.
    c. current account would be in surplus.
    d. current account would be in deficit.

25. The general plan of NAFTA is
    a. to raise tariffs on most goods so the tariffs are equal among countries.
    b. to replace tariffs with quotas.
    c. to move towards political integration among Canada, Mexico, and the United States.
    d. to remove tariffs on most goods within 15 years of signing.

Answers

1. a (1:1)	11. b (3:11)	21. b (5:9)
2. a (1:8)	12. c (3:15)	22. b (5:14)
3. c (1:11)	13. d (3:17)	23. a (6:2)
4. a (1:19)	14. a (4:1)	24. a (6:9)
5. a (2:4)	15. c (4:4)	25. d (6:15)
6. a (2:9)	16. b (4:7)	
7. b (2:15)	17. a (4:12)	
8. a (2:17)	18. d (4:16)	
9. c (3:4)	19. b (4:21)	
10. a (3:8)	20. b (5:3)	

Key: The figures in parentheses refer to multiple choice question and chapter numbers. For example (1:4) is multiple choice question 1 from chapter 4.

Chapter 7:
Economic Growth, Business Cycles, Unemployment, and Inflation

Chapter at a glance

1a. U.S. economic output has grown at an annual 2.5 to 3.5 percent rate. (158)

1b. Since 1945 the average expansion has lasted about 51 months. (163)

1c. In the 1980s and 1990s the target rate of unemployment has been between 5 percent and 6 percent. (166)

The target rate of unemployment has been called the "natural" rate of unemployment.

1d. Since World War II, the U.S. inflation rate has remained positive and relatively stable. (173)

2. Five important ingredients of growth are: (159)
1. Institutions with incentives compatible with growth;

Government policy can help or hinder growth–do you know how?

2. Technological development;

Technology not only causes growth, it changes the entire social and political dimensions of society.

3. Available resources;

Technological advances can help overcome any lack of resources.

4. Capital accumulation–investment in productive capacity; and

Can be: (1) Privately owned by business, (2) publicly owned and provided by government–our infrastructure, (3) human capital–investment in people, (4) social capital–institutions and conventions.

5. Entrepreneurship

This is the ability to get things done. It involves creativity, vision, and an ability to translate that vision into reality.

✔ *Growth is a goal because it increases the nation's absolute standard of living.*

✔ *Growth is measured as increases in real GDP from one year to the next.*

3. The four phases of the business cycle are: the peak, the downturn, the trough, and the upturn. (164)

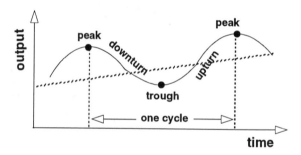

✔ *Note!*
1) *There is an overall upward secular growth trend of 2.5-3.5% shown by the dotted line.*
2) *We want to smooth out fluctuations because of the problems associated with them.*
3) *2 problems with a downturn (recession) are (a) cyclical unemployment and (b) low growth rate.*
4) *1 problem with upturn (expansion) is (a) demand-pull inflation.*

4a. The unemployment rate is measured by dividing the number of unemployed individuals by the number of people in the civilian labor force and multiplying by 100. (169)

Unemployment measures are imperfect but are still a good gauge of the economy's performance.

4b. Some microeconomic categories of unemployment are: reason for unemployment, demographic unemployment, duration of unemployment, and unemployment by industry. (172)

✔ *Know the different types of unemployment.*
✔ *Target rate of unemployment (5-6%) is the lowest rate of unemployment that policymakers believe is achievable under existing conditions (where inflation is not accelerating).*

5. Potential income is defined as the output that will be achieved at the target rate of unemployment and the target level of capacity utilization. It is difficult to know precisely where potential output is.(171)

Recession: Actual output (income) < Potential output.
Expansion: Actual output (income) > Potential output.

6a. Inflation is a continual rise in the price level. (173)

Price indexes are used to measure inflation; The most often used are the Producer Price Index (PPI), GDP deflator, and the Consumer Price Index (CPI).

6b. The "real" amount is the nominal amount divided by the price index. It is the nominal amount adjusted for inflation. (176)

Real means "inflation-adjusted."

7a. Cost-push inflation involves a rise in the price level resulting from restrictions on supply in a large number of markets When excess demand causes prices to rise it is referred to as demand-pull inflation. (177)

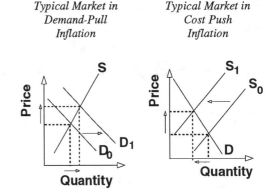

Typical Market in Demand-Pull Inflation   *Typical Market in Cost Push Inflation*

Both result in a higher price level. But, note the different directions in quantity (output).

7b. Expected inflation is the amount of inflation that people expect. Unexpected inflation is a surprise to them. (178)

We adjust to expected inflation by raising our prices or wages. However, this can create still more inflation. Demand-pull and cost-push inflation can feed on each other.

8. While inflation may not make the nation poorer, it does cause income to be redistributed and it can reduce the amount of information that prices are supposed to convey. (179)

Inflation hurts some, but benefits others.

Short-answer questions

1. What is the average rate of real growth in output in the United States since 1890 to the present? (LO1)

2. How long has the average expansion since mid-1945 lasted? (LO1)

3. In the 1980s and 1990s, what has been the target rate of unemployment? (LO1)

4. How did the inflation rate in the U.S. change in this century from pre-World War II to the post-World War II period (1950 to the present)? (LO1)

5. You've been called in by a political think tank to develop a strategy to improve growth in the U.S. What five things would you recommend that they concentrate on that would contribute positively to economic growth? (LO2)

6. Label the four phases of the business cycle in the graph to the right. (LO3)

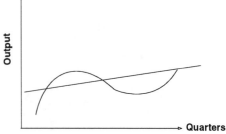

7. How is the unemployment rate calculated? (LO4)

8. Who in the United States does not work and is nevertheless not counted as unemployed? (LO4)

9. State two categories of unemployment for which microeconomic policies are appropriate. Why are such categories important to follow? (LO4)

10. How is the target rate of unemployment related to potential income? (LO5)

11. Define inflation. If there were no inflation what would happen to the distinction between a real concept and a nominal concept? (LO6)

12. Suppose the price of a Maserati in 1975 was $75,000 and the price of a Maserati in 1995 was $200,000. Your parents exclaim that the prices of Maserati's have risen by 166%! Wow! You tell them that the price of a Maserati really hasn't risen that much. They are confusing real and nominal concepts. Explain what you mean. (LO6)

13. What is the difference between cost-push and demand-pull inflation? (LO7)

14. Which of the two curves below better demonstrates a single market making a contribution to cost-pull inflation? To demand-pull inflation? (LO7)

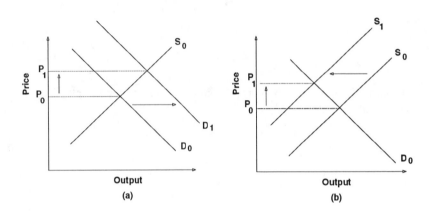

15. What is the difference between expected and unexpected inflation? (LO7)

16. What are two important costs of inflation? (LO8)

Word Scramble

1. _____ _____ 2._____ 3._____ _____
   b e i n s s s u   c c e l y   a f i i l n n o t   e e l m m n n o p t u y   a e r t

Match the Terms and Concepts to Their Definitions

_____ 1. business cycle

_____ 2. capacity utilization rate

_____ 3. Consumer Price Index

_____ 4. cyclical unemployment

_____ 5. demand-pull inflation

_____ 6. discouraged workers

_____ 7. frictional unemployment

_____ 8. full employment

_____ 9. GDP deflator

_____ 10. human capital

_____ 11. hyperinflation

_____ 12. inflation

_____ 13. leading indicators

_____ 14. Okun's rule of thumb

_____ 15. potential output

_____ 16. real output

_____ 17. recession

_____ 18. structural readjustments

_____ 19. structural unemployment

_____ 20. unemployment rate

a. A downturn that persists for more than two consecutive quarters.
b. A continual rise in the price level.
c. A one-percent change in the unemployment rate will cause income to change in the opposite direction by 2.5 percent.
d. An economic climate in which almost everyone who wants a job has one.
e. Index of inflation measuring prices of a fixed "basket" of consumer goods, weighted according to each component's share of an average consumer's expenditures.
f. Index of the price level of aggregate output of the average price of the components in GDP relative to a base year.
g. Indicators that tell us what's likely to happen in 12 -15 months.
h. Inflation resulting from the pressure exerted when the majority of markets in the economy experience increases in demand.
i. Inflation that hits triple digits (100 percent) or more per year.
j. Modifications in the types of goods produced and the methods of production.
k. Output that would materialize at the target rate of unemployment and the target rate of capacity utilization.
l. People who do not look for a job because they feel they don't have a chance of finding one.
m. People's knowledge.
n. Rate at which factories and machines are operating compared to the maximum rate at which they could be used.
o. The total amount of goods and services produced, adjusted for price level changes.
p. The upward or downward movement of economic activity that occurs around the growth trend.
q. The percentage of people in the labor force who can't find a job.
r. Unemployment caused by new entrants to the job market and people who have left their jobs to look for and find other jobs.
s. Unemployment resulting from changes in the economy itself.
t. Unemployment resulting from fluctuations in economic activity.

Problems and Exercises

1. For each of the following increases in the unemployment rate, state what will likely happen to income in the United States:

    a. Unemployment rate falls 2 percentage points.

    b. Unemployment rate falls 1 percentage point.

    c. Unemployment rate increases 3 percentage points.

2. For each, state whether the unemployment is structural or cyclical.

    a. Unemployment rises as output in the economy falls.

    b. The demand for workers to make typewriters falls as more consumers switch to computers.

    c. As the United States becomes a more high-tech producer, labor-intensive factories relocate to low-wage countries. Factory workers lose their jobs and the unemployment rate rises.

    d. As it becomes more acceptable for mothers to work, more women enter the labor market looking for work. The unemployment rate rises.

    e. Foreign economies slow and demand fewer U.S. exports. Unemployment rate rises.

3. Calculate the following given the information about the economy in the table:

Total population	260 million
Noninstitutional population	200 million
Incapable of working	60 million
Not in the labor force	66 million
Employed	134 million
Unemployed	10 million

    a. Labor force.

    b. Unemployment rate.

4. Create a price index for Green Bay Packer fans using the following basket of goods with 1997 prices as the base year.

Quantities in 1997	Prices 1997	1998
90 lbs of cheese	$2.50/lb	$2.00/lb
12 flannel shirts	$15/shirt	$20/shirt
16 football tickets	$25/ticket	$30/ticket

a.   What is the price of the basket of goods in each year? Show how the price index is 100 in the base year 1997.

b.   Using 1997 as the base year, what is the price index in 1998? By how much have prices risen?

c.   What are some potential flaws of this price index?

5.   Calculate the following given the following information about the economy in 1975, 1985, and 1995:

	1975	1985	1995
Nominal GDP (in billions of dollars)	1,630.6	4,180.7	_____
GDP deflator (index, 1992=100)	42.2	78.6	108
Real GDP (in billions of 1992 dollars)	_____	_____	6,756.48

a.   Nominal GDP in 1995.

b.   Real GDP in 1992 dollars in 1975 and 1985.

c.   Rise in prices from 1975 to 1985.

d.   Growth in nominal output from 1975 to 1985.

6.   Answer each of the following questions about nominal output, real output, and inflation:

a.   Nominal output increased from $6.5 trillion to $6.9 trillion from 1993 to 1994. The GDP deflator rose over that same year by 2.3%. By how much did real output increase?

b.   Real output increased from $4.9 trillion to $5.1 trillion from 1992 to 1993. The GDP deflator rose over that same year by 3%. By how much did nominal output increase?

c. Real output decreased from $4.8 billion in 1990 to $4.7 billion in 1991. Nominal output rose by 2%. By how much did the price level rise from 1990 to 1991?

7. For each of the following scenarios, state whether it is describing demand-pull or cost-push inflation.

a. The money supply has been expanding rapidly. Consumers can't seem to find all the goods they want.

b. The economy is operating above full employment. Workers are beginning to demand higher wages and firms are raising their prices (knowing that they will have no trouble selling their goods).

c. Even though there are no shortages of goods, firms are finding that the prices of inputs to production are rising rapidly. Firms are forced not only to cut back production but to raise their prices to cover costs.

d. In expectation of higher prices in the future, consumers stock up on goods now. Firms raise their prices just to keep pace with general inflation. They also see their inventories dwindle and increase production levels.

Multiple Choice Questions

1. The secular trend growth rate in the United States is approximately
    a. 1 to 1.5 percent per year.
    b. 2.5 to 3.5 percent per year.
    c. 5 to 5.5 percent per year.
    d. 7 to 7.5 percent per year.

2. Some people have argued that the two goals of (1) environmental protection and (2) economic growth that involves increased material consumption by individuals do not necessarily contradict each other because spending on the environment can create growth and jobs. This argument
    a. offers great hope for the future.
    b. is incorrect because environmental issues are not as important as material consumption.
    c. is correct because material consumption is not as important as the environment.
    d. is incorrect because the environmental projects will use the resources generated from growth, leaving little or nothing for increased personal consumption.

3. Important ingredients of growth include all the following except
    a. technological development.
    b. significant resources.
    c. institutions and incentives compatible with growth.
    d. strong government.

4. Technological change increases output by
   a. increasing the amount of capital.
   b. decreasing the amount of capital.
   c. changing the nature of capital.
   d. increasing the amount of resources we have.

5. The business cycle characterized by the Great Depression occurred in the early
   a. 1900s.
   b. 1930s.
   c. 1950s.
   d. 1960s.

6. Leading indicators include
   a. manufacturing and trade sales volume.
   b. number of employees on non-agricultural payrolls.
   c. industrial production.
   d. new orders for goods and materials.

7. Under pure capitalism, the main deterrent of unemployment was
   a. pure government intervention.
   b. pure market intervention.
   c. the fear of hunger.
   d. immigration.

8. In the 1980s and 1990s the target rate of unemployment generally has been
   a. between 2 and 3 percent.
   b. between 3 and 5 percent.
   c. between 4 and 6 percent.
   d. between 7 and 8 percent.

9. Keynesians
   a. generally favor activist government policies.
   b. generally favor laissez-faire policies.
   c. believe that frictional unemployment does not exist.
   d. believe that all unemployment is cyclical unemployment.

10. Classicals
   a. generally favor activist government policies.
   b. generally favor laissez-faire policies.
   c. believe that frictional unemployment does not exist.
   d. believe that all unemployment is cyclical unemployment.

11. The level of output that would materialize at the target rate of unemployment and the target rate of capital
    utilization is called
   a. nominal output.
   b. actual output.
   c. potential output.
   d. utilized output.

12. Okun's rule of thumb states that
   a. a 1 percentage point change in the unemployment rate will cause income to change in the same direction by
      2.5 percent.
   b. a 1 percentage point change in the unemployment rate will cause income to change in the opposite direction
      by 2.5 percent.
   c. a 2.5 percentage point change in the unemployment rate will cause income to change in the same direction
      by 1 percent.
   d. a. 2.5 percentage point change in the unemployment rate will cause income to change in the opposite
      direction by 1 percent.

13. Using Okun's rule of thumb, if unemployment rises from 5 to 6 percent, one would expect total output of $5 trillion to
    a. rise by $5 billion.
    b. rise by $125 billion.
    c. fall by $125 billion.
    d. fall by $5 billion.

14. A one-time rise in the price level is
    a. inflation if that rise is above 5 percent.
    b. inflation if that rise is above 10 percent.
    c. inflation if that rise is above 15 percent.
    d. not inflation.

15. Food and beverages make up about 20 percent of total expenditure. If food and beverage prices rise by 10 percent while the other components of the price index remain constant, approximately how much will the price index rise?
    a. 1 percent.
    b. 2 percent.
    c. 20 percent.
    d. 25 percent.

16. Real output is
    a. total amount of goods and services produced.
    b. total amount of goods and services produced adjusted for price level changes.
    c. total amount of goods produced, adjusted for services that aren't real.
    d. total amount of goods and services that are really produced as opposed to ones that are resold.

17. If the price level rises by 20 percent and real output remains constant, by how much will nominal output rise?
    a. 1 percent.
    b. 5 percent.
    c. 20 percent.
    d. 40 percent.

18. If inflation occurs when the economy significantly exceeds full employment, it is likely
    a. demand-pull inflation.
    b. cost-push inflation.
    c. commodity price inflation.
    d. consumer price index inflation.

19. If inflation occurs when the economy significantly falls below full employment, it is likely
    a. demand-pull inflation.
    b. cost-push inflation.
    c. commodity price inflation.
    d. consumer price index inflation.

20. A cost of inflation is that
    a. it makes everyone poorer.
    b. it makes the poor poorer but the rich richer.
    c. There are no costs of inflation because inflation does not make the society as a whole poorer.
    d. it reduces the informational content of prices.

Answers

Short-Answer Questions

1. The average rate of real growth in output in the United States from 1890 to the present is 2.5 - 3.5% per year. (158)

2. The average expansion since mid-1945 lasted has lasted 51 months. (163)

3. In the 1980s and 1990s, the target rate of unemployment has been between 5 and 6 percent. (167)

4. The inflation rate in the U.S. before World War II fluctuated and was sometimes positive and sometimes negative. Since World War II the price level has continually risen. (173-174)

5. I would tell them: (1) To promote institutions with incentives compatible with growth. Institutions that encourage hard work will lead to growth. (2) To promote institutions that foster creative thinking and lead to technological development; (3) To be creative in recognizing available resources. Growth requires resources and although it may seem that the resources are limited, available resources depend upon existing technology. New technology is a way of overcoming lack of resources. (4) To invest in capital. This would include not only buildings and machines, but also human and social capital. (5) To encourage entrepreneurship. An economy deficient in the other four areas can still grow if its population can translate vision into reality. Each of these will contribute to growth. (159-161)

6. The four phases of the business cycle are: the peak, the downturn, the trough, and the upturn. They are labeled in the graph to the right. (163)

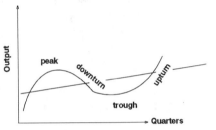

7. Unemployment is calculated by dividing the number of unemployed individuals by the number of people in the civilian labor force, and multiplying the result by 100. (165-169)

8. Those who are not in the labor force and those incapable of working are not employed and are not counted as unemployed. They include students, retirees, homemakers, those incapable of working, and those who choose not to participate in the labor force. (169)

9. Two microeconomic subcategories of unemployment include how people become unemployed and demographic unemployment. Others are duration of unemployment and unemployment by industry. These categories are important to follow because policies affect different types of unemployment differently and sometimes macro policies should be supplemented by micro policies. (172)

10. Potential income is that level of output that will be achieved at the target rate of unemployment. (171)

11. Inflation is a continual rise in the price level. If there were no inflation there would be no difference between real and nominal concepts. A real concept is the nominal concept adjusted for inflation. (176-177)

12. Yes, nominally Maseratis have risen by 166% from 1975 to 1995, but all other prices have risen during that time period too, including wages. You must adjust the rise in the aggregate price level to find out how much Maseratis have risen in real terms. From 1975 to 1995, the price level rose by 156%. (We used the *Economic Report of the President* to find this information.) So, the real price of the Maserati rose by only approximately 10% from 1975 to 1995. (176-177)

13. Cost-push inflation involves a rise in the price level resulting from restrictions on supply due to some sort of legal or social pressure. Demand-pull inflation involves excess demand resulting in price increases. (177-178)

14. Graph (a) demonstrates demand-pull inflation and graph (b) demonstrates cost-pull inflation. Graph (a) shows demand shifting to the right and equilibrium prices rising. Graph (b) shows supply contracting, leading to higher prices. (178)

15. Expected inflation is the amount of inflation that people expect. Unexpected inflation is inflation that is a surprise. (178)

16. Two important costs of inflation are that it redistributes income from people who do not raise their price to people who do raise their price; and it can reduce the amount of information that prices are supposed to convey. (179)

Word Scramble   1. business cycle   2. inflation   3. unemployment rate

Match the Terms and Concepts to Their Definitions
1-p; 2-n; 3-e; 4-t; 5-h; 6-l; 7-r; 8-d; 9-f; 10-m; 11-i; 12-b; 13-g; 14-c; 15-k; 16-o; 17-a; 18-j; 19-s; 20-q.

Problems and Exercises

1. Okun's law states that a 1-percentage point change in unemployment rate will cause income in the economy to change in the opposite direction by 2.5 percent.
   a. Income rises 5 percent. (171)
   b. Income rises 2.5 percent. (171)
   c. Income falls 7.5 percent. (171)

2. a. Cyclical because it is unemployment due to a change in economic activity. (165-166)
   b. Structural because this is a structural change in the economy. (165-166)
   c. Structural because this is a change in labor allocation. (165-166)
   d. Structural because this is a change in social structure. (165-166)
   e. Cyclical because this is unemployment due to a change in economic activity. (165-166)

3. a. Labor force = employed + unemployed = 144 million. (169)
   b. Unemployment rate = (unemployed/labor force)$\times$100 = 6.9%. (169)

4. a. The price of the basket in 1997 is $805 and in 1998 is $900. Since 1997 is the base year, the index must be 100. This is calculated as (price of the basket in 1997)/(price of the basket in 1997) = $805/$805 $\times$ 100=100. (174)
   b. The price index in 1998 is (price of the basket in 1998)/(price of the basket in 1997) = $900/$805 $\times$ 100= 112. Prices rose by 12%. (174)
   c. Some potential flaws are that (1) the basket of goods is small and might not reflect the true basket of goods purchased by Green Bay Packer fans, (2) the basket of goods is fixed (since the price of cheese fell, fans might be buying more cheese and fewer football tickets), (3) the basket does not reflect quality improvements (since the Green Bay Packers won the Super Bowl in 1997, the quality of subsequent games in 1998 might improve, but the tickets are counted as if they were the same as in 1997).

5. a. Nominal GDP in 1995 is $7,297 billion dollars. Calculate this by multiplying real GDP in 1995 by the GDP deflator and dividing by 100. (176)
   b. Real GDP in 1992 dollars in 1975 is $3,8634 billion and in 1985 $5,319 billion. Calculate these by dividing nominal GDP by the GDP deflator and multiplying by 100. (176)
   c. The price level rose by 86% from 1975 to 1985. Calculate this by dividing the change in the GDP price deflator by the base year deflator and multiplying by 100: (78.6 − 42.2)/42.2 $\times$ 100. (176)
   d. Nominal output grew by 156% from 1975 to 1985. Calculate this by dividing the change in nominal GDP from 1975 to 1985 by the base year nominal GDP and multiplying by 100: (4180.7 − 1630.6)/1630.3 $\times$ 100. (176)

6. a. Nominal output increased by 6.1% from 1993 to 1994. Since the GDP deflator rose over that same year, we know that real output increased 3.8% from 1993 to 1994. Subtract inflation from the change in nominal output to get the change in real output: 6.1% − 2.3% = 3.8%. (176)
   b. Real output increased 4.1% from 1992 to 1993. Since the GDP deflator rose 3% over that same year, we know that nominal output increased 7.1% from 1992 to 1993. Add inflation to the change in real output to find the change in nominal output: 3% + 4.1% = 7.1%. (176)

c. Real output fell 2.1% from 1990 to 1991. Since nominal output rose by 2%, we know the price level rose 4.1% from 1990 to 1991. Subtract the change in real output from the change in nominal output to find the inflation rate: 2.0%- (-2.1%) = 4.1%. (176)

7. a. Demand-pull inflation. (177)
   b. Demand-pull inflation. (177)
   c. Cost-push inflation. (177)
   d. Initial cause of inflation is unclear, but turned into demand-pull inflation. (177)

Multiple Choice Questions

1. b. See page 158.

2. d. As more material goods made available by growth are used for antipollution equipment, less is available for personal consumption. The added material goods have already been used. See page 158.

3. d. Strong government may or may not be an important ingredient of growth. The other three definitely are ingredients of growth. See page 158-161.

4. c. Technological change definitely changes the nature of capital, making it more productive; it does not necessarily increase the total amount of capital. It is also possible that one could see technological change as increasing the effective resources, but what it does is to increase *available* resources—resources are fixed. Since d didn't say effective resources, c is the better answer. This is a hard question. When presented with two answer you think might be right, choose the one you are most sure of. See pages 159-160.

5. b. See page 162.

6. d. The others are coincidental indicators. Even if you didn't remember this, you should be able to figure out that the change in inventory predicts what firms think will be happening in the future, whereas the others tell what is happening now. See page 164.

7. c. As discussed on pages 165-166, the fear of hunger was the main deterrent to unemployment. A second deterrent would have been emigration, but that would not be as good an answer. Since d says immigration (the flowing in of people), not emigration, d is definitely wrong.

8. c. See page 167.

9. a. See page 167.

10. b. See page 167.

11. c. As discussed on page 171, the statement that begins the question is the definition of potential output.

12. b. See page 171.

13. c. Total output moves in the opposite direction by 2.5% times $5 trillion, which equals a fall of $125 billion. See page 171.

14. d. As the text points out on page 173, inflation is an *ongoing* rise in the price level, so the use of the term "one-time" should have clued you that d is the answer.

15. b. To determine the price level rise you multiply each component by its price rise. Since only 20% of the total rose, you get 10% times 20% = 2% . See page 174.

16. b. See page 176. A reminder: A service is considered just as much a good and a component of real output as is a physical good.

17. c. If real output remains constant, then the nominal output must also rise by 20%, as discussed on page 176.

18. a. As discussed on page 177, demand-pull inflation occurs above full employment. Commodity price inflation was not discussed in the text, and could be either cost-push or demand-pull inflation.

19. b. As discussed on page 177, cost-push inflation occurs below full employment. Commodity price inflation was not discussed in the text, and could be either cost-push or demand-pull.

20. d. Inflation does not make society richer or poorer, and the distributional consequences of inflations differ, eliminating answers a and b. While the second part of c is true, that doesn't mean that there are no costs of inflation and, as discussed on page 179, one of those costs is the reduction in the informational content of prices.

Chapter 8:
National Income Accounting

Chapter at a glance

1. National income accounting enables us to measure and analyze how much a nation is producing and consuming. (184)

   GDP:
   - *(1) Most common measure of a nation's output (income)*
   - *(2) Calculated by either:*
      - *a) expenditures approach, or*
      - *b) income approach*

2a. Gross domestic product (GDP): Aggregate final output of residents and businesses in an economy in a one-year period. (184)

   GDP is total market ($) value of all <u>final</u> goods and services produced in a one-year period.

2b. Gross national product (GNP): Aggregate final output of citizens and businesses of an economy in a one-year period. (184)

   ✔ *GDP is output produced within a country's borders; GNP is output produced by a country's citizens wherever they may be in the world.*

   ✔ *GNP = GDP + Net foreign factor income where: Net foreign factor income => Add the foreign income of one's citizens and subtract the income of residents who are not citizens.*

2c. National income (NI) is the total income earned by citizens and businesses in a country. (188)

   See Appendix A for more details concerning national income accounting.

   Hint: In most "non-technical" discussions of "output" (GDP) and "income" (NI) are used interchangeably—that is, GDP is assumed to be equal to NI for purposes of simplification.

3. To avoid double counting, you must eliminate intermediate goods, either by calculating only final output (expenditures approach), or by calculating only final income (income approach) by using the value added approach. (186)

Know what is and is not included in calculating GDP.
<u>*GDP does not include:*</u>
1) *intermediate goods (sold for resale or further processing);*
2) *second-hand sales;*
3) *government transfers, housespouse production or any other non-market activity;*
4) *underground economic activity.*

4. GDP = C + I + G + (X − M) is an accounting identity because it is defined as true. (190)

   The above identity is really the expenditures approach, which states:

   Total output = Total expenditures
   Total output = GDP; Total expenditures=C+I+G+(X − M)

   By substitution: GDP = C + I + G + (X − M)
   ✔ *Know what C, I, G, X − M stand for!*

   Also note:
   $X_n = (X − M) =$ *Net exports.*
   If X_n is positive, then X>M => Trade surplus.
   If X_n is negative, then X<M => Trade deficit.
   If X_n is zero, then X=M => Trade balance.

5. A real concept is a nominal concept adjusted for inflation. (193)

   GDP is a price times quantity $(P \times Q)$ phenomenon. GDP can ↑ due to an ↑ in P (price level) and/or an ↑ in Q (real quantity of output). Real GDP, in essence, holds prices (P) constant. Hence, real GDP is inflation (or deflation) adjusted.

6. Limitations of national income accounting include: (193)
   1. Measurement problems.
   2. GDP measures national activity, not welfare; and
   3. Subcategories are often interdependent.

   ✔ *GDP is not and was never intended to be a measure of social well-being.*

   See also, Appendix A: "National Income Accounting in Detail."

Short-answer questions

1. What is the purpose of national income accounting? (LO1)

2. What is GDP? (LO2)

3. What is GNP? In words, how does it differ from GDP? (LO2)

4. What is NI? What are the four components that comprise NI? (LO2)

5. Calculate the contribution of Chex cereal (from seeds to consumer) to GDP, using the following information: (LO3)

Participants	Cost of materials	Value of Sales
Farmer	0	200
Chex factory	200	500
Distributor	500	800
Grocery store	800	1000

6. What are the four components of gross domestic product and why does their sum equal national income? (LO4)

7. Say the price level rises 10% from an index of 1 to an index of 1.1 and nominal GDP rises from $4 trillion to $4.6 trillion. What is nominal GDP in the second period? What is real GDP in the second period? (LO5)

8. As pointed out by the quotation that begins the chapter on national income accounting, statistics can be misleading. In what way can national income statistics be misleading? Given your answer, why use them at all? (LO6)

Word Scramble

1. _____ _____
     a e l r   D G P

2. _____ _____
     a i l m n n o   D P G

3. _____ _____
     a e l u v   d e a d d

Match the Terms and Concepts to Their Definitions

___ 1. disposable personal income

___ 2. gross domestic product

___ 3. gross national product

___ 4. intermediate products

___ 5. national income (NI)

___ 6. national income accounting

___ 7. net domestic product

___ 8. net foreign factor income

___ 9. nominal concepts

___ 10. nominal GDP

___ 11. real GDP

___ 12. value added

___ 13. Wealth Accounts

a. National income minus personal taxes plus transfer payments made to individuals.

b. Economic concepts specified in monetary terms (current dollars) with no adjustment for inflation.

c. GDP calculated at existing prices.

d. Aggregate final output of residents and businesses in an economy in a one-year period.

e. Total income earned by citizens and businesses of a country.

f. GDP adjusted to take account of depreciation.

g. Aggregate final output of citizens and businesses of an economy in a one-year period.

h. Income from foreign domestic factor sources minus foreign factor incomes earned domestically.

i. Nominal GDP adjusted for inflation.

j. Products of one firm used in some other firm's production of another firm's product.

k. A balance sheet of an economy's stock of assets and liabilities.

l. The increase in value that a firm contributes to a product or service.

m. A set of rules and definitions for measuring economic activity in the aggregate economy.

Problems and Exercises

1. For each of the following, calculate how much the action described has added to GDP:

    a. A used car dealer buys a car for $3,000 and resells it for $3,300.

    b. A company sells 1,000 disks for $500 each. Of these, it sells 600 to other companies and 400 to individuals.

    c. A company sells 50 computers at a retail price of $1,000 apiece and 100 software packages at a retail price of $50 apiece to consumers. The same company sells 25 computers at $800 and 50 software packages at $30 apiece to wholesalers. The wholesalers then sell the 25 computers at $1,250 apiece and the 50 software packages at $75 apiece.

    d. Fred purchases 100 stock certificates valued at $5 apiece and pays a 10% commission. When the price declines to $4.50 apiece, Fred decides to sell all 100 certificates, again at a 10% commission.

    e. Your uncle George receives $600 in social security each month for one year.

2. Use the following table showing the production of 500 boxes of Wheaties cereal to calculate the contribution to GDP using the value-added approach.

Participants	Cost of materials	Value of sales
Farmer	$ 0	$ 150
Mill	$ 150	$ 250
Cereal maker	$ 250	$ 600
Wholesaler	$ 600	$ 800
Grocery store	$ 800	$ 1,000

a. Calculate the value added at each stage of production.

b. What is the total value of sales?

c. What is the total value added?

d. What is the contribution to GDP for the production of those Wheaties?

3. There are three firms in an economy: X, Y, and Z. Firm X buys $200 worth of goods from firm Y and $300 worth of goods from firm Z, and produces 250 units of output at $4 per unit. Firm Y buys $150 worth of goods from firm X, and $250 worth of goods from firm Z, and produces 300 units of output at $6 per unit. Firm Z buys $75 worth of goods from X, and $50 worth goods from firm Y, and produces 300 units at $2 per unit. All other products are sold to consumers. Answer the following:

a. What is GDP?

b. How much government revenue would a value added tax of 10% generate?

c.   How much government revenue would an income tax of 10% generate?

d.   How much government revenue would a 10% sales tax on final output generate?

4.   Use the following table to answer the questions:

Year	Real output in (billions of 1992 dollars)	Nominal output (billions of dollars)	GDP deflator (1992=100)
1991	6079.0	5916.7	_____
1992	6244.4	6244.4	100.0
1993	6383.8	_____	102.6
1994	_____	_____	105.0
1995	_____	7297.2	108.0

a. What is output for 1995 in 1992 dollars?

b. What is the output in nominal terms in 1993?

c. What is the GDP deflator (1992=100) in 1991?

d. Real output grew by 3.5% from 1993 to 1994. By how much did nominal output grow in 1994?

A1. You have been hired as a research assistant and are given the following data about the economy:
All figures are in billions of dollars.

Transfer payments	$70
Interest paid by consumers	5
Net exports	10
Indirect business taxes	44
Net foreign factor income	3
Corporate income tax	69
Contribution for social insurance	37
Personal tax and non-tax payments	92
Undistributed corporate profits	49
Gross private investment	200
Government purchases	190
Personal consumption	550
Depreciation	65

You are asked to calculate the following:

a. GDP.

b. GNP.

c. NNP.

d. NDP.

e. NI.

f. Personal income.

g. Disposable personal income.

A2. You have been hired as a research assistant and are given the following data about another economy (profits, wages, rents, and interest are measured nationally):

Corporate income tax	$200
Proprietors' income	225
Profits	250
Wages	800
Rents	30
Depreciation	20
Indirect business taxes	110
Undistributed corporate profits	50
Net foreign factor income	-5
Interest	175
Social security contribution	0
Transfer payments	0
Personal taxes	150

Calculate the following:

a. GDP.

b. GNP.

c. NDP.

d. NNP.

e. National income.

f. Domestic income.

g. Personal income.

h. Disposable personal income.

Multiple Choice Questions

1. If inflation is 10 percent and nominal GDP goes up 20 percent, real GDP goes up approximately
   a. 1 percent.
   b. 10 percent.
   c. 20 percent.
   d. 50 percent.

2. To move from GDP to GNP, one must
   a. add net foreign factor income.
   b. subtract inflation.
   c. add depreciation.
   d. subtract depreciation.

3. If a firm's cost of materials is $100 and its value of sales is $500, its value added is
   a. $100.
   b. $400.
   c. $500.
   d. $600.

4. If you, the owner, sell your old car for $600, how much does GDP increase?
   a. By $600.
   b. By the amount you bought it for, minus the $600.
   c. By zero.
   d. By the $600 you received and the $600 the person you sold it to paid, or $1,200.

5. The size of the U.S. federal government budget is approximately $1.7 trillion. The federal government's contribution in the GDP accounts is approximately
   a. $660 billion.
   b. $1 trillion.
   c. $1.7 trillion.
   d. $5.6 trillion.

6. If a woman divorces her housespouse and hires him to continue cleaning her house for $20,000 per year, GDP will
   a. remain constant.
   b. increase by $20,000 per year.
   c. decrease by $20,000 per year.
   d. remain unchanged.

7. The national income identity shows that
   a. the value of factor services is equal to the value of goods plus investment.
   b. the value of factor services is equal to the value of goods plus savings.
   c. the value of factor services is equal to the value of goods sold to individuals.
   d. the value of consumption goods is equal to the value of factor services.

8. The four components of expenditures in GDP are
   a. consumption, investment, government spending, and net exports.
   b. consumption, depreciation, investment, and government expenditures.
   c. consumption, investment, gross exports, and government expenditures.
   d. durable goods, nondurable goods, services, and government expenditures.

9. The largest component of expenditures in GDP is
   a. consumption.
   b. investment.
   c. net exports.
   d. government purchases of goods and services.

10. The largest component of national income is
    a. rents.
    b. net interest.
    c. profits.
    d. compensation to employees.

11. Switching from the exchange rate approach to the purchasing power parity approach for comparing GDP among countries generally
    a. does not make a significant difference for a developing country's GDP relative to a developed country's GDP.
    b. generally increases a developing country's GDP relative to a developed country's GDP.
    c. generally decreases a developing country's GDP relative to a developed country's GDP.
    d. changes the relative GDP of developing country's GDP, but not in a predictable fashion.

12. If the price level rises by 2 percent and nominal GDP increases from $5 trillion to $6 trillion, by approximately how much has real GDP increased?
    a. 0%.
    b. 2%.
    c. 18%.
    d. 48%.

13. If nominal GDP rises
    a. welfare has definitely increased.
    b. welfare has definitely decreased.
    c. welfare may have increased or decreased.
    d. welfare most likely has increased.

14. Estimates of the importance of the underground economy in the United States
    a. are that it is very small—under 1 percent.
    b. are that it's somewhere between 1.5 percent and all the way to 20 percent.
    c. are that it's somewhere between 1.5 percent and all the way to 60 percent.
    d. are that it is as large as the non-underground economy.

A1. The largest component of U.S. consumption expenditures is
    a. durable goods.
    b. nondurable goods.
    c. services.
    d. investment.

A2. Gross investment differs from net investment by
    a. net exports.
    b. net imports.
    c. depreciation.
    d. transfer payments.

A3. GDP differs from net domestic product by
    a. depreciation.
    b. exports.
    c. imports.
    d. consumption.

A4. Whenever investment increases in a country its productive capital
    a. definitely increases.
    b. will likely increase, but may not.
    c. definitely decreases.
    d. will likely decrease, but may not.

Answers

Short-answer questions

1. The purpose of national income accounting is to measure and analyze how much the nation is producing and consuming. National income accounting defines the relationship among the sub-aggregates of aggregate production. (184)

2. GDP is the aggregate final output of *residents* and businesses *in* an economy in a one-year period. (184)

3. GNP is aggregate final output of *citizens* and businesses *of* an economy in a one-year period. GDP is output produced within a country's borders while GNP is output produced by a country's citizens. Add net foreign factor income to GDP to get GNP. (184)

4. NI is total income earned by citizens and businesses of a country. The four components that comprise NI are compensation to employees, rents, interest, and profits. (188-189)

5. $1,000. We could use either the value added approach or the final output approach. Summing the value added at each stage of production — the difference between cost of materials and value of sales —we get $1,000. (186)

Participants	Cost of materials	Value of Sales	Value Added
Farmer	$0	$200	$200
Chex factory	200	500	300
Distributor	500	800	300
Grocery store	800	1000	200
Sum (total output)			1000

6. The four components of gross domestic product are consumption, investment, government expenditures, and net exports. Their sum equals national income because it is an accounting identity — the definitions are chosen so that equality cannot be false. (190)

7. A real value is a nominal value adjusted for inflation. So, nominal GDP in the second period is $4.6 trillion, but real GDP is $4.6 trillion divided by the price index, 1.1, or $4.18 trillion. (193)

8. National income accounting statistics can be misleading. They are subject to measurement error; they are based on samples of data and assumptions about behavior. For example, the measurement of inflation is widely believed to overestimate true inflation. Also, GDP does not include non-market activities such as housework. It measures national activity, not welfare; output could rise but welfare fall. Its subcategories are often interdependent; that is, arbitrary decisions were made when determining what goes in which subcategory. Nevertheless, national income accounting makes it possible to discuss the aggregate economy. It is important to be aware of the limitations of the data in those discussions. (193-196)

Word Scramble   1. real GDP   2. nominal GDP   3. value added

Match the Terms and Concepts to Their Definitions
1-a; 2-d; 3-g; 4-j; 5-e; 6-m; 7-f; 8-h; 9-b; 10-c; 11-i; 12-l; 13-k.

Problems and Exercises

1. a. $300. Only the value added by the sale would be added to GDP, which in this case is the difference between the purchase price and the sale price. (186-187)

b. $200,000. Total output produced is $1,000 \times \$500 = \$500,000$. Of this intermediate goods valued at $600 \times \$500 = \$300,000$. So, the company's contribution to GDP is ($500,000-$300,000) = $200,000. (186-187)

c. Only that amount that is sold to the consumer is counted in GDP. This is $50 \times 1,000 + 100 \times 50 = \$55,000$ sold by the first company plus the sales of the wholesaler, which is $25 \times \$1250 + 50 \times \$75 = \$35,000$. Total contribution to GDP is $90,000. (186-187)

d. Only the commissions of $50 and $45 are counted in GDP. Together they contribute $95. (186-187)

e. Nothing has been added to GDP. Government transfers are not included in GDP. (186-187)

2.

Participants	Cost of materials	Value of sales	Value added
Farmer	$ 0	$ 150	150
Mill	$ 150	$ 250	100
Cereal maker	$ 250	$ 600	350
Wholesaler	$ 600	$ 800	200
Grocery store	$ 800	$ 1,000	200

a. The value added at each stage of production is shown in the table above. (186-187)

b. The total value of sales is $2,800. Find this by adding the rows of the value of sales column. (186-187)

c. The total value added is $1,000. Find this by adding the value added at each stage of production. (186-187)

d. The contribution to GDP for the production of those Wheaties is $1,000. Value added at each stage of production is the contribution to GDP. This avoids double-counting. (186-187)

3. a. $2375: GDP is the sum of the value added by the three firms = 500 + 1,400 + 475. (186-187)

b. $237.50: A 10% value added tax would generate = (.10)($2,375) = $237.50 of revenue. (186-187)

c. $237.50: A 10% income tax would generate the same revenue as a 10% value added tax. (186-187)

d. $340: A 10% sales tax on final output would generate = $340 of revenue: (.10) (1,000 + 1,800 + 600). (186-187)

4. a. $6756.6 billion 1992 dollars: Real output = (Nominal output/deflator) $\times$ 100 = 7297.2/108 $\times$ 100.

b. $6549.7 billion: Nominal output = (real output $\times$ deflator) / 100 = (6383.8 $\times$ 102.6)/100.

c. 97.3: Deflator = (Nominal output/real output) $\times$ 100 = (5916.7/6079.0) $\times$ 100.

d. Real output grew by 3.5% and inflation rose by 2.3%, so nominal output grew by 5.8%.

A1. a. $950: GDP = $C + I + G + (X\text{-}M)$ = 550 + 200 + 190 + 10 = 950. (202)

b. $953: GNP = GDP + net foreign factor income = 953. (184)

c. $888: NNP = GNP $-$ depreciation = 953 $-$ 65 = 888. (203)

d. $885: NDP = GDP $-$ depreciation = 950 $-$ 65 = 885. (202)

e. $844 : NI = NNP $-$ indirect business taxes = 888 $-$ 44 = 844. (203-204)

f. $759: PI = NI + transfers from government $-$ corporate retained earnings $-$ corporate income taxes $-$ social security taxes = 844 + 70 $-$ 49 $-$ 69 $-$37 = 759. (204)

g. $667: DPI = PI $-$personal income tax = 759 $-$92 = 667. (204)

A2. a. $1,615: GDP = NDP + Depreciation = NNP $-$ net foreign factor income + depreciation = NI + indirect business tax $-$ net foreign factor income + depreciation = wages + rents + interest + profits + proprietors' income + indirect business taxes $-$ net foreign factor income + depreciation = 800 + 30 + 175 + 250 - (-5) + 225 + 110 + 20 = 1615. (199-203)

b. $1,610: GNP = GDP + net foreign factor income = 1615+(-5). (184, 199-203)

c. $1,595: NDP = GDP $-$ depreciation = 1615 $-$ 20. (199-203)

d. $1,590: NNP = GNP $-$ depreciation = 1610 $-$ 20. (184, 199-203)

e. $1,480: NI = NNP $-$ indirect business taxes = 1590 $-$ 110. (199-203)

f. $1,485: DI = NI $-$ net foreign factor income = 1480 $-$ (−5) . (199-203)

g. $1,230: PI = NI + transfers $-$ corporate income taxes $-$ undistributed corporate profits $-$ social security contributions = 1480 + 0 $-$ 200 $-$ 50 $-$ 0. (199-203)

h. $1,080: DPI = PI $-$ personal taxes = 1230 $-$ 150. (199-203)

Multiple Choice Questions

1. b. As discussed on page 193, real concepts are nominal concepts adjusted for inflation. As a first approximation you can simply subtract one from the other, giving you 10%.

2. a. As discussed on page 184, GDP + net foreign factor income = GNP.

3. b. Value added equals value of sales minus cost of materials. See page 186.

4. c. As discussed on page 187, sales of used goods do not contribute to GDP except to the degree that they are sold by a second hand dealer. Then the dealer's profit would be the value added.

5. a. It is not $1.7 trillion because the only part of the government budget that goes in GDP accounts is spending on goods and services. The portion of the budget for redistribution is not included in the GDP accounts. See page 187.

6. b. As discussed on page 187, GDP measures market transactions. The divorce-and-hire changes the housecleaning activities from nonmarket to market and hence increases GDP.

7. c. The equality can be seen in Exhibit 3 on page 189. The basis of the equality is the double entry bookkeeping upon which the national income accounts are based.

8. a. See page 190.

9. a. Consumption makes up 69% of expenditures. See Exhibit 5, page 190.

10. d. As you can see in Exhibit 4 on page 189, compensation to employees is the largest percent of national income.

11. b. In developing countries, living expenses are generally lower than in developed countries. Thus moving towards a purchasing power parity approach generally increases GDP in a developing country. In the example of China given on page 192, the switch increased China's GDP by more than 400 percent.

12. c. If nominal GDP has increased from $5 trillion to $6 trillion, it has increased 20%. Real GDP growth equals nominal GDP growth minus inflation, or 20-2=18%. See page 193.

13. c. Nominal GDP must be adjusted by inflation to arrive at real GDP before one can even start to make welfare comparisons. And even if real GDP increases, it is not clear that welfare has increased, as discussed on page 194.

14. b. See page 194.

A1. c. In 1994 services were approximately 57 percent of GDP, compared to much smaller percentages for the others. See Exhibit A3, page 200.

A2. c. See pages 199-201.

A3. a. See page 201.

A4. b. As discussed on page 201, investment is not a perfect measure of increase in productive capital. So of the two possible answers, a and b, the better is b.

Chapter 9:
Money, Banking, and the Financial Sector

Chapter at a glance

1. The financial sector is central to almost all macroeconomic debates because behind every real transaction, there is a financial transaction that mirrors it. (208)

   If the interest rate does not perfectly translate savings (flows out of the spending stream) into investment (flows into the spending stream), then the economy will either expand or contract.

2. Money is a financial asset that makes the real economy function smoothly by serving as a medium of exchange, a unit of account, and a store of wealth. (209)

   Money is any financial asset which serves the functions of money.

3. The three functions of money are: (210)
   1. Medium of exchange;

   As long as people are confident that the purchasing power of the dollar will remain relatively stable over time (by the Fed controlling the money supply) then people will continue to swap real goods, services, and resources for money and vice versa.

   2. Unit of account; and

   Money acts as a measuring stick of the relative value (relative prices) of things. Therefore, the value of money itself must remain relatively stable over time.

   3. Store of wealth.

   Money's usefulness as a store of wealth also depends upon how well it maintains its value.

   ✔ *The key is for the Fed to keep the purchasing power of money (and therefore prices) relatively stable over time. Inflation can be a problem!*

4a. M1 is the component of the money supply that consists of cash in the hands of the public plus checking accounts and traveler's checks. (213)

   M1 is the narrowest definition of the money supply. It is also the most liquid.

4b. M2 is the component of the money supply that consists of M1 plus other relatively liquid assets. (213)

   ✔ *M2 is the definition of the money supply most used by the Fed to measure the money supply in circulation. This is because M2 is most closely correlated with the price level and economic activity.*

   ✔ *Anything which changes M2 changes the money supply.*

4c. The broadest definition of the money supply is L (which stands for liquidity). It consists of almost all short-term financial assets. (213)

5. Banks "create" money because a bank's liabilities are defined as money. So when a bank incurs liabilities it creates money. (215)

   Banks "create" money (increase the money supply) whenever they make loans. Whenever a person borrows from a bank they are swapping a promissory note to repay the loan (which is really an IOU; and an individual's IOU is not money because it doesn't meet the criteria of serving the functions of money) in exchange for cash or funds put in his/her checking account. Cash and checking account balances are money! Therefore, the money supply increases.

   Also Note: When a loan is repaid, the money supply (M2) decreases.

6a. The money multiplier is the measure of the amount of money ultimately created by the banking system per dollar deposited. When people hold no cash it equals 1/r, where r is the reserve ratio. (218)

A single bank is limited in the amount of money it may create. The limit is equal to its excess reserves–the maximum amount of funds which it can legally loan out. However, when considering an entire banking system, where any bank's loans, when spent, may end up being deposited back into that bank or another bank, then the entire banking system ends up being able to increase the money supply by a multiple of its initial excess reserves (the initial maximum amount of funds which can legally be loaned out) because of the money multiplier.

Simple money multiplier = 1/r.

(<u>Initial change</u> in money supply) × (money multiplier) = change in the money supply

6b. When people hold cash the approximate money multiplier is 1/ (r + c). (219)

Approximate real-world money multiplier = 1/(r+c), where c is the ratio of money people hold in currency to the money hold as deposits.

The approximate real-world money multiplier is less than the simple money multiplier because some of the funds loaned out are held as cash and therefore do not return to the banks as deposits.

7. Financial systems are based on trust that expectations will be fulfilled. Banks borrow short and lend long, which means that if people lose faith in banks, the banks cannot keep their promises. (221)

✔ *It is important to maintain the public's confidence in the banking system.*

✔ *Government guarantees of financial institutions can have 2 effects:*
1) *They can prevent the unwarranted fear that causes financial crises.*
2) *They can also eliminate <u>warranted</u> fears and hence eliminate a market control of bank loans.*

See also,
Appendix A: "The Value of a Financial Asset."
Appendix B: "A Closer Look at Financial Institutions and Financial Markets."
Appendix C: "Creation of Money Using T-Accounts."
Appendix D: "Precise Calculation of the Money Multiplier When People Hold Currency."

Short-answer questions

1. At lunch you and your friends are arguing about the financial sector. One friend says that real fluctuations are measured by real economic activity in the goods market and therefore the financial sector has nothing to do with the business cycle. You know better and set him straight. (LO1)

2. You are having another stimulating lunchtime conversation, this time about money. Your friend says "I know what money is; it's cash, the dollar bills I carry around." What is your response? (LO2)

3. You continue the conversation and begin to discuss why we have money. Your friend states that the function of money is to buy things like the lunch he has just bought. Another friend says that because she has money she is able to compare the cost of two types of slacks. Still another offers that she holds money to make sure she can buy lunch next week. What is the function of money that each has described? Are there any others? (LO3)

4. What are the two most liquid definitions of money? What are the primary components of each? (LO4)

5. What is the broadest measure of money? What does it consist of? (LO4)

6. Your friends are curious about money. At another lunchtime discussion, they ask each other two questions: Is all the money deposited in the bank in the bank's vaults? Can banks create money? Since they are stumped, you answer the questions for them. (LO5)

7. Using the simple money multiplier, what will happen to the money supply if the reserve ratio is 0.2 and high powered money is increased by $100? (LO6)

8. Using the equation for the approximate real-world money multiplier, what will happen to the money supply if the reserve ratio is 0.2, cash to deposit ratio is 0.3, and high powered money is increased by $100? (LO6)

9. How does the interest rate regulate the flow of savings into the flow of expenditures during normal times? (LO7)

10. What would happen if everyone simultaneously lost trust in their banks and ran to withdraw their deposits? (LO7)

11. What is the potential problem with government guarantees to prevent bank-withdrawal panics? (LO7)

Word Scramble

1. _____   2._____   3._____ _____
    e e e r r s s v   e n y o m   v e s r r e e   t r o i a

Match the Terms and Concepts to Their Definitions

___ 1. approximate real-world money multiplier

___ 2. asset management

___ 3. bond

___ 4. excess reserves

___ 5. Federal Reserve Bank (the Fed)

___ 6. L

___ 7. liability management

___ 8. M_1

___ 9. M_2

___ 10. money

___ 11. reserve ratio

___ 12. reserves

___ 13. simple money multiplier

___ 14. spread

a. Broad definition of "money" that includes almost all short-term assets.

b. Cash that a bank keeps on hand that is sufficient to manage the normal cash inflows and outflows.

c. Component of the money supply that consists of M_1 plus savings deposits, small-denomination time deposits, and money market mutual fund shares, along with some esoteric relatively liquid assets.

d. Component of the money supply that consists of cash in the hands of the public, checking account balances, and travelers' checks.

e. Difference between banks' costs plus the interest they pay out and the interest they take in minus bad loans.

f. How a bank attracts deposits and what it pays for them.

g. How a bank handles its loans and other assets.

h. Measure of the amount of money ultimately created by the banking system, per dollar deposited, when cash holdings of individuals and firms are treated the same as reserves of banks. The mathematical expression is $1/(r + c)$.

i. Measure of the amount of money ultimately created by the banking system per dollar deposited, when people hold no cash. The mathematical expression is $1/r$.

j. Ratio of cash or deposits a bank holds at the central bank to deposits a bank keeps as a reserve against withdrawals of cash.

k. Reserves above what banks are required to hold.

l. The U.S. central bank. Its liabilities serve as cash in the United States.

m. A highly liquid financial asset that is generally accepted in exchange for other goods and is used as a reference in valuing other goods and as a store of wealth.

n. A promise to pay a certain amount of money plus interest in the future.

Problems and Exercises

1. For each, state whether it is a component of M_1 or M_2, both, or neither:

   a. Money market mutual funds.

   b. Savings deposits.

   c. Travelers' checks.

   d. Stocks.

   e. Twenty-dollar bills.

2. Assuming individuals hold no cash, calculate the simple money multiplier for each of the following reserve requirements:

   a. 15%

   b. 30%

   c. 60%

   d. 80%

   e. 100%

3. Assuming individuals hold 10% of their deposits in the form of cash, recalculate the *approximate* real-world money multipliers from question 2.

   a. 15%

   b. 30%

   c. 60%

   d. 80%

   e. 100%

4. While Jon is walking to school one morning, a helicopter flying overhead drops $300. Not knowing how to return it, Jon keeps the money and deposits it in his bank. (No one in this economy holds cash.) If the bank keeps only 10 percent of its money in reserves and is fully loaned out, calculate the following:

   a. How much money can the bank now lend out?

   b. After this initial transaction, by how much has the money in the economy changed?

   c. What's the money multiplier?

d. How much money will eventually be created by the banking system from Jon's $300?

A1. Choose which of the following offerings you would prefer having. (Refer to the present value table on page 226.)

a. $1,500 today or $2,000 in 5 years. The interest rate is 5%.

b. $1,500 today or $2,000 in 5 years. The interest rate is 10%.

c. $2,000 today or $10,000 in 10 years. The interest rate is 15%.

d. $3,000 today or $10,000 in 15 years. The interest rate is 10%.

B1. A bond has a face value of $5,000 and a coupon rate of 10 percent. It is issued in 1997 and matures in 2006. Using this information, calculate the following:

a. What is the annual payment for that bond?

b. If the bond is currently selling for $6,000, what is its yield?

c. If the bond is currently selling for $4,000, what is its yield?

d. What do your answers to (b) and (c) tell you about what the bond must sell for, relative to its face value, if the interest rate is 10%? Rises above 10%? Falls below 10%?

B2. For each, state whether a financial asset has been created. What gives each financial asset created its value?

a. Your friend promises to pay you $5 tomorrow and expects nothing in return.

b. You buy an apple at the grocery store.

c. The government sells a new bond with a face value of $5,000, a coupon rate of 8%, and a maturity date of 2006.

d. A firm issues stock.

e. An existing stock is sold to another person on the stock market.

B3. For each of the following financial instruments, state for whom it is a liability and for whom it is an asset. Also state, if appropriate, whether the transaction occurred on the capital or money market and whether a financial asset was created.

a. First Bank grants a mortgage to David.

b. First Bank sells David's mortgage to Financial Services, Inc.

c. Broker McGuill sells existing stocks to client Debreu.

d. An investment broker sells 100 shares of new-issue stock to client Debreu.

e.   U.S. government sells a new three-month T-bill to Corporation X.

f.   Corporation X sells a 30-year government bond to Sally Quinn.

C1. Assume that Textland Bank Balance Sheet looks like this:

Assets		Liabilities	
Cash	30,000	Demand Deposits	150,000
Loans	300,000	Net Worth	350,000
Phys. Assets	170,000		
Total Assets	500,000	Total Liabilities and net worth	500,000

a.   If the bank is not holding any excess reserves, what is the reserve ratio?

b.   Show the first three steps in money creation using a balance sheet if Jane Foundit finds $20,000 in cash and deposits it at Textland.

Step #1

Step #2

Step #3

    c.   After the first three steps, how much in excess reserves is the bank holding?

    d.   Show Textland's balance sheet at the end of the money creation process.

D1. Assuming individuals hold 10% of their money in the form of cash, calculate the actual money multiplier for each of the following reserve requirements.

    a.   15%

    b.   30%

    c.   60%

    d.   80%

    e.   100%

Multiple Choice Questions

1. For every financial asset
    a. there is a corresponding financial liability.
    b. there is a corresponding financial liability if the financial asset is financed.
    c. there is a real liability.
    d. there is a corresponding real asset.

2. Using economic terminology, when an individual buys a bond, that individual
    a. is investing.
    b. is saving.
    c. is buying a financial liability.
    d. is increasing that individual's equities.

3. Which of the following is not a function of money?
    a. Medium of exchange.
    b. Unit of account.
    c. Store of wealth.
    d. Equity instrument.

4. Rational individuals
    a. would hold no money, because it pays no interest.
    b. would prefer to change all their money into bonds, which pay interest.
    c. would prefer to hold all money and no bonds.
    d. would prefer a combination of bonds and money.

5. Which of the following is not included in the M_1 definition of money?
    a. checking accounts.
    b. currency.
    c. traveler's checks.
    d. savings accounts.

6. Which of the following components is not included in the M_2 definition of money?
    a. M_1.
    b. savings deposits.
    c. small-denomination time deposits.
    d. bonds.

7. In an advertisement for credit cards, the statement is made, "Think of a credit card as smart money." An economist's reaction to this would be
    a. a credit card is not money.
    b. a credit card is dumb money.
    c. a credit card is simply money.
    d. a credit card is actually better than money.

8. Using a credit card creates
    a. a financial liability for the holder and a financial asset for the issuer.
    b. a financial asset for the holder and a financial liability for the issuer.
    c. a financial liability for both the holder and issuer.
    d. a financial asset for both the holder and issuer.

9. Modern bankers
    a. focus on asset management.
    b. focus on liability management.
    c. focus equally on asset management and liability management.
    d. are unconcerned with asset and liability management and instead are concerned with how to make money.

10. Assuming individuals hold no cash, the reserve requirement is 20 percent, and banks keep no excess reserves, an increase in an initial $100 of money will cause an increase in total money of
    a. $20.
    b. $50.
    c. $100.
    d. $500.

11. Assuming individuals hold no cash, the reserve requirement is 10 percent, and banks keep no excess reserves, an increase in an initial $300 of money will cause an increase in total money of
    a. $30.
    b. $300.
    c. $3,000.
    d. $30,000.

12. Assuming the ratio of money people hold in cash to the money they hold in deposits is .3, and the reserve requirement is 20 percent, and that banks keep no excess reserves, an increase in an initial $100 of money will cause an increase in total money of _____. (Use the approximate real world money multiplier.)
    a. $50.
    b. $100.
    c. $200.
    d. $500.

13. If banks hold excess reserves whereas before they did not, the relative money multiplier
    a. will become larger.
    b. will become smaller.
    c. will be unaffected.
    d. might increase or might decrease.

14. A sound bank will
    a. always have money on hand to pay all depositors in full.
    b. never borrow short and lend long.
    c. never borrow long and lend short.
    d. keep enough money on hand to cover normal cash inflows and outflows.

15. FDIC is an acronym for
    a. major banks in the United States.
    b. major banks in the world.
    c. U.S. government program that guarantees deposits.
    d. types of financial instruments.

16. The textbook author's view of government guarantees of deposits is
    a. they don't make sense.
    b. stronger ones are needed.
    c. it depends.
    d. it should be a private guarantee program.

A1. If the interest rate falls, the value of a fixed interest rate bond
    a. rises.
    b. falls.
    c. remains the same.
    d. cannot be determined as to whether it rises or falls.

B1. A secondary financial market is a market in which
    a. minor stocks are sold.
    b. minor stocks and bonds are sold.
    c. previously issued financial assets can be sought and sold.
    d. small secondary mergers take place.

B2. If you are depositing money at a bank, the bank is likely
   a. an investment bank
   b. a commercial bank.
   c. a municipal bank.
   d. a government bank.

B3. Liquidity is
   a. a property of water stocks.
   b. the ability to turn an asset into cash quickly.
   c. the ability to turn an asset into liquid quickly.
   d. a property of over-the-counter markets.

B4. A financial market in which financial assets having a maturity of more than one year are bought and sold is called a
   a. money market.
   b. capital market.
   c. commercial paper market.
   d. commercial bank market.

B5. Two bonds, one a 30-year bond and the other a 1-year bond, have the same interest rate. If the interest rate in the economy falls, the value of the
   a. long-term bond rises by more than the value of the short-term bond rises.
   b. short-term bond rises by more than the value of the long-term bond rises.
   c. long-term bond falls by more than the value of the long-term bond falls.
   d. short-term bond falls by more than the value of the long-term bond falls.

C1. The demand deposits in a bank would go on
   a. the asset side of its balance sheet.
   b. the liabilities side of its balance sheet.
   c. the net worth part of its balance sheet.
   d. on both sides of its balance sheet.

C2. The cash that a bank holds would go on
   a. the asset side of its balance sheet.
   b. the liabilities side of its balance sheet.
   c. the net worth part of its balance sheet.
   d. on both sides of its balance sheet.

D1. Using the precise complex money market multiplier, determine how much total money will increase if there is an increase of $1,000 in high-powered money when people hold cash, c equals 20 percent, and r equals 30 percent.
   a. $1,200.
   b. $2,400.
   c. $2,600.
   d. $2,800.

D2. Using the precise complex money market multiplier, determine how much total money will increase if there is an increase of $1,000 in high-powered money when people hold cash, c equals 30 percent, and r equals 20 percent.
   a. $1,200.
   b. $2,400.
   c. $2,600.
   d. $2,800.

Answers

Short-answer questions

1. The financial sector is important to the business cycle because the financial sector channels the flow of savings out of the circular flow back into the circular flow either as consumer loans, business loans, or government loans. If the financial sector did not translate enough of the savings out of the spending stream back into the spending stream, output would decline and a recession might result. Likewise, if the financial sector increased flows into the spending stream (loans) that exceeded flows out of the spending stream (savings) an upturn or boom might result and inflation might rise. It is this role of the financial sector that Keynesians focused on to explain why production and expenditures might not be equal, resulting in fluctuations in output. (208-209).

2. In one sense your friend is right; cash is money. But money is more than just cash. Money is a highly liquid financial asset that is accepted in exchange for other goods and is used as a reference in valuing other goods. It includes such things as CDs and traveler's checks. (209-210)

3. The first friend has described money as a medium of exchange. The second has described money as a unit of account. And the third has described money as a store of wealth. These are the three functions of money. There are no others. (210-212)

4. The two most liquid definitions of money are M_1 and M_2. M_1 consists of currency, checking accounts, and traveler's checks. M_2 consists of M_1 plus savings deposits, small-denomination time deposits, money market mutual funds, and a few esoteric financial instruments not discussed in the text. (213)

5. The broadest measure of money is L. L consists of almost all short-term financial assets. (213-214)

6. No, banks do not hold all their deposits in the vault. They keep a small percentage of it for normal withdrawal needs and lend the remainder out. This maintenance of checking accounts is the essence of how banks create money. You count your deposits as money since you can write checks against them and the money that is lent out from bank deposits is counted as money. Aha! The bank has created money. (215-219)

7. The equation for the simple money multiplier is $(1/r)$ where r is the reserve ratio. Plugging in the values into the equation, we see that the money multiplier is 5, so the money supply increases by $500. (218)

8. The equation for the approximate real-world money multiplier is $1/(r+c)$ where r is the reserve ratio and c is the ratio of cash to deposits. Plugging the values into the equation, we see that the money multiplier is 2, so the money supply increases by $200. (219-220)

9. Just as price equlibrates supply and demand in the real sector, interest rates equilibrate supply and demand for savings. The supply of savings comes out of the spending stream. The financial sector transforms those savings back into the spending stream in the form of loans that are then used to purchase consumer or capital goods. (208-209)

10. If everyone lost their trust in banks, a financial panic could occur. The bank holds only a small portion of total deposits as reserves so that if everyone withdraws their money, the bank cannot meet its promises. (222-221)

11. The potential problem with government guarantees to prevent bank-withdrawal panics is that guarantees might lead to unsound lending and investment practices by banks. Also, depositors have less of a reason to monitor the practices of their banks. (222)

Word Scramble   1. reserves   2. money   3. reserve ratio

Match the Terms and Concepts to Their Definitions

1-h; 2-g; 3-n; 4-k; 5-l; 6-a; 7-f; 8-d; 9-c; 10-m; 11-j; 12-b; 13-i; 14-e.

Problems and Exercises

1. a. M_2. (213)
   b. M_2. (213)
   c. Both. (213)
   d. Neither. (213)
   e. Both. (213)

2. a. 6.67. multiplier = (1/.15). (218)
   b. 3.33. multiplier = (1/.30). (218)
   c. 1.67. multiplier = (1/.6). (218)
   d. 1.25. multiplier = (1/.8). (218)
   e. 1. multiplier = (1/1). (218)

3. a. $4 = 1/(.10+.15)$. (220)
   b. $2.5 = 1/(.1+ .3)$. (220)
   c. $1.43 = 1/(.1+ .6)$. (220)
   d. $1.11 = 1/(.1+ .8)$. (220)
   e. 0.91. In reality a multiplier less than one would be highly unlikely. Recall that this is the approximate real-world multiplier. In Appendix D the precise complex multiplier is given. See pages 242-244.

4. a. $270. (217-219)
   b. $570: the initial $300 in new deposits plus .9×300 in loans that are then deposited. (217-219)
   c. 10: $1/r = 1/.1$. (217-219)
   d. $3,000: money multiplier×initial deposit = 10×300. (217-219)

A1. Using the table to calculate the present value of $100 to be received in the future, we find that the better value is
   a. $2,000 in 5 years, valued today at $1,568. (226)
   b. $1,500 today. $2,000 in 5 years when the interest rate is 10% is worth only $1,242 today. (26)
   c. $10,000 in 10 years, valued at $2,470 when the interest rate is 15%. (226)
   d. $3,000 today. $10,000 in 15 years when the interest rate is 10% is worth only $2,390 today. (226)

B1. a. The annual payment for that bond is $5,000×.10 = $500 annually. (237-238)
   b. If the bond is currently selling for $6,000, its yield is $500/$6,000 = 8.3%. (237-238)
   c. If the bond is currently selling for $4,000, its yield is $500/$4,000 = 12.5%. (237-238)
   d. My answers to (b) and (c) tell me that the bond must sell for its face value if interest rate is 10%, less than face value if interest rates rise above 10%, and more than face value if interest rates fall below 10%. (237-238)

B2. a. A financial asset has been created. Your friend's promise to pay you $5 is what gives that asset its value. (228)
   b. No, a financial asset has not been created, although a financial transaction did occur. (228)
   c. Yes, a financial asset has been created. The government's promises to pay you $5,000 at maturity and $400 each year until then are what give that asset its value. (228)
   d. Yes, a financial asset has been created. A claim to future profits is what gives that asset its value. (228)
   e. No, a financial asset has not been created. The financial asset already existed. (228)

B3. a. The mortgage is an asset for First Bank and a liability for David. The transaction occurred on the capital market. A financial asset was created. (228-232)
   b. The mortgage is an asset for Financial Services, Inc., and a liability for David. The transaction occurred on the capital market. A financial asset was not created. (228-232)
   c. The stocks are an asset for client Debreu and a liability for the broker's firm. The transaction occurred on the capital market. A financial asset was not created. (228-232)
   d. The stocks are an asset for client Debreu and a liability for the firm. The transaction occurred on the capital market. A financial asset was created. (228-232)
   e. The T-bill is a liability for the U.S. government and an asset for Corporation X. The transaction occurred on the money market. A financial asset was created. (228-232)
   f. The bond is a liability for the U.S. government and an asset for Sally Quinn. The transaction occurred on the capital market. A financial asset was not created. (228-232)

C1. a. .2: cash/deposits = 30,000/150,000. (242-244)
   b. Step 1: Increase of $20,000 in demand deposits and cash:

Assets		Liabilities	
Cash	30,000	Demand Deposits	150,000
Cash from Jane	20,000	Jane's deposit	20,000
Total cash	50,000	Total deposits	170,000
Loans	300,000	Net Worth	350,000
Phys. Assets	170,000		
Total Assets	520,000	Total Liabilities	
		and net worth	520,000

Step 2: Assuming the reserve ratio is .2 as calculated in (a), the bank can now lend out 80% of the $20,000 received in cash. It lends $16,000 to Sherry: (242-244)

Assets		Liabilities	
Cash	50,000	Demand Deposits	170,000
Cash to Sherry	16,000		
Total cash	34,000		
Begin. Loans	300,000	Net Worth	350,000
Loan to Sherry	16,000		
Total loans	316,000		
Phys. Assets	170,000		
Total Assets	520,000	Total Liabilities	
		and net worth	520,000

Step 3: Sherry uses the loan to purchase a car from John. John deposits the cash in the bank (242-244):

Assets		Liabilities	
Cash	34,000	Demand Deposits	170,000
Cash from John	16,000	Deposit from John	16,000
Total cash	50,000	Total Deposits	186,000
Begin. Loans	316,000	Net Worth	350,000
Phys. Assets	170,000		
Total Assets		536,000	Total Liabilities
		and net worth	536,000

c. The bank is holding $12,800 in excess reserves. Required reserves for $186,000 in deposits is .2*186,000 = $37,200. The bank has $50,000 in reserves, $12,800 higher than required. (242-244)

d. The ending balance sheet will look like this (242-244):

Assets		Liabilities	
Cash	50,000	Demand Deposits	250,000
Loans	380,000	Net Worth	350,000
Phys. Assets	170,000		
Total Assets	600,000	Total Liabilities	
		and net worth	600,000

D1. We use the equation from the money multiplier found in Appendix D. (242-244)

    a. $4.4 = (1+.1)/(.1+.15).$ b. $2.75 = (1+.1)/(.1+.30).$ c. $1.57 = (1+.1)/(.1+.60).$

    d. $1.22 = (1+.1)/(.1+.80).$ e. $1 = (1+.1)/(.1+1.00).$

Multiple Choice Questions

1. a. The very fact that it is a financial asset means that it had a financial liability, so the qualifier in b is unnecessary. See pages 208-209.

2. b. In economic terminology, buying a financial asset, which is what buying a bond is, is a form of saving. Investing occurs when a firm or an individual buys a real asset. See page 209.

3. d. See pages 210-211.

4. d. Even though money does not pay interest, it is useful as a medium of exchange. Thus, only d is acceptable. See page 210.

5. d. See page 213 and Exhibit 2 on page 214.

6. d. See page 213 and Exhibit 2 on page 214.

7. a. A credit card is not money and thus a would be the best answer. A credit card replaces money, making the same amount of money able to handle many more transactions. See page 214.

8. a. One is borrowing money when one uses a credit card, thereby incurring a financial liability. See page 214.

9. c. As discussed on page 215, banks are concerned with both asset management and liability management. The second part of answer d is obviously true, but it's through management of assets and liabilities that they make money, so the first part is wrong.

10. d. The simple money multiplier is $1/r = 1/.2 = 5$, which gives an increase in total money of $500. See page 218.

11. c. The simple money multiplier is $1/r = 1/.1 = 10$ which gives an increase of total money of $3,000. See page 218.

12. c. The approximate real-world money multiplier is $1/(r+c) = 1/.5 = 2$, which gives an increase in total money of $200. See pages 219-220.

13. b. Holding excess reserves would be the equivalent to increasing the reserve requirement, which would decrease the multiplier. See pages 217-218.

14. d. Banks earn income by managing their assets and liabilities. To follow any policy other than d would cost them income. See page 217.

15. c. FDIC stands for Federal Deposit Insurance Corporation. See page 221.

16. c. For this textbook author, just about everything depends; you can't get him to take a firm position on anything. See page 223.

A1. a. The present value formula tells us that the value on any fixed interest rate bond varies inversely with the interest rate in the economy. See page 226.

B1. c. See page 230.

B2. b. Investment banks don't take deposits, and who knows what the last two types of banks are; we certainly don't. See page 229.

B3. b. Answers a and c are total gifts to you — water stocks; give us a break — and it's unclear what d means. The b option is the definition given on page 231.

B4. b. See page 232.

B5. a. Since bond values vary inversely with interest rate changes, the answer must be a or b. Judging between a and b will be hard for you at this point unless you have studied present value in another course. However, based on the discussion in the text on pages 237 and 238, you can deduce that since a long-term bond is not paid back for a long time, it will be much more strongly affected by interest rate changes.

C1. b. Demand deposits at banks are liabilities for those banks and hence go on the liability side. (241)

C2. a. The cash that banks hold is an asset for them; hence it goes on the asset side. See page 240.

D1. b. The precise complex money multiplier is $(1+c)/(r+c)$ or $1.2/.5 = 2.4$, so the increase in total money is $2,400. See pages 242-243.

D2. c. The precise complex money multiplier is $(1+c)/(r+c)$ or $1.3/.5 = 2.6$, so the increase in total money is $2,600. See pages 242-243.

Chapter 10:
The Modern Macroeconomic Debate

Chapter at a glance

1. The historical development of macro has involved a debate between laissez-faire and activist economists. Laissez-faire economists oppose government intervention. Activist economists generally favor government intervention. (247)

   Laissez-faire economists are sometimes referred to as Classical economists and activist economists are sometimes referred to as Keynesian economists. However, don't overemphasize the difference between these two camps. There is more agreement among them than disagreement. Moreover, few economists today fall solidly into either camp.

2. Say's Law—supply creates its own demand. (248)

   Say's law implies that any savings (leakage out of the spending stream—the circular flow of spending) would be re-injected back into the spending stream in the form of investment by businesses. Therefore, underspending is very unlikely and there would be no change in the level of economic activity. Moreover, if wages (and prices) are allowed to adjust, any unemployment would not last long because real wages would fall. This Classical reasoning implies there is virtually no role for government in the economy—Classicals advocate a laissez-faire approach.

   The 2 pillars of the Classical Model are:
   1. Say's Law, and
   2. The Quantity Theory of Money:
   (Say's law analysis determines real output and the quantity theory determines the price level)

   According to Clasicals: MV=PQ
   a) Velocity (V) is constant
   b) Real output (Q) is independent of the money supply (M). Moreover, Q is relatively constant and would exist at full employment (potential Q) because of flexible wages and prices
   c) Causation runs from M to P (an increase in M causes an increase in P)

   ✔ *Therefore, $M\overline{V} = P\overline{Q}$.*
   The experience of the Great Depression cast much doubt on the Classical Theory. Keynesian analysis began gaining favor.

Keynesians argue:
a) There is no guaranteed equality between savings and investment (the leakages and injections in the spending stream)
b) Given the institutional realities of relatively fixed prices and wages if people stopped spending as much, firms would decrease their production, creating some unemployment, which would cause a further decline in spending, production, and still more unemployment...

✔ *Therefore, government should increase its spending or cut taxes (fiscal policy), or increase the money supply (monetary policy) to combat unemployment. Keynesians argue for activist government policy.*

3a. The slope of the AED curve is determined by the international effect and the wealth effect (among others) and the repercussions these effects cause. (254)

   As the price level falls, the cash people hold is worth more, making people richer, so they buy more (wealth effect). Also, as the price level in the United States falls (assuming the exchange rate does not change), the price of U.S. goods relative to foreign goods goes down. U.S. exports increase and U.S. imports decrease. That is, the quantity of U.S. goods demanded rises (the international effect). Repercussions of these effects are called multiplier effects (and make the AED curve flatter than otherwise).

3b. Five important initial shift factors of the AED curve are: (256)

   1. Changes in foreign income.
   A rise in foreign income leads to an increase in U.S. exports and an increase (outward shift) of the U.S. AED curve.

   2. Changes in expectations.
   Positive (optimistic) expectations about the future state of the economy could cause an outward shift of the AED curve.

   3. Changes in exchange rates.
   A decrease in the value of the dollar relative to other currencies shifts the AED curve outward to the right.

4.   Changes in the distribution of income.
Typically, as the real wage increases, the AED curve increases (shifts out).

5.   Changes in government aggregate demand policy.
Expansionary macro policy (an increase in government spending and/or a decrease in taxes—fiscal policy; or an increase in the money supply—monetary policy) increases the AED curve, shifting it outward to the right.

✔   *Note: Anything that affects autonomous components of aggregate expenditures (AE or "total spending") is a shift factor of AED (aggregate equilibrium demand). (Recall that $AE = C + I + G + X - M$). These components are autonomous consumption (C), investment (I), government spending (G), and net exports (X − M). Any change in these components of total spending is multiplied by the multiplier effect shifting the AED curve by a multiple of the original change in spending.*

4a.   The AS path has three ranges: (260)

1.   A fixed-price range,
The flat (horizontal) portion; often referred to as "Range A" or the "Keynesian range."

2.   A partially flexible price range, and
The upward sloping portion; often referred to as "Range B" or the "intermediate range." Most economists see the economy in this range.

3.   A perfectly flexible price range.
The vertical portion; often referred to as "Range C" or the "Classical range."

These ranges are determined by empirical observations.

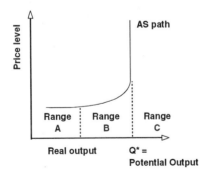

4b.   The horizontal portion of the AS path can shift up or down due to nominal price level shocks. The vertical portion of the AS path can shift left or right due to changes in productive capacity. (263)

Anything which significantly increases (decreases) costs of production or prices of goods will shift the horizontal (and upward sloping) portion of the AS path upward (downward). An increase (decrease) in perceived or actual productive capacity shifts the vertical portion of the AS path to the right (left).

5.   Activist Keynesians see the economy in the fixed-price range of the AS path. Laissez-faire Classicals see the economy in the perfectly-flexible range of the AS path. (262)

Most economists are somewhere between committed Keynesians and committed Classicals; they see the economy in the intermediate range—Range B, where real output changes some, and the price level changes some as the AED curve shifts.

6.   Shifts in aggregate equilibrium demand and the aggregate supply path can affect the price level and real output. How it does so depends upon the shift as well as where the economy is before the shift. (267)

Start at some point of intersection between the AED curve and the AS path. Given a shift of either the AED curve or AS path, simply find the new point of intersection. However, note that any initial change in the AED curve is magnified because of the multiplier effect. The impact on P and Q depends on which range of the AS path we started in and the extent of the shift. ("Problems and Applications" exercise #3 allows you to practice some of this.)

7.   Knowing where potential output is and dealing with structural change are just two reasons why macro policy is more complicated that the model makes it look. (268)

We have no way of precisely determining for sure what range the economy is in, or precisely where the correct target level of potential output is, and therefore of precisely knowing by how much we should shift the AED curve (with the use of macro—fiscal and monetary—policy). Hence, the debate between Keynesians and Classicals can be expected to remain quite lively. However, most economists are neither committed Keynesians nor committed Classicals and therefore see the economy in the intermediate range.

See also, Appendix A: "The Foundations of the Macro Policy Model."

Short-answer questions

1. What was the main difference between Classical and Keynesian economists? (LO1)

2. How does the Keynesian explanation of the Great Depression differ from the Classical explanation? (LO1)

3. What is Say's law and what is the reasoning behind Say's law? (LO2)

4. What is the quantity theory of money? (LO2)

5. What effects determine the slope of the AED curve? (LO3)

6. List some of the important initial shift factors of the AED curve. (LO3)

7. Define the aggregate supply path. What the three ranges of the AS path? (LO4)

8. What will shift the horizontal portion of the AS path up or down? What shifts the vertical portion of the AS path right or left. (LO4)

9. Why do Keynesians believe that activist policies are effective while Classicals believe they are not? Explain using the macro policy model. (LO5)

10. Show graphically the effect of increased government expenditure on real output when the economy is in the fixed price-level range and when it is in the perfectly flexible price-level range of the AS path. (LO6)

11. State two reasons why the macro policy model is more complicated than the model makes it look. (LO7)

Word Scramble

1. _____ _____ _____   2. _____ _____   3. _____ _____
   garetgage   ulpysp   atph   carom lyoipc dmloe   y'sSa   awl.

Match the Terms and Concepts to Their Definitions

____1. aggregate equilibrium demand curve

____2. aggregate supply path

____3. disinflation

____4. equilibrium income

____5. international effect

____6. macro policy model

____7. multiplier effect

____8. potential income

____9. quantity-adjusting markets

____10. quantity theory of money

____11. real business cycle theory

____12. real wage

____13. Say's law

____14. structural readjustment

____15. wealth effect

a. Supply creates its own demand.

b. Phenomenon of the economy trying to change from what it had been doing to doing something new, not to repeat what it did in the past.

c. The level of income that the economy technically is capable of producing without generating accelerating inflation.

d. A curve that shows how a change in the price level will change aggregate equilibrium demand after all the dynamic interactive effects between production and expenditures are taken into account.

e. All changes in the economy are real shifts—shifts in potential income—that reflect real causes such as technological changes or shifting tastes.

f. Markets in which firms modify their supply to bring about equilibrium instead of changing prices.

g. A curve that tells us how changes in aggregate equilibrium demand will be split between real output changes and price level changes.

h. The level of income toward which the economy gravitates in the short run because of the cumulative circles of increasing and decreasing production.

i. Model that demonstrates the effects of macro policy on output and prices.

j. Wage level relative to the price level.

k. As the price level falls, people are richer, so they buy more.

l. As the price level in a country falls the quantity of that country's goods demanded by foreigners and residents will increase.

m. Repercussions that the change in aggregate expenditures has on production and subsequently on income and expenditures.

n. The price level varies in response to changes in the quantity of money.

o. A fall in the rate at which the price level is rising.

Problems and Exercises

1. State the equation of exchange. With that equation answer the following questions:

   a. GDP is $2,000, the money supply is 200. What is the velocity of money?

   b. The velocity of money is 5.60, the money supply is $1,100 billion. What is nominal output?

   c.   Assuming velocity is constant and the money supply increases by 6%, by how much does nominal output rise?

2.   What will likely happen to the shape or position of the *AED* curve in the following circumstances?

   a.   A rise in the price level does not make people feel poorer.

   b.   Income is redistributed from poor people to rich people.

   c.   The country's currency depreciates.

   d.   The exchange rate changes from fixed to flexible.

   e.   Expectations of future rises in the price level develop without any current change in the price level.

3.   State what range of the aggregate supply path you think the economy is in, given the following information:

   a.   The economy is significantly below potential. Downward shifts in aggregate equilibrium demand do not result in falls in the price level.

   b.   Increases in aggregate equilibrium demand result in little change in real output and large increases in the price level.

c. Increases in aggregate equilibrium demand seem to be split roughly equally between increases in real output and increases in the price level.

4. Graphically demonstrate the effect of each of the following on the position of the *AS* curve. Be sure to label all axes.

a. Businesses find that they are able to produce more output without having to pay more wages nor increase their costs of capital.

b. A severe snow storm paralyzes most of the United States.

c. The country's currency appreciates dramatically.

5. What will happen to the position of the *AS* path in the following circumstances?

a. Available inputs fall.

b. A hurricane destroys productive capital.

c. The relative price of oil drops by half.

6. The government of Germany wants to expand its economy through increased spending. Show the likely effects of an activist policy in the following three cases.

a. Economists believe that the economy is in the fixed price-level range.

b.   There are some supply bottlenecks appearing in the economy and most economists think the economy is in the partially flexible price-level range.

c.   Most economists think that the high unemployment figures in Germany reflect structural unemployment.

7.   The Japanese economy has some supply bottlenecks and most economists think it is operating in the partially flexible price-level range on the aggregate supply path. Now suppose the Japanese yen appreciates.

a.   If there is no inflation in the Japanese economy (any shift in the AED is deflationary) what would the likely equilibrium price and output level be after the appreciation?

b.   If there has been inflation in the Japanese economy (any shift in the AED is disinflationary) what would the likely equilibrium price and output level be after the appreciation?

A1. Show the difference between the Classical and the Keynesian adjustment mechanism if the aggregate equilibrium demand falls.

Multiple Choice Questions

1. Classical economists
    a. generally favor government intervention.
    b. generally oppose government intervention.
    c. believe the economy is primarily directed by the invisible handshake.
    d. think unions are not responsible for unemployment.

2. Say's law states that
    a. demand creates its own supply.
    b. supply creates its own demand.
    c. supply and demand are not related.
    d. there is no such thing as a free lunch.

3. When people save, Say's law
   a. is invalidated.
   b. remains true because saving has nothing to do with Say's law.
   c. remains true as long as saving is translated back into investment.
   d. is false because saving creates unemployment.

4. Classical economists believed all the following except
   a. frictional unemployment could exist.
   b. structural unemployment could exist.
   c. cyclical unemployment could be caused by a shortage of aggregate demand.
   d. cyclical unemployment could be caused by inflexible wages.

5. The equation of exchange is
   a. $MP = VQ$.
   b. $MQ = VP$.
   c. $MV = PQ$.
   d. $PV = QM$.

6. In its simplest terms, the quantity theory of money states that
   a. the price level varies in response to changes in the quantity of money.
   b. the equation of exchange is true.
   c. if you count the money you can tell how much unemployment there will be.
   d. the only function of money is as a medium of exchange.

7. If $M = 200$, $V = 4$, P $= 2$, then $Q =$ _____.
   a. 50.
   b. 100.
   c. 200.
   d. 400.

8. Classical economists believed the equation of exchange should be read from
   a. left to right.
   b. right to left.
   c. top to bottom.
   d. bottom to top.

9. To move from the equation of exchange to the quantity theory, all the following assumptions are needed except
   a. Velocity is constant.
   b. Real output is independent of the money supply.
   c. Causation goes from money supply to prices.
   d. Velocity varies in relation to the change in the money supply.

10. The Classical economists' solution to the Great Depression was
    a. reduce the wage rate.
    b. increase aggregate demand.
    c. increase the money supply.
    d. decrease the money supply.

11. Keynes's major problem with the Classical model was that
    a. it focused too much on money.
    b. it was a short-run model.
    c. it lacked a reasonable disequilibrium adjustment mechanism.
    d. it would assume the price level constant.

12. A decrease in foreign income
    a. would likely shift the United States' AED in.
    b. would likely shift the United States' AED out.
    c. would likely make the United States' AED flatter.
    d. would likely make the United States' AED steeper.

13. Suppose there is an increase in the expected future prices in the U.S. This would likely
    a. shift the AED in.
    b. shift the AED out.
    c. make the AED flatter.
    d. make the AED steeper.

14. In the middle of 1985, the value of the Japanese yen rose. This likely:
    a. shifted its AED in.
    b. shifted its AED out.
    c. made its AED flatter.
    d. made its AED steeper.

15. The aggregate supply path is
    a. another name for the short-run aggregate supply curve.
    b. another name for the long-run aggregate supply curve.
    c. a curve based upon institutional realities.
    d. another name for the aggregate demand curve.

16. If the economy is significantly below its potential output, the aggregate supply
    path is generally considered to be
    a. flat.
    b. upward sloping.
    c. backward sloping.
    d. perfectly vertical.

17. If the economy is at its highest potential output, the aggregate supply path is generally considered to be
    a. flat.
    b. upward sloping.
    c. backward sloping.
    d. perfectly vertical.

18. The Keynesian range of the aggregate supply path is
    a. horizontal.
    b. vertical.
    c. upward sloping.
    d. backward bending.

19. Germany has some of the world's highest wage rates. It also has nationwide unions. If the government
    managed to lower labor wages by 12 percent, the aggregate supply path in Germany would likely:
    a. move right.
    b. move left.
    c. move up.
    d. move down.

20. A major technological improvement would likely cause the aggregate supply path of a country to:
    a. move right.
    b. move left.
    c. move up.
    d. move down.

21. Assuming the interdependency between expenditure and production decisions discussed in the text exists, if the economy is in the fixed price-level range and there is an increase in aggregate expenditures, aggregate output will
    a. increase by a multiple of the shift.
    b. decrease by a multiple of the shift.
    c. remain the same.
    d. increase by the amount of the shift.

22. Suppose the AED curve shifted in from AED_0 to AED_1. If there had been inflation and the price level axis is interpreted as inflation relative to expectations, i.e., the shift was disinflationary, the resulting price and output level would be at:
    a. P_1, Q_1.
    b. P_2, Q_1.
    c. P_2, Q_2.
    d. P_1, Q_3.

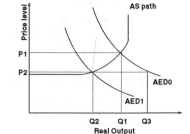

23. When an economy is in Range B of the aggregate supply path, policy making is difficult because:
    a. output cannot be increased by government action.
    b. output can be increased but the cost is price-level stability.
    c. it is impossible to reach potential output or Range C.
    d. trying to do anything might put the economy on a downward spiral.

A1. If a country changes from fixed to flexible exchange rates, one would expect the aggregate demand curve to be
    a. flatter.
    b. unaffected.
    c. steeper.
    d. backward sloping.

A2. If the price level changes one would expect
    a. the aggregate demand curve to shift to the right.
    b. the aggregate demand curve to shift to the left.
    c. the aggregate demand curve to remain unchanged.
    d. the aggregate demand curve to become flatter.

A3. The AED curve includes which of the following that the AD curve does not?
    a. the wealth effect.
    b. the price-level interest rate effect.
    c. the multiplier effect.
    d. the international effect.

A4. The graph to the right shows the first two interactive shifts in the Keynesian AS/AD model. As a result of a decline in aggregate demand, the final Keynesian equilibrium will be at point:
    a. A.
    b. B.
    c. C.
    d. None of the above.

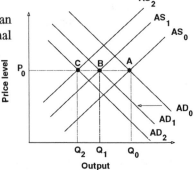

Answers

Short-Answer Questions

1. Classical economists opposed government intervention in the economy whereas Keynesian economists advocated it. (247)

2. Classical economists focused on the real wage. They explained that unemployment would decline if the real wage were allowed to decline. Political and social forces were keeping the real wage to high. Keynesians focused on insufficient aggregate expenditures that resulted in a downward spiral. The economy was at a below-potential-income equilibrium. (247-252)

3. Say's Law states that supply creates its own demand. According to Say's Law people work because they want goods; thus supply creates its own demand. Even if people save, supply still creates its own demand because savings leads to investment. (248-249)

4. The quantity theory of money holds that increases in the money supply cause increases in the price level, and that real output is independent of the money supply and hence the price level. (249-250)

5. The wealth effect, the international effect, and the repercussions these effects cause, i.e., the multiplier effect, determine the slope of the AED curve. (253-254, 256)

6. Five important initial shift factors of the AED curve are: 1. Changes in the world income. 2. Changes in expectations. 3. Changes in exchange rates. 4. Changes in the distribution of income. 5. Changes in government aggregate demand policy. (256)

7. The aggregate supply path is a curve that tells us how changes in aggregate equilibrium demand will be split between real output changes and price level changes. Its three ranges are the fixed price-level range, the partially flexible price-level range, and the perfectly flexible price-level range. (260)

8. The horizontal portion of the AS path could shift up or down due to nominal price level shocks. The vertical portion of the AS path could shift right or left due to changes in actual or perceived productive capacity. (264)

9. Activist Keynesians see the economy in the fixed price-level range of the aggregate supply path. So, the economy can be expanded through activist policies without causing any change in the price level. The Classicals believe the economy to be in the perfectly flexible price-level range of the aggregate supply path. Activist policies would only succeed in changing the price level. Real output would remain unchanged. (262)

10.

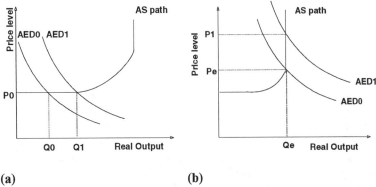

(a)   (b)

Increased government expenditures would shift the AED out to the right from AED0 to AED1 in (a). In the fixed price-level range, the price level would remain the same at P0 but real output would increase from Q0 to Q1. In the perfectly flexible price-level range, the real output would remain unchanged at Qe but the price level would rise from Pe to P1 in (b). (267)

11. Knowing where the potential output of the economy is and coping with structural changes in the economy are two reasons why the macro policy model becomes very complicated. (268)

Word Scramble   1. aggregate supply path   2. macro policy model.   3. Say's law.

Match the Terms and Concepts to Their Definitions
1-d; 2-g; 3-o; 4-h; 5-l; 6-i; 7-m; 8-c; 9-f; 10-n; 11-e; 12-j; 13-a; 14-b; 15-k.

Problems and Exercises

1. $MV = PQ$ where M = quantity of money, V = velocity of money, P = price level, Q = quantity of real output. (249)
   a. $V = 10$: $MV = PQ$; $200V = \$2,000$; $V = 10$. (249)
   b. \$6,160 billion: $MV = PQ$; $(5.6)(1,100) = \$6,160$ billion. (249)
   c. By 6%.

2. a. This would cause the wealth effect to become inoperative and the AED curve will become steeper. (254)
   b. Assuming the marginal propensity to consume of rich people is less than that of poor people, the AED curve will shift to the left. (257)
   c. As the exchange rate depreciates, exports will rise and imports will fall. This shifts the AED curve out. (257)
   d. If the exchange rate were originally assumed to be fixed and became flexible, increases in the price level will be offset by changes in the exchange rate and the international effect becomes inoperative. The *AED* curve will be steeper. (257)
   e. Expectations of future price increases without changes in the current price level will tend to cause the *AED* curve to shift to the right. (256)

3. a. Fixed price-level range. (260-261)
   b. Upwardly flexible price-level range. (260-261)
   c. Partially flexible price-level range. (260-261)

4.

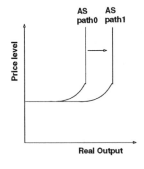   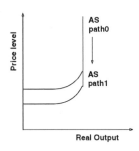

(a)   (b)   (c)

   a. The aggregate supply path shown in (a) shifts to the right from AS path0 to AS path1, because businesspeople are finding that their productive capacity is larger than they had thought. (263-264)
   b. The aggregate supply path shown in (b) shifts to the left from AS path0 to AS path1 because bad weather will hinder production. (263-264)
   c. The aggregate supply path shown in (c) above shifts down from AS path0 to AS path1, because businesses will benefit from the declining import prices to the extent that imports are used in production. The fall in input prices is passed through to the goods market. (263-264)

5. a. A decrease in available inputs shifts the *AS* path to the left. (263-264)
   b. Destruction of productive capital and will cause a shift in the AS path to the left. (263-264)
   c. Initially, to the degree that the fall in the relative price of oil causes the price level to fall, the AS path will shift down. (263-264)

6.

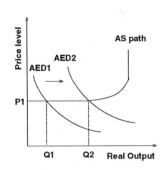

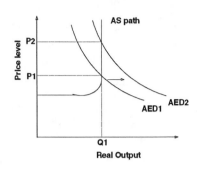

(a)   (b)   (c)

a. The economy is in the fixed price-level range of the aggregate supply path as shown in (a) above. As the AED curve shifts out, the price level remains unchanged at P1, and output increases to Q2. Government activism in this range is very effective. (263-267)

b. The economy is in the partially flexible price-level range of the aggregate supply path as shown in (b) above. As the AED curve shifts out, the price level rises from P1 to P2 and output increases from Q1 to Q2. Government activism in this range is less effective than in Range A. In this range, real output rises by less than in (a) and the economy experiences some demand-pull inflation. (263-267)

c. The economy is in the perfectly flexible price-level range of the aggregate supply path as shown in (c) above. As the AED curve shifts out, the output remains unchanged at Q1 and only the price level increases from P1 to P2. Government activism in this range is ineffective. (263-267)

7. a. The exchange rate appreciation will shift the AED curve back from AED1 to AED2. If there is no inflation in the economy the price level will remain fixed at P1 and output will fall to Q3. (263-267)

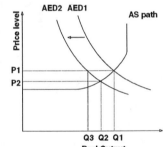

b. In this case, we interpret the vertical axis as a deviation from the expected rate of inflation. If there is inflation in the economy the price level relative to expected inflation will fall to P2 and output will fall only to Q2. (263-267)

A1. In the Keynesian model, effective aggregate demand and aggregate supply are interdependent and the AS path is assumed flat. The shift in demand causes a shift in supply and the shift in supply causes a shift in demand. Since the price level is assumed constant, the adjustment path is along arrow A in graph (a) below. In the Classical model, aggregate demand and supply are not interdependent and wages and the price level are flexible. A drop in demand will lead to a fall in prices while output remains constant as shown in graph (b) below. (277-278)

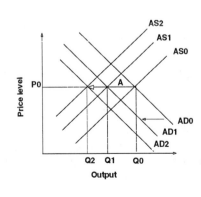

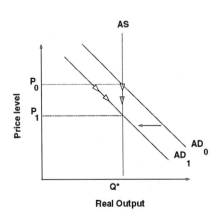

(a)   (b)

Multiple Choice Questions

1. b. See page 247.

2. b. See page 248.

3. c. See pages 249, especially Exhibit 2. The financial sector translates savings into investment.

4. c. See page 249.

5. c. See page 249.

6. a. The correct answer is the definition given in the text on page 249. The "equation of exchange" is a tautology and is true by definition; thus b can't be an answer. The quantity theory of money adds assumptions about the variables in the equation of exchange.

7. d. Since $MV=PQ$; 200 times 4 equals 800, so Q equals 800 divided by 2 or 400. See page 249.

8. a. By reading it from left to right they saw changes in the money supply *causing* changes in prices. See page 250.

9. d. Velocity is constant in the quantity theory. See page 250.

10. a. See page 250. They knew this was unpopular, but it was what their theory said.

11. c. As discussed on pages 251-252, Keynes felt the Classicals had no reasonable explanation of how the aggregate economy adjusted to equilibrium.

12. a. A decrease in foreign income would mean that foreign countries would import less from the U.S., shifting its AED in. See page 256.

13. b. An increase in expected future prices would mean that people would tend to buy more immediately instead of waiting to buy. This would likely shift the AED out. See pages 256-257.

14. a. A rise in the exchange rates would decrease exports and increase imports. This likely shifted the AED in. See page 257.

15. c. See page 258, including Exhibit 4.

16. a. See page 260.

17. d. See page 261.

18. a. See Exhibit 6, page 261.

19. d. Because of the nominal price fall, the aggregate supply path is likely to move down. See page 263.

20. a. Because productive capacity would increase, the aggregate supply path would shift to the right. See pages 263-264.

21. a. Since the price level wouldn't change at all at this range, an increase in aggregate equilibrium demand will cause aggregate output to increase by a multiple of the shift of the initial change in aggregate expenditures. See pages 266-267.

22. c. The deviation from expected inflation will fall to P_2 and the output will fall to Q_2. See pages 265-266.

23. b. Expansionary activist policy could increase income, but the price level will rise as this happens. See page 266

A1. c. The change from fixed to flexible exchange rate means that the international effect is reduced. Since the international effect is one of the reasons the AD curve slopes downward, its elimination makes the AD curve steeper. See pages 273-274.

A2. c. The change in the price level causes a movement along the existing AD curve; it does not change the slope or the position of the aggregate demand curve. See pages 272-273.

A3. c. The AED curve takes into account the interactive effects between aggregate supply and demand. See page 274.

A4. d. According to Keynes the shifts in the effective aggregate demand and the effective aggregate supply curve would continue beyond point C because of the interdependencies between expenditures and production. See pages 277-278.

Chapter 11:
The Macro Debate in Reference to the Aggregate Production/Aggregate Expenditures Model

Chapter at a glance

1. Autonomous expenditures are unrelated to income; induced expenditures are directly related to income. (284)

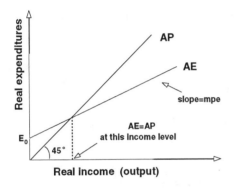

E_0 (autonomous expenditures) can change (shift the AE curve) if there is an autonomous change in any component of aggregate expenditures (AE).

Note: $AE = C + I + G + (X-M)$.

2. To determine income graphically in the Keynesian AP/AE model, you find the income level at which aggregate expenditures equal aggregate production. (287)

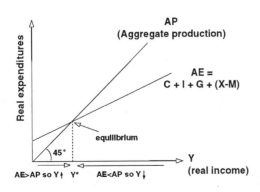

3. To determine income using the Keynesian equation you determine the multiplier and multiply it by the level of autonomous expenditures (289)

Multiplier = 1/(1 −mpe) = 1/mpw.
Y = (multiplier)(Autonomous expenditures)
ΔY = (multiplier)(ΔAutonomous expenditures)

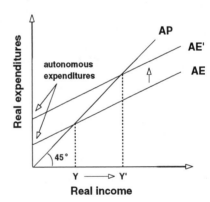

4. The multiplier process works because when expenditures don't equal production, businesspeople change planned production, which changes income, which changes expenditures, which.... (289)

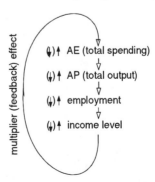

✔ *This is the income adjustment process—the multiplier effect on income given a change in spending.*

151

5a. A mechanistic Keynesian model sees the model as a direct guide for policy; it tells you what policy to follow. An interpretive Keynesian model sees the model as a guide to one's common sense; highlighting important dynamic interdependencies. Before applying the model, one must consider other interdependencies.

The interpretive approach is best. It's the approach taken in the textbook.

The Keynesian model is applied by making policy recommendations (prescriptions) to try to smooth out the business cycles. But all "medicine" should be taken with common sense.

5b. A mechanistic Classical sees the Classical model as a direct guide for policy; an interpretive Classical sees the Classical model as an aid in understanding complicated disequilibrium dynamics with interdependencies. (299)

The Classical model, like the Keynesian model, cannot be applied mechanistically; it is only a guide to common sense.

6. The macro policy model dynamics and the AP/AE model dynamics are equivalent when the price level is fixed. The AED curve can be derived from the AP/AE model. (299)

When the price level is constant (we are in Range A of the AS path) the AP/AE model tells us precisely how much the AED curve will shift when autonomous expenditures shift by a specified amount. The difference between the shift in autonomous expenditures (the AE curve) and the AED curve is due to the multiplier.

See also, Appendix A: "An Algebraic Presentation of the Expanded Keynesian Model."

Short-answer questions

1. What is the difference between induced and autonomous expenditures? (LO1)

2. Draw an AP and AE curve and show how the level of income is graphically determined in the Keynesian aggregate production/aggregate expenditures model. Describe the forces that are set in motion when income levels are above and below equilibrium? (LO2)

3. In the Keynesian model, if autonomous expenditures were $200 and the *mpe* were 0.75, what is equilibrium income? (LO3)

4. Explain the process by which the economy reaches a new equilibrium income if autonomous expenditures increase by $100. The marginal propensity to expend is 0.5. (LO4)

5.   Suppose an economist appears before Congress and states that his model has estimated the *mpe* in the U.S. to be 0.75. Given this estimate he tells the Congress that the $200 reduction in government spending will result in a decline in output of $800 billion. Another economist also testifying before Congress says that the first economist's answer is in the right direction, but too precise. She states that the U.S. economy is complicated and a simple model cannot capture the complicated disequilibrium dynamics of the U.S. economy. How would you characterize the Keynesian model used by each economist and why? (LO5)

6.   Suppose a decrease in the price level causes the AE curve to shift up. How do you show this shift in the macro policy model? (LO6)

7.   What happens to output in the AP/AE model if there is perfect price-level flexibility when the AE curve shifts up due to a shift in autonomous expenditures? (LO6)

Word Scramble

1. _____   2._____   _____
        u t r p m l l i i e   a e e i K n n s y   u t q o n i e a

3._____   _____
        u t s p o o n n m i c   c f i n n o t u

Match the Terms and Concepts to Their Definitions

____1.   aggregate expenditures

____2.   aggregate production curve

____3.   Aggregate Production/Aggregate Expenditures (AP/AE) Model

____4.   autonomous expenditures

____5.   expenditures function

____6.   income adjustment mechanism

____7.   induced expenditures

____8.   interpretive Keynesian model

____9.   Keynesian equation

____10.   marginal propensity to expend

____11.   multiplier

____12.   path-dependent equilibrium

____13.   permanent income hypothesis

____14.   real business cycle theory

a.   Chase between aggregate production and aggregate expenditures.

b.   The hypothesis that expenditures are determined by permanent or lifetime income.

c.   Expenditures that change as income changes.

d.   The theory that fluctuations in the economy reflect real phenomena—simultaneous shifts in supply and demand, not simply supply responses to demand shifts.

e.   Equation that tells us that income equals the multiplier times autonomous expenditures.

f.   Equilibrium that is influenced by the adjustment process to that equilibrium.

g.   A number that tells us how much income will change in response to a change in autonomous expenditures.

h.   In the Keynesian model, the total level of expenditures in an economy, the summation of all four components of expenditures: aggregate consumption, investment, spending by government, and net foreign spending on U.S. goods. It is expressed by the equation $AE = C + I + G + (X - M)$.

i.   In the Keynesian model, the 45° line on a graph with real income measured on the horizontal axis and real production on the vertical axis. Alternatively called the aggregate income curve.

j.   The ratio of a change in expenditures, to a change in income.

k.   Expenditures that are unaffected by changes in income.

l.   Keynesian model that is an aid in understanding complicated disequilibrium dynamics.

m.   Representation of the relationship between expenditures and income as a mathematical function ($E = E_0 + mpeY$, where $E =$ expenditures, $E_0 =$ autonomous expenditures, $mpe =$ marginal propensity to expend, $Y =$ income).

n.   Keynesian model giving "aggregate supply" the name "aggregate production" and focusing on total production changes, not on changes in output caused by price level changes, and emphasizing the difference between the Keynesian focus and the Classical focus on quantity of aggregate supply and demand changes resulting from changes in the price level.

Problems and Exercises

1.   Answer the following questions about the aggregate production curve.

   a.   Draw an aggregate production curve. Label all axes.

b.   What is the slope of the aggregate production function?

c.   Why is the slope as you have drawn it?

2.   You are given the following information about the economy:

Income	Expenditures
0	100
500	500
1000	900
2000	1700
3000	2500
4000	3300

a.   What is the level of autonomous expenditures?

b.   What is the marginal propensity to expend?

c.   What expenditures function (an equation) corresponds to the table?

d.   What is the *mpw*? Explain why it is important.

3.   Putting expenditures and production together:

a.   Graph the expenditures function from question 2 on the aggregate production curve from question 1.

b.   What is the slope of the expenditures function?

4.   Given the following equation, answer the questions: $AE = C_0 + .6Y + I + G + (X - M)$ where $C_0 = 1000$, $I = 500$, $G = 300$, $X = 300$, $M = 400$.

a.   Draw the aggregate expenditures curve.

b.   What is the slope of the curve?

c.   What is the vertical axis intercept?

d.   Add the aggregate production curve.

e.   What is the multiplier?

f.   What is equilibrium income? Label that point A on the graph.

g. What is the effect of an increase in autonomous consumption of $200 on equilibrium income? Demonstrate your answer graphically.

h. What is the effect on equilibrium income of a change in the *mpe* from .6 to .8? Demonstrate your answer graphically. How does your answer to (g) change with the new *mpe*?

5. Calculate the multiplier in each case.

    a. *mpe* = .7

    b. *mpw* = .4

6. For each of the following, state what will happen to equilibrium income.

    a. The *mpe* is 0.9 and autonomous government expenditures just rose $200 billion. Graph your analysis.

    b. The *mpe* is 0.65 and autonomous investment just fell $70 billion. Graph your analysis.

A1. You've just been appointed chairman of the Council of Economic Advisers in Textland. The *mpc* is .8, and all nonconsumption expenditures and taxes are exogenous.

    a.   How can the government increase output by $400 through a change in expenditures?

    b.   Oops! There's been a mistake. Your research assistant tells you that taxes are actually not exogenous, and that there is a marginal tax rate of .1. How can the government change expenditures to increase income by $400?

    c.   There's more new news which your research assistant just found out. She tells you that not only is there a marginal tax rate of .1; there's also a marginal propensity to import of .2. You have to change your solutions now. How can the government change expenditures to increase income by $400?

Multiple Choice Questions

1.   In the Keynesian model the aggregate production curve is
    a. a horizontal line.
    b. a vertical line.
    c. a 45° line.
    d. a downward slope line.

2.   Autonomous expenditures are
    a. expenditures that are automatically created by income.
    b. expenditures that are unrelated to income.
    c. expenditures that change as income changes.
    d. expenditures that automatically change as income changes.

3.   The equation for the expenditures function is
    a. $E = E_0 - mpeY$.
    b. $E = E_0 \times mpeY$.
    c. $E = E_0 + mpeY$.
    d. $E = E_0 + mpe + Y$.

4.   The marginal propensity to expend is the
    a. change in expenditures times change in income.
    b. change in expenditures divided by the change in income.
    c. change in expenditures divided by income.
    d. expenditures divided by the change in income.

5. *Mpe* plus *mpw* equals
    a. zero.
    b. one.
    c. ten.
    d. unknown (cannot be determined).

6. If the *mpe* is .8, what is the size of the multiplier in the Keynesian model?
    a. .5.
    b. 5.
    c. 1.
    d. 10.

7. As the *mpe* rises, the multiplier
    a. increases.
    b. decreases.
    c. remains the same.
    d. sometimes rises and sometimes falls.

8. In the Keynesian *AE/AP* model, if autonomous expenditures are $5,000 and the *mpe* equals .9, what is the level of income in the economy?
    a. $5,000.
    b. $10,000.
    c. $20,000.
    d. $50,000.

9. In the Keynesian *AE/AP* model, if autonomous exports falls by 40 and the *mpe* is .5, what happens to the income?
    a. income rises by 20.
    b. income falls by 20.
    c. income rises by 80.
    d. income falls by 80.

10. In the Keynesian *AE/AP* model if autonomous investment falls by 20 and the *mpe* is .75, what happens to the income?
    a. income rises by 15.
    b. income falls by 15.
    c. income rises by 80.
    d. income falls by 80.

11. In the Keynesian *AE/AP* model, if autonomous consumption increases by 10 and the *mpe* is .8, what happens to the income?
    a. income rises by 8.
    b. income falls by 8.
    c. income rises by 50.
    d. income falls by 50.

12. In the Keynesian *AE/AP* model, if government spending falls by 20 and the *mpe* is .66, what happens to the income?
    a. income rises by 60.
    b. income falls by 60.
    c. income rises by 126.
    d. income falls by 126.

13. In the Keynesian *AE/AP* model, if autonomous imports fall by 40 and the *mpe* is .5, what happens to the income?
    a. income rises by 20.
    b. income falls by 20.
    c. income rises by 80.
    d. income falls by 80.

14. In the Keynesian *AE/AP* model, if autonomous exports falls by 40 and government spending increases by 20, and the *mpe* is .8, what happens to the income?
   a. income rises by 25.
   b. income falls by 25.
   c. income rises by 100.
   d. income falls by 100.

15. The term paradox of thrift refers to the process by which
   a. individuals attempt to save less, but in doing so spend less causing income to decrease, ending up much less than they desired.
   b. individuals attempt to save less, but in doing so spend more causing income to decrease, ending up saving much less than desired.
   c. individuals attempt to save more, but in doing so spend less causing income to decrease, ending up saving less.
   d. individuals attempt to save more, but in doing so spend more causing income to decrease, ending up saving less.

16. The hypothesis that expenditures are determined by permanent or lifetime income (making the mpe close to zero) implies that the AE curve will be close to
   a. a flat line.
   b. a vertical line.
   c. an upward sloping 45⁰ line.
   d. something economists cannot determine.

17. When the price level falls
   a. the aggregate expenditures curve remains constant.
   b. the aggregate expenditures curve shifts down.
   c. the aggregate expenditures curve shifts up.
   d. the slope of the aggregate expenditures curve changes.

18. To derive the aggregate equilibrium demand curve from the Keynesian *AE/AP* model, one must
   a. relate the initial autonomous shifts caused by price level changes on the *AE* curve to the *AED* curve.
   b. relate the *AE/AP* equilibria at different price levels to the *AED* curve.
   c. relate the *AE/AP* equilibria at different quantity levels to the *AED* curve.
   d. relate the initial autonomous shifts caused by price level changes on the *AP* curve to the *AED* curve.

19. If there is partial price-level flexibility
   a. the Keynesian *AE/AP* model is no longer relevant.
   b. the results of the Keynesian *AE/AP* model will be reversed.
   c. the results of the Keynesian *AE/AP* model will be modified but the central point will remain the same.
   d. the Keynesian *AE/AP* model will turn into a Classical model.

20. A path-dependent equilibrium
   a. is an equilibrium that one arrives at in a supply/demand model.
   b. cannot exist since the economy would always be on a path.
   c. the type of equilibrium the Classical model arrived at.
   d. an equilibrium in which the adjustment process influences the final equilibrium.

21. The interpretive Keynesian macro model differs from the mechanistic Keynesian model in that
   a. the interpretive Keynesian model is essentially a Classical model.
   b. the interpretive model sees the Keynesian model as a guide, not a definitive result.
   c. the interpretive Keynesian model integrates the quantity theory into the *AE/AP* model.
   d. the interpretive Keynesian model integrates the quantity theory into both the Keynesian *AS/AD* and the *AE/AP* models.

22. Which group is most likely to believe that a model using autonomous expenditures is relevant?
    a. Keynesians.
    b. Classicals.
    c. Keynesians and Classicals would be equal in their belief.
    d. Neither Keynesians nor Classicals would see a model using autonomous elements as relevant.

23. In the real business cycle theory, business cycles occur because of
    a. changes in the real price level.
    b. changes in real income.
    c. technological and other natural shocks.
    d. changes in the money supply.

24. In the modern Keynesian model, Keynesians see
    a. the real business cycle as totally irrelevant.
    b. the real business cycle as expanded beyond what people desire because of TANSTAFFL.
    c. the real business cycle as exaggerated beyond what people desire because of dynamic externalities.
    d. the real business cycle as true.

A1. If the marginal tax rate increases, what would happen to the general expenditures multiplier?
    a. It would increase.
    b. It would decrease.
    c. It would remain the same.
    d. One cannot say.

A2. In the Keynesian *AE/AP* model, if a country has a very large marginal propensity to import
    a. expansionary fiscal policy would be extremely effective in expanding domestic income.
    b. expansionary fiscal policy would not be very effective in expanding domestic income.
    c. The size of the marginal propensity to import has no effect on the effectiveness of expansionary fiscal policy.
    d. The Keynesian *AE/AP* model is not relevant to a country with a very large marginal propensity to import.

A3. Assuming the marginal propensity to import is .1, the tax rate is .2, and the marginal propensity to expend is .6, the multiplier will be approximately
    a. 0.
    b. 1.2.
    c. 1.6.
    d. 2.6.

A4. Assume the marginal propensity to import is .1, the tax rate is .25, the marginal propensity to expend is .8, and that the government wants to increase income by 100. In the Keynesian model you would suggest increasing government spending by
    a. 10.
    b. 35.7.
    c. 50.
    d. 100.

A5. Assume the marginal propensity to import is .3, the tax rate is .2, the marginal propensity to expend is .5, and that the government wants to increase income by 200. In the Keynesian model you would suggest increasing government spending by
    a. 87.5.
    b. 100.
    c. 180.
    d. 200.

Answers

Short-answer questions

1. Induced expenditures depend upon the level of income. Autonomous expenditures are independent of income. (284)

2. The *AP* curve is a 45 degree line through the origin. At all points on the *AP* curve, output equals income. The *AE* curve is an upward-sloping line with a slope less than one that intersects the expenditures axis at the level of autonomous expenditures. These curves are shown in a graph to the right. Equilibrium income is where the two curves intersect. At points to the left, aggregate expenditures exceed aggregate production and businesses are finding their inventories running down faster than desired. They increase production, which increases income and expenditures, moving income toward equilibrium. At points to the right, aggregate expenditures are less than aggregate production and businesses see their inventories accumulating. They cut production, which cuts income and expenditures, moving income toward equilibrium. (287)

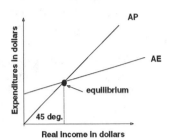

3. To determine equilibrium income multiply the sum of all autonomous expenditures by the multiplier. In this case the multiplier is 1/(1-.75) = 4, so equilibrium income is $800. (289)

4. The initial shock is $100. This increase in expenditures causes aggregate production to increase also by $100, which creates an additional $100 in income. Consumers spend $50 of this additional income on additional goods. Once again aggregate production rises by the same amount as the $50 increase in aggregate expenditures. Subsequent increases in aggregate expenditures and aggregate production are determined in a similar fashion, each time getting smaller and smaller. Equilibrium income is $200 higher at the end of this multiplier process. This is determined by calculating the multiplier, 1/(1-*mpe*) = 2 and multiplying it by the initial rise in aggregate expenditures, $100. (289)

5. The first economist is following a mechanistic Keynesian model while the second is following an interpretive Keynesian model. The mechanistic Keynesian sees the model as a direct guide for policy. An interpretive Keynesian sees the model as a guide to one's common sense, highlighting important dynamic interdependencies. (299)

6. A decline in the price level will shift the AE curve up. This is shown as a movement down along the AED curve connecting the output and price levels corresponding to equilibrium output in the AE/AP model at the two prices. (299-300)

7. In the AP/AE model, a change in autonomous expenditures will be offset entirely by a change in the price level that shifts the AE curve in a direction opposite to the initial shift. If the initial shift causes the AE curve to shift up, prices will rise sufficiently to shift the AE curve back to its initial position. (300)

Word Scramble   1. multiplier   2. Keynesian equation   3. consumption function

Match the Terms and Concepts to Their Definitions
1-h; 2-i; 3-n; 4-k; 5-m; 6-a; 7-c; 8-l; 9-e; 10-j; 11-g; 12-f; 13-b; 14-d.

Problems and Exercises

1. a. The aggregate production curve is a 45 degree line shown on the right. Production is on the vertical axis and real income is on the horizontal axis. (282-283)
   b. The slope is 1. (282-283)
   c. The slope is one because the aggregate production curve represents the identity that aggregate production must equal aggregate income. That can only be represented by a straight line through the origin with slope one. (282-283)

6. a. Income rises by $2 trillion: 200/(1-0.9). In this case the aggregate expenditures curve has a slope of 0.9 as shown in the graph to the right. The increase in government expenditures shifts the *AE* curve up from AE_0 to AE_1 and income increases by a multiple of that amount, in this case by a multiple of 10. (291-292)

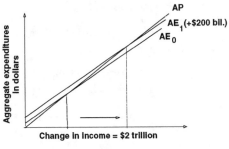

Change in Income = $2 trillion

Income in dollars

b. Income falls by $200 billion: $70/.35. In this case the aggregate expenditures curve has a slope of .65 as shown in the graph to the right. The decrease in investment shifts the *AE* curve down from AE_0 to AE_1 and income decreases by a multiple of that amount, in this case by a multiple of 2.86. (291-292)

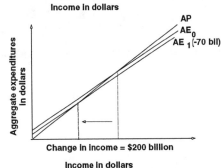

Change in Income = $200 billion

Income in dollars

A1. Given an *mpc* of .8:
   a. Increase expenditures by $80. The multiplier is $1/(1-mpc) = 1/(1-.8) = 5$. Therefore, to increase GDP by $400, government spending has to increase $80. (304-305)
   b. Increase expenditures by $112. The multiplier is $1/(1- mpc + t \times mpc) = 1/(1-.8+.1\times.8) = 3.57$. Therefore, to increase GDP by $400, government spending has to increase by $112. (304-305)
   c. Increase expenditures by $193. The multiplier is $1/(1- mpc + t \times mpc + mpm) = 1/(1-.8+.1\times.8+.2) = 2.08$. Therefore, to increase GDP by $400, government spending has to increase by $192. (304-305)

Multiple Choice Questions

1. c. See pages 282-293, including Exhibit 2.

2. b. See page 284.

3. c. See page 285.

4. b. See page 285.

5. b. See page 290.

6. b. The multiplier equals $1/(1-.8)=1/.2=5$. See pages 288-289.

7. a. You can determine this by substituting into the formula. See page 289.

8. d. The multiplier is 10 so the answer is 10 times $5,000, or $50,000. See page 288.

9. d. The multiplier is 2 so the answer is 2 times -40, or minus 80. See pages 291-292.

10. d. The multiplier is 4 so the answer is 4 times -20, or minus 80. See pages 291-292.

11. c. The multiplier is 5 so the answer is 5 times 10, or 50. See pages 291-292.

12. b. The multiplier is 3 so the answer is 3 times -20, or minus 60. See pages 291-292.

13. c. The multiplier is 2 so the answer is 2 times - (-40), or plus 80. Imports falling is expansionary. See pages 291-292.

14. d. The multiplier is 5 so the answer is 5 times (-40 + 20), or minus 100. See pages 291-292.

15 c.   See page 294.

16. a.   If the mpe is close to zero it would mean that the slope of the AE curve would also be zero, making it flat. See page 297.

17. c.   Since a lower price level makes the cash people hold worth more, people feel wealthier and the *AE* curve shifts up. See page 299.

18. b.   As discussed on pages 299-301, especially Exhibit 12, one considers the effect of different price levels on the *AE* curve to derive an *AED* curve.

19. c.   If you could follow that complicated Exhibit 12(c and d) on page 301 you would see that the results are modified. If you are following that, you're doing great. Have you thought of becoming an economist?

20. d.   As discussed on pages 297-298, in a path-dependent equilibrium the adjustment process influences the final equilibrium. The supply/demand and Classical models are definitely not path-dependent models.

21. b.   As discussed on page 298, the interpretive Keynesian model views the Keynesian model as an aid in understanding. It might integrate the Keynesian model with other models but that is not what is distinctive about it.

22. a.   Keynesians see policy as useful because some aspects of expenditures are autonomous. Classicals see everything as induced, making government policy useless. See pages 297-299.

23. c.   See page 297.

24. c.   As discussed on page 297, modern Keynesians see externalities in the adjustment process that lead to outcomes which do not reflect people's desires.

A1. b.   This is a hard question since it requires some deduction. The marginal tax rate is one of the components of the marginal propensity to expend. It is a leakage from the circular flow, so it makes the multiplier smaller. See pages 304-305.

A2. b.   A large marginal propensity to import reduces the size of the multiplier since the marginal propensity to import is one of the components of the marginal propensity to expend. See pages 304-305.

A3. c.   The multiplier for the full model is $1/(1-b+bt+m)$. Substituting in gives $1/(1-.6+.1+.12)$ or $1/.62$ or a multiplier of about 1.6. See pages 304-305.

A4. c.   First you determine the multiplier. The multiplier for the full model is $1/(1-b+bt+m)$. Substituting in gives $1/(1-.8+.1+.2)$ or $1/.5$ or a multiplier of 2. Dividing 100 by 2 gives an increase of government spending of 50. See pages 304-305.

A5. c.   First you determine the multiplier. The multiplier for the full model is $1/(1-b+bt+m)$. Substituting in gives $1/(1-.5+.3+.1)$ or $1/.9$ or a multiplier of about 1.11. Dividing 200 by 1.11 gives an increase of government spending of about 180. The multiplier is very small because the *mpc* is low and the *mpm* is high. See pages 304-305.

$\mathbb{C}$hapter 12: Demand Management, Fiscal Policy, and the Debate about Activist Demand Management Policy

Chapter at a glance

1. Expansionary fiscal policy involves decreasing taxes or increasing government spending. Contractionary fiscal policy involves increasing taxes or decreasing the government spending. (307)

✔ Use *expansionary fiscal policy* to combat cyclical unemployment and slow growth *during a recession* (a downturn in the business cycle).

✔ Use *contractionary fiscal policy* to combat demand-pull inflation *during an upturn* in the business cycle.

2a. Expansionary fiscal policy stimulates autonomous expenditures, which increases people's income, which increases people's spending even more. (309)

Any increase in autonomous C, I, G or (X-M) times the multiplier [1/(1 - mpe)] equals the change in income

2b. Expansionary fiscal policy shifts the aggregate equilibrium demand curve up. The effect on prices and output depends upon where the economy is on the aggregate supply path. (310)

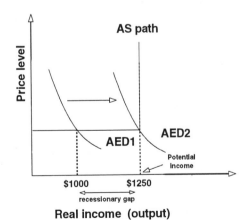

In the graph above, the AS path is simplified with only two ranges, Range A and Range C. If the multiplier is

5 *and there is a recessionary gap of $250, government must increase expenditures by $50 (since $50 × multiplier of 5 = $250) to arrive at potential income. If the AS path had a Range B, the effect of the shift in the AED curve (and the multiplier effect) would be split between increases in real output and increases in the price level.*

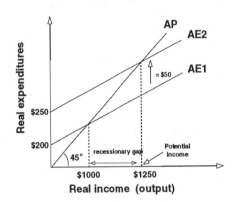

Here is the story using the AP/AE model: In the graph above, initial autonomous AE is $200 and the mpe is 0.8. The multiplier is 1/(1−0.8) = 5. Equilibrium income is $1000. Since there is a recessionary gap of $250, government increases expenditures by $50 (since $50 × multiplier of 5 = $250). This depends upon the economy being in the Keynesian range of the AS path.

Keynesians argue the economy is usually operating in Range A (the horizontal portion of the AS path). Classicals think the economy is usually operating in Range B (upward sloping portion) or Range C (vertical portion), where any increase in aggregate expenditures results in a much smaller increase in income and a much larger increase in the price level.

3. Three alternatives to fiscal policy are directed investment policies, trade policies, and autonomous consumption policies. (315)

Anything which government can do to alter components of AE (I, X-M, and C) will have a multiple impact on Y (the income-output level in the macroeconomy) because of the multiplier. For example, Rosy Scenarios, bank guarantees, reduction in interest rates, export-led growth policies, and increases in consumer credit availability could increase AE and stimulate the economy.

4. A structural deficit is a deficit that would exist at potential income. A passive deficit is the deficit that exists because income is below or above potential income. (319)

A structural deficit can be a problem because the economy cannot "grow" out of it. Passive deficits are not as much a problem because we can grow out of them. Passive deficits are expected to occur during recessions because of the automatic stabilizers.

5. Six assumptions of the model that could lead to problems with fiscal policy are: (323)

   1. Financing the deficit doesn't have any offsetting effects.
   In reality, it often does (e.g., the crowding-out effect).

   2. The government knows what the situation is.
   In reality the government must estimate what the situation is.

   3. The government knows the economy's potential income.
   In reality the government may not know what this level is.

   4. The government has flexibility in terms of spending and taxes.
   In reality, the government cannot change them quickly.

   5. The size of the government debt doesn't matter.
   In reality, the size of the debt often does matter.

   6. Fiscal policy doesn't negatively affect other government goals.
   In reality, it often does.

6. Crowding out is the offsetting effect on private expenditures caused by the government's sale of bonds to finance expansionary fiscal policy. (325)

Increases in the deficit financed by borrowing (selling bonds) leads to increases in interest rates (which increases the cost of borrowing). This leads to lower investment (business spending on capital) which offsets the rise in government spending.

✔ *So, increased deficit spending may be partially or totally offset by decreases in other spending components.*
✔ *The size of the crowding-out effect is debatable.*

7. An automatic stabilizer is any government program or policy that will counteract the business cycle without any new government action. (328)

Automatic stabilizers include:
1. Welfare payments
2. Unemployment insurance, and
3. Income tax system.

Assume a recession which is caused by too little total spending. Government expenditures automatically rise (because of increased welfare payments and unemployment claims). Taxes automatically decrease (because fewer people are earning income). The deficit increases and AE (total spending) increases. This passive deficit is good for the economy because it automatically stimulates AE which is needed during a recession. The opposite occurs during an upturn in the business cycle. <u>Automatic stabilizers help smooth out the business cycle.</u>

Short-answer questions

1. The intial policy proposal by U.S. Keynesian economists was to introduce public works programs. How did that proposal work and what was added to that policy by subsequent Keynesian policymakers? (LO1)

2. Suppose you are the featured speaker at a primer for the first-year Congresspeople. You have been asked to speak about fiscal policy. A Congressperson asks what fiscal policy tools Congress has to affect the economy, and what effect they have on the level of output. You tell her. (LO1)

3. What are contractionary and expansionary fiscal policies? (LO1)

4. How does fiscal policy affect the economy? Demonstrate an expansionary fiscal policy graphically using the macro policy model. (LO2)

5. The first-year Congresspeople are worried about how your answer to question 2. They feel they are politically unable to implement those policies. What three alternatives to fiscal policy can you offer? (LO3)

6. First-year Congresspeople are eager to pass a balanced budget amendment that will make deficits unconstitutional. You warn them about the effects of this amendment by explaining the difference between a structural deficit and a passive deficit. (LO4)

7. How do the six problems of fiscal policy limit its use? (LO5)

8. You are speaking at the Congressional conference. A Congressperson wonders whether the funding of fiscal policy by selling bonds will change the direct effect of fiscal policy. You tell her that it might and explain how. (LO6)

9. Some Classical economists argue that crowding out totally undermines the Keynesian view of fiscal policy. Explain their argument. (LO6)

10. A country has just removed its unemployment insurance program and is experiencing a recession. How will this recession differ from earlier recessions? (LO7)

Word Scramble

1. _____ _____   2._____ '_ _____   3._____ _____
   a c f i l s   y p o l i c   u s O n k   a l w   a a f i i l n n o r t y   a p g

Match the Terms and Concepts to Their Definitions

___ 1. aggregate demand (expenditure) management policy

___ 2. automatic stabilizer

___ 3. crowding in

___ 4. crowding out

___ 5. exchange rate policy

___ 6. export-led growth policy

___ 7. fine tuning

___ 8. fiscal policy

___ 9. inflationary gap

___ 10. Okun's law

___ 11. passive deficit

___ 12. recessionary gap

___ 13. Rosy Scenario policy

___ 14. structural deficit

a. Any policy that increases autonomous exports or decreases autonomous imports, thereby increasing autonomous expenditures.

b. Any government program or policy that will counteract the business cycle without any new government action.

c. Countercyclical fiscal policy designed to keep the economy always at its target or potential level of income.

d. Deliberate change in either government spending or taxes to stimulate or slow down the economy.

e. Deliberately affecting a country's exchange rate in order to affects its trade balance.

f. Government policy of making optimistic predictions and never making gloomy predictions.

g. Portion of the deficit that exists because the economy is operating below its potential level of output.

h. Positive effects of government spending on other components of spending.

i. Proportion of the budget deficit that would exist even if the economy were at its potential level of income.

j. Rule of thumb economists use to translate the unemployment rate into changes in income. "A one percentage point fall in the unemployment rate equals a 2.5 percent increase in income."

k. The offsetting effect on private expenditures caused by the government's sale of bonds to finance expansionary fiscal policy.

l. The difference between equilibrium income and potential income when equilibrium income exceeds potential income.

m. The difference between equilibrium income and potential income when potential income exceeds equilibrium income.

n. Policy aimed at changing the level of income in the economy by a combination of a change in autonomous expenditures and the multiplied induced expenditures resulting from that change.

Problems and Exercises

1. You are hired by the president who believes that the economy is operating at a level $300 billion beyond potential output. You are told that the marginal propensity to expend is 0.5.

   a. The president wants to use taxes to close the gap. What do you advise? Show your answer using the AP/AE model. (Read the Added Dimension on page 315 for a hint).

   b. The president wants to compare your plan in (a) to a plan using spending to close the inflationary gap. What do you advise? Show your answer graphically using the macro policy model.

   c.   Advisers from the council realize that the marginal propensity to expend is 0.75. Recalculate your answer to (b) and show using the macro policy model.

2.   You are called by the president to close a recessionary gap of $1,000. You are told that the mpe is 0. You estimate that the economy is in Range B of the AS path. Show why the expenditures needed to close the gap if the economy were in Range A are insufficient to close the gap when the economy is in Range B.

3.   Calculate the structural deficit and the passive deficit for each of the following:

   a.   Suppose potential income is $6 trillion and actual income is $5.7 trillion. The actual deficit is $200 billion and the marginal tax rate is .25.

   b.   Suppose potential income is $5 trillion and actual income is $4.5 trillion. The actual deficit is $400 billion and the marginal tax rate is .15.

   c.   Suppose potential income is $10 trillion and actual income is $9 trillion. The actual deficit is $500 billion and the marginal tax rate is .3.

4.   Suppose the government wants to increase income by $250 billion. The *mpe* is .6.

   a.   Assuming the economy is in Range A of the AS path, by how much must government increase spending to reach its goal? Show the effect of this action, using the macro policy model.

b. Suppose government finances this increase in spending with the sale of bonds. As a result, interest rates increase. How does this affect the analysis? Demonstrate using the AE/AP model.

5. Congratulations. You have just been appointed economic adviser to Dreamland. For each of the following, advise the president.

   a. The president wants to reduce unemployment from 8 to 6 percent. Income is $40,000 and the *mpe* is .4. What spending policy would you advise?

   b. The president wants to reduce unemployment from 8 to 6 percent. Income is $50,000 and the *mpe* is .75. What fiscal spending policy would you advise?

6. In 1995, national income was $7 trillion and unemployment was 6%. Assume the tax rate is 25%.

   a. Suppose the Chairman of the Council of Economic Advisers believed that the natural rate of unemployment was 5% while the Chairman of the Fed believed that natural rate was 5.5%. Calculate the difference in the underlying estimates of potential income.

   b. Which Chairman would estimate a lower structural deficit?

   c. What spending policy would each recommend to close the recessionary gap, assuming the *mpe* is .5?

Multiple Choice Questions

1. Expansionary fiscal policy involves
    a. increasing taxes.
    b. increasing the money supply.
    c. increasing government spending.
    d. changing the exchange rate.

2. The macro policy that followed from the Keynesian *AE/AP* and macro model is generally called
    a. aggregate supply management.
    b. aggregate demand management.
    c. price-level policy.
    d. exchange rate policy.

3. In the graph on the right, actual income is below potential income. The government is planning to use expansionary fiscal policy. This will
    a. shift the *AP* curve up.
    b. shift the *AE* curve up.
    c. shift the *AP* curve down.
    d. shift the *AE* curve down.

    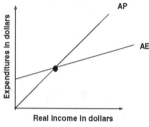

4. In the graph on the right, autonomous imports have just increased. This will cause
    a. the aggregate supply path to shift down.
    b. the aggregate supply path to shift up.
    c. the aggregate equilibrium demand curve to shift to the right.
    d. the aggregate equilibrium demand curve to shift to the left.

    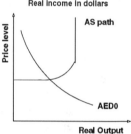

5. The economy has a fixed price level, an *mpe* of .5, and a recessionary gap of 240. Using the Keynesian *AE/AP* model, an economist would advise government to
    a. increase autonomous expenditures by 120.
    b. increase autonomous expenditures by 240.
    c. increase autonomous expenditures by 480.
    d. increase autonomous expenditures by 620.

6. The economy is in Range A of the aggregate supply path, the *mpe* is .8, and there is a recessionary gap of 600. Using the macro policy model, an economist would advise government to
    a. increase autonomous expenditures by 120
    b. increase autonomous expenditures by 480.
    c. increase autonomous expenditures by 600.
    d. increase autonomous expenditures by 3000.

7. The economy has a fixed price level, an *mpe* of .66, and a recessionary gap of 900. Using the Keynesian *AE/AP* model, an economist would advise government to
    a. increase autonomous expenditures by about 30.
    b. increase autonomous expenditures by about 300.
    c. increase autonomous expenditures by about 600.
    d. increase autonomous expenditures by about 2700.

8. The economy has an inflationary gap in the macro policy model at point A. In the graph on the right, the government should shift
    a. the *AS* path up.
    b. the *AS* path down.
    c. the *AED* curve to the right.
    d. the *AED* curve to the left.

    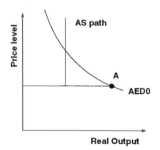

9. Which of the following is true in the late 1990s?
    a. Keynesian economists support fine tuning.
    b. Classical economists support fine tuning.
    c. Both Keynesian and Classical economists generally support fine tuning.
    d. Both Keynesian and Classical economists generally oppose fine tuning.

10. Expansionary aggregate demand policy includes all of the following except
    a. increasing government spending.
    b. increasing autonomous expenditures.
    c. increasing imports.
    d. decreasing taxes.

11. Contractionary aggregate demand policy includes all of the following except
    a. decreasing autonomous investment.
    b. decreasing imports.
    c. decreasing exports.
    d. decreasing government spending.

12. Exchange rate policy is
    a. increasing the size of the government deficit.
    b. deliberately affecting the country's exchange rate in order to affect its trade balance.
    c. deliberately affecting the country's money supply in order to affect its trade balance.
    d. deliberately affecting the country's tax rate in order to affect its trade balance.

13. When there are induced elements of taxes and imports and an expansionary fiscal policy of 100 is run, at the new equilibrium
    a. the government deficit will increase by precisely 100.
    b. the budget deficit will increase by less than 100.
    c. the government deficit will increase by more than 100.
    d. there will be no budget deficit.

14. In an economy the trade deficit is 20. When there are induced elements of taxes and imports and an expansionary fiscal policy is run, at the new equilibrium
    a. the trade deficit will be more than 20.
    b. the trade deficit will be less than 20.
    c. the trade deficit will remain at 20.
    d. the trade deficit will be zero.

15. The portion of the budget deficit that would exist even if the economy were at its potential level of income is called the
    a. structural deficit.
    b. passive deficit.
    c. primary deficit.
    d. secondary deficit.

16. Crowding out occurs when
    a. the government runs a deficit and sells bonds to finance that deficit.
    b. the government prints money.
    c. the government runs a surplus and sells bonds and the people who buy those bonds sell their older bonds to the government.
    d. the tendency for new workers to replace more expensive older workers is a factor.

17. Generally, the U.S. economy is in
    a. a Keynesian range of the price-level flexibility curve.
    b. a Classical range of the price-level flexibility curve.
    c. the intermediate range of the price-level flexibility curve.
    d. an unemployment rate of over 25 percent.

Answers

Short-Answer Questions

1. Keynes's policy proposals worked by starting the multiplier process that got the economy in a low income equilibrium in reverse. It increases aggregate expenditures. Businesses produce more to meet the additional demand which creates additional income. The additional income results in a further increase in ependitures. The process continues until a new equilibrium level of income is reached. Later Keynesians added to that policy: (1) another way to stimulate the economy by reducing taxes, (2) a way to slow down the economy when called for by decreasing spending or increasing taxes, (3) policies to change the money supply as a way of controlling the economy, and (4) general policies to influence components of aggregate expenditures. (307-309)

2. The tools of fiscal policy are changing taxes and changing government spending. Increasing taxes and low-ering spending contract the economy; decreasing taxes and expanding spending expand the economy. (307)

3. Contractionary fiscal policies involve increasing taxes or decreasing government spending. Expansionary fiscal policies involve decreasing taxes or increasing government spending. (309-314)

4. Fiscal policy affects the economy by changing aggregate expenditures, which changes people's incomes, which increases people's spending even more. Expansionary fiscal policy shifts the aggregate equilibrium curve to the right by a multiple of the increase in government spending, as shown in the accompanying diagram. The change in income equals the multiplier times the change in government expenditures. (308-309, 311)

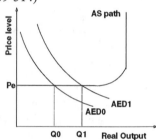

5. Three alternatives to fiscal policy are directed investment policies, trade policies, and autonomous consumption policies. Directed investment policies include talking up the economy so that businesses will invest in expectation of better days and protecting the financial system by guarantees. Trade policies would include government assistance to promote exports. Autonomous consumption policies would include creating institutions conducive to easy credit. (315)

6. A structural deficit is a deficit that would exist at potential income. A passive deficit is the part of the deficit that exists because income is below potential income. (319)

7. The six problems with fiscal policy limit its use in the following ways: (1) Financing the deficit might have offsetting effects, reducing the net effect. (2) The government doesn't always know the current state of the economy and where it is headed, meaning these must be forecast; if you don't know the state of the economy you don't know what fiscal policy to use. (3) The government doesn't know what potential income is, mean-ing it must be estimated; if you estimated it wrong, you get the wrong fiscal policy. (4) The government cannot implement policy easily; if you can't implement it you can't use it. (5) The size of the debt might matter and since deficits create debt, you might not want to use it. And (6) fiscal policy often negatively affects other government goals; if it does you might not use the policy even though it would change the economy in the direction you want. The bottom line is: In extreme cases, the appropriate fiscal policy is clear, but in most cases, the situation is not extreme. (323-327)

8. This first-year Congressperson is sharp! What she has described is crowding out. Crowding out is the offset-ting effect on private expenditures caused by the government's sale of bonds to finance expansionary fiscal policy. If the government finances expansionary fiscal policy through the sale of bonds, interest rates will tend to rise. This will cause investment to decline, offsetting the initial stimulus. (323-325)

9. If crowding out is so strong that the reduced investment totally offsets the expansionary effect of fiscal spend-ing, the net effect of fiscal policy can be zero. (325)

10. Unemployment insurance is an automatic stabilizer, a government program that counteracts the business cycle without any new governtment action. If the income falls, automatic stabilizers will increase aggregate expenditures to counteract that decline. Likewise with increases in income: when income increases, automatic stabilizers decrease the size of the deficit. Eliminating unemployment insurance will eliminate this stabilization aspect of the policy and will contribute to making the recession more severe than it otherwise would have been. However, it would also make people more likely to accept lower wages and search harder for a job, thereby reducing the amount of unemployment. As usual, the answer depends. (328)

Word Scramble   1. fiscal policy   2. Okun's law   3. inflationary gap

Match the Terms and Concepts to Their Definitions
1-n; 2-b; 3-h; 4-k; 5-e; 6-a; 7-c; 8-d; 9-l; 10-j; 11-g; 12-m; 13-f; 14-i.

Problems and Exercises

1. a. The spending multiplier is 2, 1/(1-.5), but only a fraction of the increase in taxes reduces spending. Taxes must be increased by $300 to reduce income by $300 billion. We calculate this by solving the following for change in taxes: change in taxes $\times mpe \times 1/(1-mpe)) =$ $300 billion. (312-315)

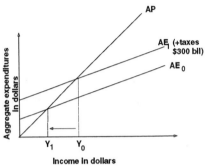

b. The spending multiplier is 2. Spending must be decreased by $150 to reduce income by $300 billion. We calculate this by solving the following for change in government spending: change in government spending $\times (1/(1-mpe)) = -300$ billion. This is shown in the graph on the right. (312-315)

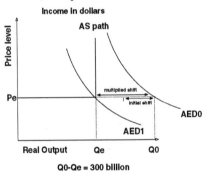

c. The spending multiplier is now 4, 1/(1-.75). Government spending must be decreased by $75 billion to reduce income by $300 billion. We calculate this by solving the following for change in government spending: change in government spending $\times 4 = -300$ billion. This is shown in the graph to the right. Notice that the initial shift in the AED curve is smaller than in (b). If (b) and (c) had been shown using the AE/AP model, the *AE* curve in (c) would be steeper than the AED curve for (b). (312-315)

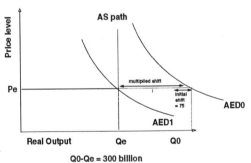

2. To close the recessionary gap in Range A, government expenditures need to rise by the full amount of the gap because the multiplier is 1. This is shown as a shifting from AED0 to AED1. However, given that the economy is in Range B, the same shift of $1000 from AED1 to AED2 will not close the gap because the increase in expenditures is split between an increase in the price level and an increase in output. When expenditures rise by $1,000, a recessionary gap of Q3-Q2 remains. (312-315)

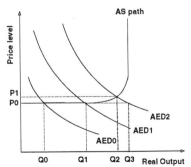

3. a. There is an income shortfall of $300 billion ($6 - $5.7 trillion). If the economy were at potential, tax revenue would be $75 billion higher and the deficit would be $125 billion. The structural deficit is $125 billion. The $75 billion (.25×300 billion) is the passive deficit. (319-320)

   b. There is an income shortfall of $500 billion ($5 - $4.5 trillion). If the economy were at potential, tax revenue would be $75 billion higher and the deficit would be $325 billion. The structural deficit is $325 billion. The $75 billion (.15×500 billion) is the passive deficit. (319-320)

   c. There is an income shortfall of $1 trillion ($10 - $9 trillion). If the economy were at potential, tax revenue would be $300 billion higher and the deficit would be $200 billion. The structural deficit is $200 billion. The $300 billion (.3×1 trillion) is the passive deficit. (319-320)

4. The spending multiplier is 2.5 (1/(1-.4)). (310-314)

   a. Assuming the economy is in range A of the AS path government must increase spending on goods and services by $100 billion to increase income by $250 billion. This is shown to the right as a rightward shift in the *AED* curve of $100 billion from *AED*$_0$ to *AED*$_1$. Income increases by a multiple of that amount, by 2.5×100 = $250 billion. If the economy is in range B, the increase in expenditures will be split between increases in real output and the price level. To increase income by $250, expenditures must increase by some amount more than $100 billion. (310-314)

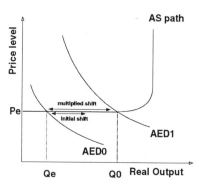

   b. Again, we're assuming the economy is in Range A of the AS path. Since interest rates have risen, investment declines and the *AE* curve shifts down, partially offsetting the initial increase in aggregate expenditures. The net effect of the spending increase is smaller than $250 billion. This is shown by a shift down in the *AE* curve from *AE*$_1$ to *AE*$_2$ resulting in income Y_2, lower than Y_1. (310-314, 323-324)

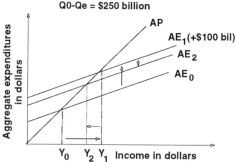

5. a. Increase spending by $1,200. According to Okun's Law, to decrease unemployment by 2 percent income must rise 5 percent, which in this case is $2,000. With an *mpe* of .4 and thus a multiplier of 1.67, the government needs to increase spending by $2,000/1.67 or $1,200 (325-326)

   b. Increase spending $625. According to Okun's Law to decrease unemployment by 2 percent income must rise 5 percent, which is $2,500. With an *mpe* of .75 and thus a multiplier of 4, the government needs to increase spending by $2,500/4 or $625. (325-326)

6. a. Since a 1 percent decrease in the unemployment rate means an increase in income of 2.5%, or, in 1995, $175 billion, the difference in their estimates of potential is $87.5 billion (.5×175). The Chairman of the CEA believed potential income was $7.175 trillion while the Chairman of the Fed believed potential income was $7.0875 trillion. (319-320, 325-326)

   b. Since the Chairman of the CEA believed the natural rate of unemployment was lower, his estimate of the structural deficit would be lower by $21,875 million. According to the Chairman of the CEA, the shortfall in income was $175 billion. According to the Chairman of the Fed, the shortfall in income was $87.5 billion. The difference in these shortfalls times the tax rate, 25%, is the amount by which their estimates differed. (319-320, 325-326))

   c. The spending multiplier is (1/(1-*mpe*)) = 2. The Chairman of the CEA would suggest an increase in spending of $175/2 = $87.5 billion while the Chairman of the Fed would suggest an increase in spending of $87.5/2 = $43.75 billion. (319-320, 325-326))

Multiple Choice Questions

1. c.   See page 309.

2. b.   See page 309.

3. b.   See Exhibit 1, page 310.

4. d.   See Exhibit 1, page 310. Also remember from earlier chapters that an increase in imports is a decrease in autonomous expenditures.

5. a.   To determine how much to increase expenditures in the Keynesian *AE/AP* model to reach potential income, you divide the recessionary gap of 240 by the multiplier of 2. See pages 311-312.

6. a.   To determine how much to increase expenditures in the macro policy model in Range A of the AS path, you divide the recessionary gap, 600, by the multiplier, 5. See pages 311-312.

7. b.   To determine how much to increase expenditures in the Keynesian *AE/AP* model to reach potential income, you divide the recessionary gap of 900 by the multiplier of 3. See pages 311-312.

8. d.   Aggregate demand management policies do not affect the AS, so a and b are out. With an inflationary gap you want to decrease output, so the answer is d. See Exhibit 3 on page 313.

9. d.   As discussed on page 314, while earlier Keynesian economists supported fine tuning, modern Keynesian economists do not.

10. c.   Increasing imports is contractionary. See pages 312-314.

11. b.   Decreasing imports is expansionary. See pages 312-314.

12. b.   See page 318.

13. b.   When there are induced elements of taxes, the increase in income will bring in more taxes, reducing the actual deficit at the new equilibrium. See page 319.

14. a.   When there are induced elements of imports, the increase in income will increase imports, increasing the trade deficit at the new equilibrium. See page 319.

15. a.   See page 319.

16. a.   See page 323. Answer c, if you could follow it, is nonsensical.

17. c.   When it is not in this range there is a consensus of action that brings it back into this range. See page 329.

Chapter 13:
Monetary Policy and the Debate about Macro Policy

Chapter at a glance

1. Monetary policy is a policy that influences the economy through changes in the money supply and available credit. (333)

   Expansionary (contractionary) monetary policy shifts the AED curve to the right (left). The effect on real income depends upon the range of the AS path the economy is operating in.

2a. The Fed is a semiautonomous organization composed of 12 regional banks. It is run by the Board of Governors. (335)

   The Fed (Federal Reserve Bank) is in charge of monetary policy (changing the money supply, credit availability, and interest rates).

2b. Congress gave the Fed six explicit duties. The most important is conducting monetary policy. (336)

   6 Functions of the Fed:
   1. *Conducting monetary policy (influencing the supply of money and credit in the economy).*
   2. *Supervising and regulating financial institutions.*
   3. *Serving as a lender of last resort to financial institutions.*
   4. *Providing banking services to the U.S. government.*
   5. *Issuing coin and currency.*
   6. *Providing financial services (such as check clearing) to commercial banks, savings and loan associations, savings banks, and credit unions.*

3. The three tools of monetary policy are: (338)

   1. Changing the reserve requirement;
   This is the least-used tool. It is a potentially very powerful tool (could be a case of overkill) because it changes (1) banks, excess reserves and (2) the money multiplier.

   2. Changing the discount rate; and
   The discount rate is the interest rate the Fed charges banks for loans. It is the least powerful tool.

   ✔ *Banks don't usually like to borrow from the Fed any more than we do from our parents.*

   3. Executing open market operations.
   Open market operations are the Fed's buying and selling of U.S. government securities. This is the most frequently used and most important tool to change the money supply.

   ✔ *Assume a recession:*
   The Fed should increase the money supply (pursue an expansionary monetary policy) by doing any one or more of the following:
   1. Decrease the reserve requirement.
   2. Decrease the discount rate.
   3. Buy government securities.

4. The Federal funds rate is the interest rate banks charge one another for overnight bank reserve loans. The Fed determines whether monetary policy is loose or tight depending upon what's happening to the Fed funds rate. The Fed funds rate is an important intermediate target. (343)

   The Fed targets a range for the Fed funds rate. If the Fed funds rate goes above (below) that target range, it buys (sells) bonds. These are "defensive" actions by the Fed.

5. In the Keynesian model, monetary policy works as follows: (344)
   Contractionary monetary policy:
   $$M\downarrow \Rightarrow i\uparrow \Rightarrow I\downarrow \Rightarrow Y\downarrow$$
   Used during an upturn in the economy to close an inflationary gap.

   Expansionary monetary policy:
   $$M\uparrow \Rightarrow i\downarrow \Rightarrow I\uparrow \Rightarrow Y\uparrow$$
   Used during a downturn in the economy to close a recessionary gap.

To increase the money supply (M2), the Fed must first increase banks' excess reserves and therefore bank loans.

Keynesians emphasize interest rates because it is changes in interest rates (i) which change investment (I) and eventually change income (Y).

6. In the Classical model, monetary policy works through the quantity theory: $MV = PQ$. It has short-run effects on real output, Q, but in the long run it affects only the price level, P. (346)

Three assumptions Classicals make in the quantity theory of money:
1. Velocity (V) is constant.
2. Real output (Q) is independent of the money supply (M).
3. Causation goes from money (M) to prices (P). That is, an increase (decrease) in M causes an increase (decrease) in P.

Classicals argue:
1. The short-run impact of changes in M are unpredictable because of the effects on inflationary expectations, and therefore interest rates.
2. In the long run we're already at full employment, so Q is fixed. Because V is constant any increase in M will only increase P (the price level).

✔ *The short-run effects of monetary policy are uncertain. The long-run effect is negative. So don't change M. Keep M constant, or increase it at a constant rate equal to the potential annual growth rate of the economy. That is, follow a monetary rule.*

7. Five problems of monetary policy: (345)

    1. Knowing what policy to use.
    Need to know the potential income level first.

    2. Understanding what policy you're using.
    Fed only indirectly controls M.

    3. Lags in monetary policy.
    It takes time to work.

    4. Political pressure.
    Fed is not totally insulated from political pressures.

    5. Conflicting international goals.
    We live in a global economy. The desired domestic policy may adversely affect the exchange rate value of the dollar and our trade balance.

See also,
Appendix A: "The Effect of Monetary Policy Using T-Accounts."
Appendix B: "Keynesian and Classical Theories of interest and Their Implications for Monetary Policy."

Short-answer questions

1. You have been asked to speak to the first-year Congresspeople. Your talk is about the Fed. They want to know what monetary policy is. You tell them. (LO1)

2. To clarify your answer to question 1 tell when the Fed was created and what its specific duties are. (LO2)

3. Another Congressperson asks what monetary policy actions the Fed can take. You answer. (LO3)

4. You are asked to elaborate on your answer to question 3. Now that you have listed each of the tools of monetary policy, how does each work? (LO3)

5. One Congressperson realizes that the Fed does not have complete control over the money supply. She states that people could demand more cash, which will reduce the money supply. How does the Fed know whether its buying and selling of bonds is having the desired effect? You answer by explaining the Fed's intermediate target. (LO4)

6. Another Congressperson asks how monetary policy can keep the economy from overheating. You reply from a Keynesian perspective. (LO5)

7. Suppose the economy is below potential output. Now how can monetary policy boost output? You reply again from a Keynesian perspective. (LO5)

8. Someone from the audience speaks up after your answers to the last two questions. "That's not what I remember from my college economics course." After some discussion you realize that her professor was a Classical economist. You explain to everyone how your answers to 6 and 7 change if answered from a Classical perspective. (LO6)

9. You take one final question at the conference and it is a difficult one: "It doesn't seem that the Fed is doing a good job. I read in the paper that the Fed has followed too contractionary a policy and has caused a recession or that it is not even sure what policy it is following." How do you respond to those concerns? (LO7)

Word Scramble

1. _____ _____   2. _____   3. _____ _____ _____
     a e m n o r t y   c y p o l i   e F d   p o n e   a e k m r t   t s r p o o n i e a

Match the Terms and Concepts to Their Definitions

_____ 1. central bank

_____ 2. contractionary monetary policy

_____ 3. discount rate

_____ 4. equation of exchange

_____ 5. expansionary monetary policy

_____ 6. Federal Open Market Committee (FOMC)

_____ 7. Federal funds rate

_____ 8. monetary base

_____ 9. nominal interest rate

_____ 10. open market operations

_____ 11. quantity theory of money

_____ 12. real interest rate

_____ 13. reserve requirement

_____ 14. veil of money assumption

_____ 15. velocity of money

a. The theory that the price level varies in direct response to change in the quantity of money.

b. Interest rate you actually see and pay.

c. Interest rate adjusted for expected inflation.

d. Assumption that holds that real output is not influenced by changes in the money supply.

e. Rate of interest the Fed charges on loans it makes to banks.

f. The Fed's day-to-day buying and selling of government securities.

g. The number of times per year, on average, a dollar goes around to generate a dollar's worth of income.

h. The percentage the Federal Reserve System sets as the minimum amount of reserves a bank must have.

i. A banker's bank; it conducts monetary policy and supervises the financial system.

j. The vault cash plus reserves that banks have at the Fed.

k. Monetary policy aimed at raising the money supply and raising the level of aggregate demand.

l. Monetary policy aimed at reducing the money supply and reducing the level of aggregate demand.

m. The Fed's chief policy making body.

n. The interest rate banks charge one another for Fed funds.

o. An equation for "quantity of money times velocity of money equals the price level times the quantity of real goods sold."

Problems and Exercises

1. The Fed wants to change the reserve requirement in order to change the money supply (which is currently $3,000). For each situation below, calculate the current reserve requirement and the amount by which the Fed must change the reserve requirement to achieve the desired change in the money supply. Assume no cash holdings.

   a. Money multiplier is 3 and the Fed wants to increase money supply by $300.

   b. Money multiplier is 2.5 and the Fed wants to increase the money supply by $300.

  c. Money multiplier is 4 and the Fed wants to decrease the money supply by $500.

  d. Money multiplier is 4 and the Fed wants to increase the money supply by $1,000.

2. How do your answers change for 1 (a) - (d) if instead of changing the reserve requirement, the Fed wants to use an open market operation to change the money supply? Assume the reserve requirement remains unchanged. What should the Fed do to achieve the desired change? (The multiplier and desired change in money supply for each are listed.)

  a. Money multiplier is 3 and the Fed wants to increase money supply by $300.

  b. Money multiplier is 2.5 and the Fed wants to increase the money supply by $300.

  c. Money multiplier is 4 and the Fed wants to decrease the money supply by $500.

  d. Money multiplier is 4 and the Fed wants to increase the money supply by $1000.

3. Instead of changing the reserve requirement or using open market operations, the Fed wants to change the discount rate to achieve the desired change in the money supply. Assume that for each 1 percentage point fall in the discount rate, banks borrow an additional $20. How do your answers change to from answers 1 (a)-(d)? (The multiplier and desired change in money supply for each are listed.)

  a. Money multiplier is 3 and the Fed wants to increase money supply by $300.

  b. Money multiplier is 2.5 and the Fed wants to increase the money supply by $300.

  c. Money multiplier is 4 and the Fed wants to decrease the money supply by $500.

d. Money multiplier is 4 and the Fed wants to increase the money supply by $1,000.

4. a. What are the three assumptions that translate the equation of exchange into the quantity theory of money?

   b. State the equation of exchange and show how the three assumptions lead to the conclusion that inflation is always and everywhere a monetary phenomenon.

5. Answer the following questions about the quantity theory of money: Assume the money supply is $1,200 billion, the price level is $1.25, and the velocity of money is 6.

   a. What is the level of real output?

   b. What is the level of nominal output?

   c. Assuming the velocity of money remains at 6, what will nominal output be if the money supply increases by 7%?

   d. Assuming the velocity of money remains at 6, by how much will prices rise if the money supply increases by 7%?

6. Fill in the blanks in the following table:

	Inflation rate	Nominal Interest Rate	Real Interest rate
a.	5%	10%	____
b.	____	15%	7%
c.	-3%	____	9%
d.	4%	____	10%

7. Suppose the Fed decides to pursue an expansionary monetary policy. The money supply is currently $1 billion. Assume people hold no cash, the reserve requirement is 10 percent, and there are no excess reserves.

   a. By how much must the Fed change the reserve requirement to increase the money supply by $100 million?

   b. What would the Fed do to increase the money supply by $100,000 through open market operations?

8. The money supply is currently $1 billion. Assume people hold 25 percent of their money in the form of cash balances, the reserve requirement is 25 percent, and there are no excess reserves.

   a. By how much must the Fed change the reserve requirement to increase the money supply by $200 million?

   b. What would the Fed do to increase the money supply by $200 million through open market operations?

A1. Suppose the money multiplier is 2.5 and there are no cash holdings. Textland Bank is the only bank in the country. The Fed wants to decrease the money supply by $10,000. The initial balance sheet is shown below.

Initial Balance Sheet

Assets		Liabilities	
Cash	20,000	Demand Deposits	50,000
Loans	120,000	Net Worth	100,000
Phys. Assets	10,000		
Total Assets	150,000	Total Liabilities and net worth	150,000

a. What open market operations must the Fed execute to reduce the money supply by $10,000?

b. Using T-accounts show the first two steps of the effects of the Fed open market operation reducing the money supply by $10,000.

Step #1

Assets	Liabilities

Step #2

Assets	Liabilities

c. Show the final balance sheet for Textland bank.

Final Position

Assets	Liabilities

A2. Using T-accounts, show the effect of a decrease in the reserve ratio from .2 to .1 given the following initial position of Textland. Again, Textland is the only bank, no one holds cash, and there are no excess reserves. Show the first two steps and the then the final position.

Initial Position

Assets		Liabilities	
Cash	40,000	Demand Deposits	200,000
Loans	230,000	Net Worth	100,000
Phys. Assets	30,000		
Total Assets	300,000	Total Liabilities	
		and net worth	300,000

Step #1

Assets	Liabilities

Step #2

Assets	Liabilities

Final Position

Assets	Liabilities

Multiple Choice Questions

1. The central bank of the United States is
    a. the Treasury.
    b. the Fed.
    c. the Bank of the United States.
    d. Old Lady of Threadneedle Street.

2. Monetary policy is
    a. a variation of fiscal policy.
    b. undertaken by the Treasury.
    c. undertaken by the Fed.
    d. the regulation of monetary institutions.

3. There are seven Governors of the Federal Reserve, who are appointed for terms of
    a. 5 years.
    b. 10 years.
    c. 14 years.
    d. 17 years.

4. Explicit functions of the Fed include all the following except
    a. conducting monetary policy.
    b. conducting fiscal policy.
    c. providing banking services to the U.S. government.
    d. serving as a lender of last resort to financial institutions.

5. FOMC stands for
    a. Federal Open Money Committee.
    b. Federal Open Market Committee.
    c. Fixed Open Market Commitments.
    d. Federation of Open Monies Committee.

6. Tools of monetary policy include all the following except
    a. changing the reserve requirement.
    b. changing the discount rate.
    c. executing open market operations.
    d. running deficits.

7. Assuming $c = .2$ and $r = .1$, the approximate real-world money multiplier would be
    a. 1.33.
    b. 2.33.
    c. 3.33.
    d. 4.33.

8. The discount rate refers to
    a. the lower price large institutions pay for government bonds.
    b. the rate of interest the Fed charges for loans to banks.
    c. the rate of interest the Fed charges for loans to individuals.
    d. the rate of interest the Fed charges for loans to government.

9. The primary tool of monetary policy is
    a. open market operations.
    b. changing the discount rate.
    c. changing the reserve requirement.
    d. imposing credit controls.

10. The Fed wants to increase the money supply.
    a. It should buy bonds.
    b. It should sell bonds.
    c. It should pass a law that the interest rates rise.
    d. It should pass a law that the interest rates fall.

11. When the Fed sells bonds, the money supply is
    a. expanded.
    b. contracted.
    c. Selling bonds does not have any effect on the money supply.
    d. sometimes raised and sometimes lowered

12. An open market purchase
    a. raises bond prices and reduces interest rates.
    b. raises both bond prices and interest rates.
    c. reduces bond prices and raises interest rates.
    d. reduces both bond prices and interest rates.

13. The Federal funds rate is
    a. the interest rate the government charges banks for Fed funds.
    b. the interest rate the Fed charges banks for Fed funds.
    c. the interest rate the banks charge individual investors for Fed funds.
    d. the interest rate the banks charge each other for Fed funds.

14. If the Fed undertakes expansionary monetary policy the effect will be to
    a. shift the AED curve to the right.
    b. shift the AED curve to the left.
    c. shift the AS path up.
    d. shift the AS path down.

15. If the Fed undertakes contractionary monetary policy the effect will be to
    a. shift the AED curve to the right.
    b. shift the AED curve to the left.
    c. shift the AS path up.
    d. shift the AS path down.

16. Which of the following is the path through which contractionary monetary policy works?
    a. money down implies interest up implies investment down implies income down.
    b. money down implies interest down implies investment down implies income down.
    c. money down implies interest up implies investment up implies income down.
    d. money down implies interest down implies investment up implies income down.

17. In the Classical model, monetary policy works through the quantity theory, which is designed around the equation of exchange. This equation of exchange is
    a. $MV = PM$.
    b. $MV = PQ$.
    c. $AE = AP$.
    d. $MF = CE$.

18. In 1997 nominal GDP in the U.S. was approximately $7.5 trillion, and the money supply was approximately $3.75 trillion. The velocity of money was
    a. 1/2
    b. 2
    c. $7.5 \times $3.75
    d. cannot be determined.

19. An economist has just said she favors "steady as you go" monetary policy. This economist
    a. is most likely a Keynesian.
    b. is most likely a Classical.
    c. could equally be either a Keynesian or a Classical.
    d. must be neither a Keynesian nor a Classical, since neither group favors such a policy.

20. Expected inflation is 4 percent; nominal interest rates are 7 percent; the real interest rate is
    a. 1 percent.
    b. 2 percent.
    c. 3 percent.
    d. 7 percent.

21. The real interest rate is 3 percent; the nominal interest rate is 7 percent. It is likely that one could deduce an expected inflation rate of
    a. 1%.
    b. 2%.
    c. 3%.
    d. 4%.

22. The Fed most directly controls
    a. M_1.
    b. M_2.
    c. the monetary base.
    d. the amount of credit in the economy.

B1. The Keynesian theory of the interest rate says that the interest rate is determined primarily in the
    a. money market.
    b. saving/investment market.
    c. real economy.
    d. exogenously.

B2. The Classical theory of the interest rate says that the interest rate is determined primarily in the
    a. money market.
    b. saving/investment market.
    c. foreign exchange market
    d. exogenously.

Answers

Short-answer questions

1. Monetary policy is a policy that influences the economy through changes in the money supply and available credit. The Fed conducts U.S. monetary policy. (333)

2. The Fed was created in 1913. Its six explicit duties are (1) conducting monetary policy, (2) regulating financial institutions, (3) serving as a lender of last resort, (4) providing banking services to the U.S. government, (5) issuing coin and currency, and (6) providing financial services to financial institutions. (336-337)

3. The three tools of monetary policy at the disposal of the Fed are (1) changing the reserve requirement, (2) changing the discount rate, and (3) executing open market operations (buying and selling bonds). (338)

4. Changing the reserve requirement changes the amount of reserves the banks must hold and thus changes the amount of loans they can make. This changes the money supply. Changing the discount rate changes the willingness of banks to borrow from the Fed to meet reserve requirements, thus changing the amount of loans they are willing to make. This changes the money supply. Open market operations change the reserves banks hold by directly increasing or decreasing cash held by banks and simultaneously decreasing or increasing their holdings of government bonds. This changes the amount of loans banks can make and changes the money supply. (338-341)

5. Economists and policymakers keep a close eye on the Fed funds rate, the rate banks charge one another for loans of reserves, as an intermediate target to determine the effect of an open market operation—whether it indeed was expansionary or contractionary. An expansionary action will lower the Fed funds rate and contractionary action will raise the Fed funds rate. In effect, the Fed chooses a range for the Fed funds rate and buys and sells bonds to keep the Fed funds rate within that range. If the Fed funds rate is below (above) the target, the Fed sells (buys) bonds. (343)

6. Contractionary monetary policy in the Keynesian model increases interest rates, lowers investment, and reduces income. (344)

7. Expansionary monetary policy in the Keynesian model decreases interest rates, raises investment, and increases income. (344)

8. Contractionary monetary policy in the Classical model works through the quantity theory of money, $MV = PQ$. Classicals believe that V is relatively constant, Q is determined by forces outside the model, and causation goes from MV to PQ. In the short run, it can lead to decreases in output, but in the long run, it only leads to decreases in the price level. Expansionary monetary policy in the Classical model works through the quantity theory of money, $MV = PQ$. In the short run, it can lead to increases in output, but in the long run, it only leads to inflation. (346-349)

9. You tell the Congressperson that conducting monetary policy is difficult. Five problems often encountered in conducting monetary policy are: (1) Knowing what potential income is. No one has the magic number. It must be estimated. (2) Knowing whether the policy you are using is contractionary or expansionary. The Fed does not directly control the money supply. (3) There are significant lags in the effect of monetary policy in the economy. (4) The Fed is subject to political pressure. And (5) often domestic goals differ from international goals when deciding which policy to follow. (350-351)

Word Scramble   1. monetary policy   2. Fed   3. open market operations

Match the Terms and Concepts to Their Definitions

1-i; 2-l; 3-e; 4-o; 5-k; 6-m; 7-n; 8-j; 9-b; 10-f; 11-a; 12-c; 13-h; 14-d; 15-g.

Problems and Exercises

1. a. Current $r = 1/3$; New $r = .3$, so it must be changed by .03. To find the reserve requirement solve $1/r = 3$ for r. $r = 1/3$. These calculations are based on the formula $M = (1/r) \times MB$, where M is the money supply, r is the reserve ratio, and MB is the monetary base (here it equals reserves). We first find out the cash (monetary base) that supports \$3,000 money supply with a money multiplier of 3. It is \$1,000. We want the money supply to be \$3,300. So the multiplier we want is \$3,300/1,000= 3.3. Again solving $1/r = 3.3$ we find r must be 0.3. (339)
    b. To find the reserve requirement solve $1/r = 5/2$ for r. $r = .4$. Cash must be \$1,200 to support money supply of \$3,000. The Fed must reduce the reserve requirement to .3636 to increase the money supply by \$300. Use the method described in (a) to find the answer. (339)
    c. To find the reserve requirement solve $1/r = 4$ for r. $r = .25$. Cash must be \$750 to support money supply of \$3,000. The Fed must increase the reserve requirement to .3 to decrease the money supply by \$500. Use the method described in (a) to find the answer. (339)
    d. To find the reserve requirement solve $1/r = 4$ for r. $r = .25$. Cash must be \$750 to support money supply of \$3,000. The Fed must reduce the reserve requirement to .1875 to increase the money supply by \$1,000. Use the method described in (a) to find the answer. (339)

2. These calculations are based on the formula $M = (1/r) \times MB$, where M is the money supply, r is the reserve ratio, and MB is the monetary base (here it equals reserves).
    a. The Fed should buy bonds to increase reserves in the system by \$100. We find this by dividing the desired increase by the money multiplier. (338-339, 341)
    b. The Fed should buy bonds to increase reserves in the system by \$120. We find this by dividing the desired increase by the money multiplier. (338-339, 341)
    c. The Fed should sell bonds to decrease reserves in the system by \$125. We find this by dividing the desired increase by the money multiplier. (338-339, 341)
    d. The Fed should buy bonds to increase reserves in the system by \$250. We find this by dividing the desired increase by the money multiplier. (338-339, 341)

3. These calculations are based on the formula $M = (1/r) \times MB$, where M is the money supply, r is the reserve ratio, and MB is the monetary base (here it equals reserves). Find out how much reserves must be changed and divide by 20 to find how much the discount rate must be lowered (if reserves are to be raised) or increased (if reserves are to lowered).
    a. To increase reserves in the system by \$100, the discount rate should be reduced by 5 points. We find how much reserves must be increased by dividing the desired increase in the money supply by the money multiplier. We find how much the discount rate must be lowered by dividing the desired increase in reserves by 20 (the amount reserves will increase with each percentage point decline in the discount rate). (339-340)
    b. To increase reserves in the system by \$120, the discount rate should be reduced by 6 points. See introduction to answer number 3 for how to calculate this. (339-340)
    c. To decrease reserves in the system by \$125, the discount rate should be increased by 6.25 points. See introduction to answer number 3 for how to calculate this. (339-340)
    d. To increase reserves in the system by \$250, the discount rate should be reduced by 12.5 points. See introduction to answer number 3 for how to calculate this. (339-340)

4. a. 1. Velocity is constant, 2. Real output is independent of the money supply, 3. Causation goes from money supply to prices. (346-348)
    b. $MV = PQ$ is the equation of exchange. Since V is constant and Q exogenous, the only remaining variables that change within the system are M and P. Since the causation runs from M to P, to keep the equation balanced, a rise in M must lead to a rise in P (and only P since Q is exogenous). (346-348)

5. a. \$5,760 billion: $MV = PQ$; $6 \times 1200 = 1.25Q$. Solve for Q. (346-348)
    b. \$7,200 billion: $MV = PQ = 6 \times 1200$. (346-348)
    c. \$7,704: $MV = PQ = 6 \times 1284$. (346-348)
    d. 7%. (346-348)

6.

Inflation rate	Nominal Interest Rate	Real Interest rate	
a. 5%	10%	5% :	Real rate = nominal - inflation. (349)
b. 8%	15%	7%:	Inflation = nominal - real rate. (349)
c. -3%	6%	9%:	Nominal = inflation + real. (349)
d. 4%	14%	10%:	Nominal = inflation + real. (349)

7. These calculations are based on the formula $M = (1/r) \times MB$, where M is the money supply, r is the reserve ratio, and MB is the monetary base (here it equals reserves).
   a. The money multiplier is $1/r = 10$. Reserves must be $100 million to support a money supply of $1 billion. The reserve ratio to support $1.1 billion money supply with $100 million reserves is about 9.1%. We find this by dividing reserves by the desired money supply. (339-343)
   b. The Fed would have to buy $10,000 worth of bonds to increase the money supply by $100,000. Calculate this by dividing the desired increase in the money supply by the money multiplier. (339-343)

8. In this case, the approximate real-world money multiplier is $1/(r + c) = 1/(.25+.33) = 1.72$. The cash-to-deposit ratio is .33 since people hold 25% of their money in cash and the remainder, 75%, in deposits.
   a. The reserve requirement must be lowered to about 15%. We find this by first calculating the monetary base: $1 billion /1.72 = $580 million (Money supply/ multiplier). For the money supply to increase to $1.2 billion, the money multiplier must be $1.2/.580 = 2.07. To find the new reserve ratio solve $1/(r+c) = 2.07$ for r. We find that $r = .15$. (339-343)
   b. The Fed must buy $116,280,000 in bonds to increase the money supply by $200 million Calculate this by dividing the desired increase in the money supply by the money multiplier: $200 million / 1.72. (339-343)

A1. This calculations are based on the formula $M = (1/r) \times MB$, where M is the money supply, r is the reserve ratio, and MB is the monetary base (here it equals reserves).
   a. The Fed must sell bonds worth $4,000 to reduce reserves by $4,000. We calculate this by dividing the desired reduction in the money supply by the money multiplier. (354-355)
   b. Step 1: An individual or group of individuals buy $4,000 in Treasury bonds from the Fed. Individuals withdraw the funds from the bank. (354-355)

Assets		Liabilities	
Cash	20,000	Demand Deposits	50,000
Payment to individuals	(4,000)	Withdrawals	(4,000)
Total cash	16,000	Total demand deposits	46,000
Loans	120,000	Net Worth	100,000
Phys. Assets	10,000		
Total Assets	146,000	Total Liabilities and net worth	146,000

Step 2: Reserves are now too low to meet the reserve requirement of .4. (We calculated the reserve requirement by solving the equation $1/r = 2.5$ for r.) The bank must call in $2,400 in loans ($46,000 \times .4 - 16,000$). This shows up as loans repaid. But the individuals repaying the loans must get the money from somewhere. Since no one holds cash and Textland bank is the only bank, the individuals must withdraw the $2,400 from the bank. This is shown as a withdrawal on the liability side and a payment to individuals on the asset side. Again reserves are too low, this time by $1,440. (354-355)

Assets		Liabilities	
Cash	16,000	Demand Deposits	46,000
Loans repaid	$2,400	Withdrawals	(2,400)
Payment to inds.	(2,400)	Total demand deposits	43,600
Total cash	16,000		

Loans	120,000	Net Worth	100,000
loans called in	(2,400)		
Loans	117,600		
Phys. Assets	10,000	Total Liabilities	
Total Assets	143,600	and net worth	143,600

c. Final balance sheet: Banks continue to call in loans to meet reserve requirements until the multiplier process is finished. The money supply is now $10,000 less. At last, the balance sheet is as shown: (354-355)

Assets		Liabilities	
Cash	16,000	Demand Deposits	40,000
Loans	114,000	Net Worth	100,000
Phys. Assets	10,000		
Total Assets	140,000	Total Liabilities	
		and net worth	140,000

A2. Step 1: The bank makes $20,000 in new loans. This money is spent and then deposited into Textland by other individuals. (354-355)

Assets		Liabilities	
Cash	40,000	Demand Deposits	200,000
Payments out	(20,000)	New deposits	20,000
Payments in	20,000	Total deposits	220,000
Total cash	40,000		
Loans	230,000	Net Worth	100,000
New loans	20,000		
Total loans	250,000		
Phys. Assets	30,000	Total Liabilities	
Total Assets	320,000	and net worth	320,000

Step 2: Textland still has excess reserves (40,000/220,000 > .1) by $18,000 so it makes $18,000 in new loans. Calculate excess reserves by reserves - total deposits×reserve ratio. (354-355)

Assets		Liabilities	
Cash	40,000	Demand Deposits	220,000
Payments out	(18,000)	New deposits	18,000
Payments in	18,000	Total deposits	238,000
Total cash	40,000		
Loans	250,000	Net Worth	100,000
New loans	18,000		
Total loans	268,000		
Phys. Assets	30,000		
Total Assets	338,000	Total Liabilities	
		and net worth	338,000

Final position: The previous steps continue until the money creation process ends as shown below. (354-355).

Assets		Liabilities	
Cash	40,000	Demand Deposits	400,000
Loans	430,000	Net Worth	100,000
Phys. Assets	30,000		
Total Assets	500,000	Total Liabilities and net worth	500,000

Multiple Choice Questions

1. b. See pages 333-335.

2. c. The correct answer is "policy undertaken by the Fed." The last answer, d, involves regulation, which is also done by the Fed, but such regulation generally does not go under the name "monetary policy." Given the accuracy of answer c, answer d should be avoided. See pages 333-334, 336-337.

3. c. See page 335.

4. b. Fiscal policy is definitely not a function of the Fed. See pages 336-337.

5. b. See the text, Exhibit 2, page 336, and page 338.

6. d. Deficits are a tool of fiscal policy. See page 338.

7. c. The approximate real-world money multiplier is $1/(r + c) = 1/.3 = 3.33$. See page 339.

8. b. The Fed makes loans only to other banks, and the discount rate is the rate of interest the Fed charges for these loans. See page 335, 340.

9. a. See pages 338-341.

10. a. The last two answers, c and d, cannot be right, because the Fed does not pass laws. When the Fed buys bonds, it lowers the interest rate but it does not lower interest rates by law. Therefore, only a is correct. See page 341.

11. b. People pay the Fed for those bonds with money—FED IOUs-—so the money supply in private hands is reduced. See page 341.

12. a. As the Fed buys bonds and reduces their supply, their price rises. Since bond prices and interest rates are inversely related, interest rates will fall. See pages 341-342.

13. d. See page 342.

14. a. See pages 334 and 342.

15. b. Contractionary monetary policy increases interest rates which reduces investment, a component of aggregate expenditures. The AED curve shifts to the left by a multiple of the decline in investment. See pages 334 and 342.

16. a. Contractionary monetary policy increases interest rates which decreases investment, thereby decreasing income by a multiple of that amount. See pages 344, 342, and 344.

17. b. See page 346.

18. b. Velocity of money equals nominal GDP divided by the money supply (7.5/3.75). See page 347.

19. b. While it could be either, it is most likely a Classical; Keynesians tend to favor more activist policy. See page 348.

20. c. To determine real interest rate, you subtract expected inflation from nominal interest rates. 7-4=3. See page 349.

21. d. To determine expected inflation you subtract real interest rates from nominal interest rates. 7-3=4. See page 349.

22. c. The monetary base is the vault cash and the reserves banks have at the Fed. It is the one variable the Fed can directly control. See page 350.

B1. a. The Keynesian theory of the interest rate focuses on the supply and demand for money. See page 356.

B2. b. See page 356.

Pretest II
Chapters 7 - 13

Take this test in test conditions, giving yourself a limited amount of time to complete the questions. Ideally, check with your professor to see how much time he or she allows for an average multiple choice question and multiply this by 33. This is the time limit you should set for yourself for this pretest. If you do not know how much time your teacher would allow, we suggest 1 minute per question, or about 35 minutes.

1. The secular trend growth rate in the United States is approximately
    a. 1 to 1.5 percent per year.
    b. 2.5 to 3.5 percent per year.
    c. 5 to 5.5 percent per year.
    d. 7 to 7.5 percent per year.

2. In the 1980s and 1990s the target rate of unemployment generally has been
    a. between 2 and 3 percent.
    b. between 3 and 5 percent.
    c. between 4 and 6 percent.
    d. between 7 and 8 percent.

3. Okun's rule of thumb states that
    a. a 1 percentage point change in the unemployment rate will cause income to change in the same direction by 2.5 percent.
    b. a 1 percentage point change in the unemployment rate will cause income to change in the opposite direction by 2.5 percent.
    c. a 2.5 percentage point change in the unemployment rate will cause income to change in the same direction by 1 percent.
    d. a. 2.5 percentage point change in the unemployment rate will cause income to change in the opposite direction by 1 percent.

4. Real output is
    a. total amount of goods and services produced.
    b. total amount of goods and services produced adjusted for price level changes.
    c. total amount of goods produced, adjusted for services that aren't real.
    d. total amount of goods and services that are really produced as opposed to ones that are resold.

5. If inflation is 10 percent and nominal GDP goes up 20 percent, real GDP goes up approximately
    a. 1 percent.
    b. 10 percent.
    c. 20 percent.
    d. 50 percent.

6. If you, the owner, sell your old car for $600, how much does GDP increase?
    a. By $600.
    b. By the amount you bought it for, minus the $600.
    c. By zero.
    d. By the $600 you received and the $600 the person you sold it to paid, or $1,200.

7. The four components of expenditures in GDP are
   a. consumption, investment, government spending, and net exports.
   b. consumption, depreciation, investment, and government expenditures.
   c. consumption, investment, gross exports, and government expenditures.
   d. durable goods, nondurable goods, services, and government expenditures.

8. The largest component of national income is
   a. rents.
   b. net interest.
   c. profits.
   d. compensation to employees.

9. For every financial asset
   a. there is a corresponding financial liability.
   b. there is a corresponding financial liability if the financial asset is financed.
   c. there is a real liability.
   d. there is a corresponding real asset.

10. Assuming individuals hold no cash, the reserve requirement is 20 percent, and banks keep no excess reserves,
    an increase in an initial $100 of money will cause an increase in total money of
    a. $20.
    b. $50.
    c. $100.
    d. $500.

11. If banks hold excess reserves whereas before they did not, the relative money multiplier
    a. will become larger.
    b. will become smaller.
    c. will be unaffected.
    d. might increase or might decrease.

12. A sound bank will
    a. always have money on hand to pay all depositors in full.
    b. never borrow short and lend long.
    c. never borrow long and lend short.
    d. keep enough money on hand to cover normal cash inflows and outflows.

13. Classical economists
    a. generally favor government intervention.
    b. generally oppose government intervention.
    c. believe the economy is primarily directed by the invisible handshake.
    d. think unions are not responsible for unemployment.

14. When people save, Say's law
    a. is invalidated.
    b. remains true because saving has nothing to do with Say's law.
    c. remains true as long as saving is translated back into investment.
    d. is false because saving creates unemployment.

15. If $M = 200$, $V = 4$, P = 2, then $Q =$ _____.
    a. 50.
    b. 100.
    c. 200.
    d. 400.

16. A decrease in foreign income
    a. would likely shift the United States' AED in.
    b. would likely shift the United States' AED out.
    c. would likely make the United States' AED flatter.
    d. would likely make the United States' AED steeper.

17. If the economy is significantly below its potential output, the aggregate supply path is generally considered to be
    a. flat.
    b. upward sloping.
    c. backward sloping.
    d. perfectly vertical.

18. Suppose the AED curve shifted in from AED_0 to AED_1. If there had been inflation and the price level axis is interpreted relative to expectations, i.e., the shift was disinflationary, the resulting price and output level would be at:
    a. P_1, Q_1.
    b. P_2, Q_1.
    c. P_2, Q_2.
    d. P_1, Q_3.

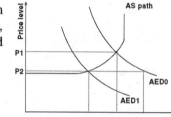

19. The marginal propensity to expend is the
    a. change in expenditures times change in income.
    b. change in expenditures divided by the change in income.
    c. change in expenditures divided by income.
    d. expenditures divided by the change in income.

20. If the *mpe* is .8, what is the size of the multiplier in the Keynesian model?
    a. .5.
    b. 5.
    c. 1.
    d. 10.

21. In the Keynesian *AE/AP* model, if autonomous exports falls by 40 and the *mpe* is .5, what happens to the income?
    a. income rises by 20.
    b. income falls by 20.
    c. income rises by 80.
    d. income falls by 80.

22. In the Keynesian *AE/AP* model, if autonomous exports falls by 40 and government spending increases by 20, and the *mpe* is .8, what happens to the income?
    a. income rises by 25.
    b. income falls by 25.
    c. income rises by 100.
    d. income falls by 100.

23. To derive the aggregate equilibrium demand curve from the Keynesian *AE/AP* model, one must
    a. relate the initial autonomous shifts caused by price level changes on the *AE* curve to the *AED* curve.
    b. relate the *AE/AP* equilibria at different price levels to the *AED* curve.
    c. relate the *AE/AP* equilibria at different quantity levels to the *AED* curve.
    d. relate the initial autonomous shifts caused by price level changes on the *AP* curve to the *AED* curve.

24. Which group is most likely to believe that a model using autonomous expenditures is relevant?
    a. Keynesians.
    b. Classicals.
    c. Keynesians and Classicals would be equal in their belief.
    d. Neither Keynesians nor Classicals would see a model using autonomous elements as relevant.

25. The economy has a fixed price level, an *mpe* of .5, and a recessionary gap of 240. Using the Keynesian *AE/AP* model, an economist would advise government to
    a. increase autonomous expenditures by 120.
    b. increase autonomous expenditures by 240.
    c. increase autonomous expenditures by 480.
    d. increase autonomous expenditures by 620.

26. Expansionary aggregate demand policy includes all of the following except
    a. increasing government spending.
    b. increasing autonomous expenditures.
    c. increasing imports.
    d. decreasing taxes.

27. The portion of the budget deficit that would exist even if the economy were at its potential level of income is called the
    a. structural deficit.
    b. passive deficit.
    c. primary deficit.
    d. secondary deficit.

28. Crowding out occurs when
    a. the government runs a deficit and sells bonds to finance that deficit.
    b. the government prints money.
    c. the government runs a surplus and sells bonds and the people who buy those bonds sell their older bonds to the government.
    d. the tendency for new workers to replace more expensive older workers is a factor.

29. Explicit functions of the Fed include all the following except
    a. conducting monetary policy.
    b. conducting fiscal policy.
    c. providing banking services to the U.S. government.
    d. serving as a lender of last resort to financial institutions.

30. Tools of monetary policy include all the following except
    a. changing the reserve requirement.
    b. changing the discount rate.
    c. executing open market operations.
    d. running deficits.

31. Assuming $c = .2$ and $r = .1$, the approximate real-world money multiplier would be
    a. 1.33.
    b. 2.33.
    c. 3.33.
    d. 4.33.

32. When the Fed sells bonds, the money supply is
    a. expanded.
    b. contracted.
    c. Selling bonds does not have any effect on the money supply.
    d. sometimes raised and sometimes lowered

33. An economist has just said she favors "steady as you go" monetary policy. This economist
    a. is most likely a Keynesian.
    b. is most likely a Classical.
    c. could equally be either a Keynesian or a Classical.
    d. must be neither a Keynesian nor a Classical, since neither group favors such a policy.

Answers

1. b (7:1)	12. d (9:14)	23. b (11:18)
2. c (7:8)	13. b (10:1)	24. a (11:22)
3. b (7:12)	14. c (10:3)	25. a (12:5)
4. b (7:16)	15. d (10:7)	26. c (12:10)
5. b (8:1)	16. a (10:12)	27. a (12:15)
6. c (8:4)	17. a (10:16)	28. a (12:16)
7. a (8:8)	18. c (10:22)	29. b (13:4)
8. d (8:10)	19. b (11:4)	30. d (13:6)
9. a (9:1)	20. b (11:6)	31. c (13:7)
10. d (9:10)	21. d (11:9)	32. b (13:11)
11. b (9:13)	22. d (11:14)	33. b (13:19)

Key: The figures in parentheses refer to multiple choice question and chapter numbers. For example (1:4) is multiple choice question 1 from chapter 4.

Chapter 14:
Inflation and Its Relationship to Unemployment and Growth

Chapter at a glance

1. High inflation rates are inevitably accompanied by high money growth and high inflationary expectations. The reason is that the velocity of money generally cannot increase enormously and people's expectations of the future are determined in large part by what is occurring now. (359)

   Inflation can either be cost-push or demand-pull and these can feed on each other because of adaptive expectations.

2. The long-run Phillips curve is vertical; it takes into account the feedback of inflation on expectations of inflation. The short-run Phillips curve does not take this feedback into account. (364)

   In the long run when expectations of inflation are met, changes in the rates of inflation have no effect on the level of unemployment. Classicals believe the long-run Phillips curve is fixed at the natural rate of unemployment. This is shown as LR in the accompanying graph.

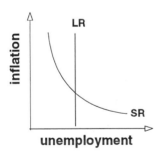

   The short-run Phillips curve reflects the empirically observed trade-off between inflation and unemployment. Expectations of inflation are constant along the short-run (SR) Phillips cuve. Increases (decreases) in inflationary expectations shift the short-run Phillips curve to the right (left).

Classicals believe that inflation undermines long-run growth and that there is an inverse relation between inflation and long-run growth.

In the long run we have more time to adjust our expectations to actual inflation. In the short run we may be fooled–we may expect less (more) inflation than actually occurs when inflation is accelerating (decelerating).

3. The Classical theory of inflation is summarized by the sentence: Inflation is everywhere and always a monetary phenomenon. (367)

$$\textit{Long Run: } M\overline{V} \overset{\uparrow}{} = P\overline{Q} \overset{\uparrow}{}$$

Note: The price level rises because the money supply rises.

Short Run: An increase in the money supply may also increase real output (employment and income), but only for awhile–for as long as people are fooled into thinking increases in nominal income are increases in their real income.

4. Classical economists favor a monetary rule because they believe the short-run effects of monetary policy are unpredictable and the long-run effects of monetary policy are on the price level, not on real output. (369)

Monetary Rule: Increase the money supply by a constant rate year after year equal to the potential annual growth rate in real GDP (about 2.5-3.5%).

5. The Keynesian theory of inflation holds that institutional and structural aspects of inflation, as well as increases in the money supply, are important causes of inflation. (370)

   The "insider" versus "outsider" situation creates imperfect markets. Imperfect markets provide an opportunity for "insiders" to increase their wages and prices even when unemployment and excess capacity exists in the overall economy, thereby creating inflation.

6a. Classicals view the long-run Phillips curve as vertical; the short-run trade-off is only a temporary illusion. (370)

   The Classical view of the Phillips curve trade-off centers around the natural rate of unemployment. Any attempts to maintain unemployment at a rate below the natural rate is unsustainable because doing so would cause accelerating inflation.

✔ *To stop an inflation, Classicals say the Fed must reduce the rate of growth of the money supply.*

6b. Keynesians believe that institutional factors play a major role in determining inflation, and that expected inflation need not precisely equal actual inflation. Within a range of output levels, a trade-off is possible. (372)

   So, whenever inflation is not really out of control then there is a long-run trade-off between inflation and unemployment (the Phillips curve is downward sloping).

✔ *To stop an inflation, Keynesians favor contractionary monetary policy along with a combination of other policies that directly slow down inflation such as an incomes policy. Exhibit 6 shows how an incomes policy works.*

   In sum, Keynesians see inflation as an institutional phenomenon; Classicals see it as a monetary phenomenon.

Short-answer questions

1. If there is a high inflation, most economists are willing to accept that a rough approximation of the quantity theory holds true. Why? (LO1)

2. Which of the two curves in the graph on the right is a short-run Phillips curve, and why? (LO2)

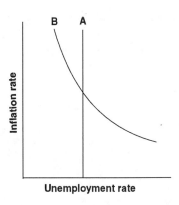

3. What is the Classical view of inflation and how does it relate to long-run growth? (LO3)

4. Are Classical economists or Keynesian economists more likely to favor a monetary rule? Why? (LO4)

5. How does the Keynesian theory of inflation differ from the Classical theory of inflation? (LO5)

6. Would Keynesians or Classicals be more likely to see a long-run trade-off between inflation and unemployment? Why? (LO6)

7. Why would a Keynesian be more likely to support the introduction of an incomes policy than a Classical would be? (LO6)

Word Scramble

1. _____ 2._____ _____ 3._____
   tonnliifa   sPplliih   vurec   ttsonligfaa

Match the Terms and Concepts to Their Definitions

____ 1. adaptive expectations

____ 2. cost-push inflation

____ 3. demand-pull inflation

____ 4. expectations of inflation

____ 5. incomes policy

____ 6. inflation

____ 7. just-noticeable difference

____ 8. long-run Phillips curve

____ 9. monetary rule

____ 10. natural rate of unemployment

____ 11. Phillips curve

____ 12. short-run Phillips curve

____ 13. stagflation

a. A threshold below which our senses don't recognize that something has changed.

b. A prescribed monetary policy to be followed regardless of what is happening in the economy.

c. A representation of the relation between inflation and unemployment.

d. A policy placing direct pressure on individuals to hold down their nominal wages and prices.

e. A curve showing the trade-off between inflation and unemployment when expectations of inflation are constant.

f. A curve showing the trade-off (or complete lack thereof) between inflation and unemployment when expectations of inflation equal actual inflation.

g. Classical term for the unemployment rate in long-run equilibrium when expectations of inflation equal the actual level of inflation.

h. Combination of high and accelerating inflation and high unemployment.

i. Expectations of the future based on what has been in the past.

j. Inflation where money supply increases cause price increases.

k. Inflation where price increases cause money supply increases.

l. The rise in the price level that the average person expects.

m. A continuous rise in the price level.

Problems and Exercises

1. Suppose the economy is operating at potential output. Inflation is 3% and expected inflation is 3%. Unemployment is 5.5%.

    a. Draw a long-run Phillips curve and a short-run Phillips curve consistent with these conditions.

    b. The government implements an expansionary monetary policy. As a result, unemployment falls to 4.5% and inflation rises to 6%. Expectations do not adjust. Show where the economy is on the graph you drew for 1(a). What happens to the short-run Phillips curve? Inflation? Unemployment?

    c. Expectations now fully adjust. Show this on the graph drawn for 1(a). What happens to the short-run Phillips curve?

2. Redraw the long-run Phillips curve and a short-run Phillips curve consistent with the conditions of the economy described in question #1 above and explain the effect of the following on inflation and unemployment using the curves you have drawn.

    a. The government implements a contractionary monetary policy. As a result, unemployment rises to 6.5% and inflation falls to 0%. Expectations do not adjust.

    b. Expectations now fully adjust.

3. For each of the following points that represents the economy on the Phillips curve, make a prediction for unemployment and inflation.

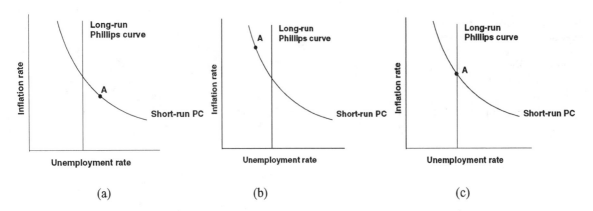

| (a) | (b) | (c) |

4. Suppose inflation is 12% and unemployment is 5.5% and the natural rate of unemployment is 5.5%. The president believes inflation and unemployment are both too high.

    a. Assume you are a Classical economist. What policy would you recommend to improve the situation?

    b. Show the short-run effect of this policy on unemployment and inflation using the Phillips curve analysis. Will the president be satisfied? What is your response?

c. Show the long-run effect of this policy on unemployment and inflation using the Phillips curve analysis. Will the president be satisfied? What is your response? (In that response, discuss the issue of long-run growth).

Multiple Choice Questions

1. Assuming velocity is relatively constant and real income is relatively stable, an increase in the money supply of 40 percent will bring about an approximate change in the price level of
   a. 4 percent.
   b. 40 percent.
   c. 80 percent.
   d. zero percent.

2. When there is cost/push inflation
   a. price increases tend to lead the money supply increases.
   b. price increases tend to lag the money supply increases.
   c. price increases tend to have no relation to the money supply increases.
   d. price increases sometimes lead and sometimes lag the money supply increases.

3. The Phillips curve represents a relationship between
   a. inflation and unemployment.
   b. inflation and real income.
   c. money supply and interest rates.
   d. money supply and unemployment.

4. The short-run Phillips curve shifts around because of
   a. changes in the money supply.
   b. changes in expectations of employment.
   c. changes in expectations of inflation.
   d. changes in expectations of real income.

5. The slope of the long-run Phillips curve is thought by many economists to be
   a. horizontal.
   b. vertical.
   c. downward sloping.
   d. backward bending.

6. An economist has just said, "Inflation is everywhere and always a monetary phenomenon." You would deduce this economist
   a. is likely to be a Keynesian economist.
   b. is likely to be a Classical economist.
   c. could be either a Keynesian economist or a Classical economist.
   d. must be neither a Keynesian economist nor a Classical economist, because neither of these groups would ever say that.

7. Classicals generally favor a monetary rule that has
   a. money supply not changing at all.
   b. money supply increasing by a predetermined percentage of about 3 percent.
   c. money supply increasing by a predetermined percentage of about 10 percent.
   d. monetary policy tied to whether the economy is in a recession or a boom.

8. Classicals see the economy gravitating towards
   a. the stagflation rate of unemployment.
   b. the natural rate of unemployment.
   c. the inflation rate of unemployment.
   d. the Phillips rate of unemployment.

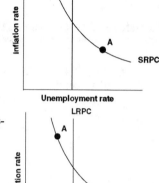

9. If the economy is at Point A in the Phillips curve graph to the right, what prediction would you make for inflation?
   a. It will increase.
   b. It will decrease.
   c. It will remain constant.
   d. It will explode.

10. If the economy is at Point A in the Phillips curve graph to the right, what prediction would you make for inflation?
    a. It will increase
    b. It will decrease.
    c. It will remain constant.
    d. It will immediately fall to zero.

11. Stagflation is
    a. a combination of low and decelerating inflation and low unemployment.
    b. a combination of low and decelerating inflation and high unemployment.
    c. a combination of high and accelerating inflation and low unemployment.
    d. a combination of high and accelerating inflation and high unemployment.

12. An economist has just made the statement that institutional and structural aspects of inflation are important. You would deduce that this economist
    a. is likely a Keynesian economist.
    b. is likely a Classical economist.
    c. could be either a Keynesian economist or a Classical economist.
    d. must not be an economist, since no economist would make such a statement.

13. One explanation of why the long-run Phillips curve might not be perfectly vertical is
    a. the just noticeable difference explanation.
    b. the supply shock explanation.
    c. the demand shock explanation.
    d. the monetary explanation.

14. An individual has said that she favors an incomes policy. She
    a. is likely a Keynesian economist.
    b. is likely a Classical economist.
    c. could be either a Keynesian economist or a Classical economist.
    d. is not an economist, because no economist could ever support an incomes policy.

15. Classicals generally see supply price shocks
    a. as a cost-push pressure.
    b. as a demand-pull pressure.
    c. as a relative price change.
    d. as an institutional change.

Answers

Short-answer questions

1. The quantity theory is based on the equation of exchange, $MV=PQ$. The quantity theory adds the following assumptions: (1) that velocity is relatively constant; (2) that real output is relatively constant; and (3) that changes in money supply cause changes in prices. In reality, velocity and real output can change sufficiently to make it questionable whether this theory is useful. However, when there is significant inflation—say 100% or more—the relative changes in velocity and real output that are reasonable to assume possible are much smaller than that 100%, leaving a rough correlation between changes in the money supply and changes in the price level.

   The debate between economists does not concern the relationships between money growth and inflation; it concerns the direction of causation. Classicals tend to believe that the causation goes from money to prices, and hence they are willing to accept the existence of a long-run vertical Phillips curve. Keynesians tend to believe that the causation goes from changes in prices and expectations of prices to changes in the money supply—the government is accommodating the higher prices. Thus they favor more institutionally-oriented theories of inflation. (367-372)

2. The Phillips curve represents a trade-off between inflation and unemployment. It is an empirically determined phenomenon, and based on that empirical evidence economists generally believe that the downward sloping curve (curve B) represents the short-run Phillips curve: Whenever unemployment decreases, inflation increases, and vice versa. They explain that this empirical occurrence is due to slowly adjusting expectations and institutions. In the long run, expectations and institutions can change and hence the reason for the trade-off is eliminated, making the vertical line represent the long-run Phillips curve—it represents the lack of a trade-off between inflation and unemployment in the long run. (362-365)

3. The Classical view of inflation is best summarized by the phrase "Inflation is everywhere and always a monetary phenomenon." Essentially, it is that increases in the money supply are the cause of inflation, and all other supposed causes are simply diversions from the key monetary cause. They see a long-run inverse relationship between inflation and growth. (367-370)

4. Classical economists are more likely to favor a monetary rule, because they see the economy gravitating toward a natural rate of unemployment regardless of monetary policy. Thus expansionary monetary policy can lead only to inflation. A monetary rule will limit the government's attempt to expand the economy with monetary policy and hence will achieve the natural rate of unemployment and low inflation. Keynesian economists are less likely to see the economy gravitating toward the natural rate of unemployment, so they would favor some discretionary policy to improve the operation of the macro economy. (368-370, 372)

5. The Keynesian theory of inflation differs from the Classical in that it is more likely to include institutional and social aspects as part of the theory. The insider/outsider model is a Keynesian model of inflation. Another way of stating the difference is that the Keynesian theory of inflation sees the equation of exchange as being read from right to left, rather than from left to right. (370-372)

6. Keynesian economists see institutional and social aspects of the price setting process as more important than do Classicals. They also see individuals as having a cost of rationality, so individuals may not notice small amounts of inflation. These aspects of the Keynesian theory make it more likely that there is a long-run trade-off between inflation and unemployment since, in their absence, we would expect that money is essentially a veil and real forces predominate. (372-374)

7. An incomes policy is a policy designed to put direct downward pressure on the nominal price setting process. Keynesian economists see institutional and social aspects of the price setting process as more important than do Classicals. It is these social aspects of the price setting process which place a direct upward pressure on the price level that will require an incomes policy to offset. Therefore, Keynesians are more likely to support an incomes policy. (374-375)

Word Scramble   1. inflation   2. Phillips curve   3. stagflation

Match the Terms and Concepts to Their Definitions

1-i; 2-k; 3-j; 4-l; 5-d; 6-m; 7-a; 8-f; 9-b; 10-g; 11-c; 12-e; 13-h.

Problems and Exercises

1. a. The long-run Phillips curve is vertical at the rate of unemployment consistent with potential output, here at 5.5%. The short-run Phillips curve is the downward sloping curve shown in the graph to the right as PC_1. In this case, we drew a short-run Phillips curve where expected inflation equals 3%, actual inflation. It intersects the long-run Phillips curve at 5.5% unemployment and 3% inflation. The economy is at point A. (362-365)

   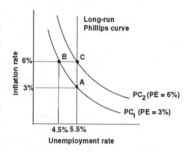

   b. The economy moves along the short-run Phillips curve up and to the left to point B. The short-run Phillips curve does not shift since inflation expectations have not changed. At point B, inflation is 6% and unemployment rate is 4.5%. (362-365)

   c. Now that expectations fully adjust, the short-run Phillips curve shifts to the right to PC_2 so that it intersects the long-run Phillips curve at inflation rate of 6%. The unemployment rate returns to 5.5% and inflation remains at 6%. (362-365)

2. a. The economy moves along the short-run Phillips curve down and to the right to point B. The short-run Phillips curve does not shift since inflation expectations have not changed. At point B, inflation is 0% and unemployment rate is 6.5%. (362-365)

   b. Now that expectations fully adjust, the short-run Phillips curve shifts to the left to PC_2 so that it intersects the long-run Phillips curve at inflation rate of 0%. The unemployment rate returns to 5.5% and inflation remains at 0%. (362-365)

   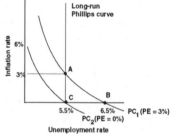

3. a. Inflation is below expected inflation and unemployment is higher than the natural rate of unemployment. As expectations adjust, the short-run Phillips curve shifts to the left and both unemployment and inflation will fall. (362-365)

   b. Inflation is above expected inflation and unemployment is lower than the natural rate of unemployment. As expectations adjust, the short-run Phillips curve shifts to the right and both unemployment and inflation will rise. (362-365)

   c. Inflation equals expected inflation and unemployment equals the target rate of unemployment. Inflation and unemployment will not change. (362-365)

4. a. I assume that in the long run, only inflation can be improved, so I ignore the higher-than-desired rate of unemployment and focus on fighting inflation. A contractionary monetary policy will improve the inflation rate. (368-370)

   b. The economy begins at point A, where unemployment is 5.5% and inflation is 12%. Inflation expectations equal actual inflation. This is shown to the right. With contractionary monetary policy, the economy moves along the short-run Phillips curve down and to the right to point B. The short-run Phillips curve does not shift since inflation expectations have not changed. At point B, inflation is lower than 12% and the unemployment rate is higher than 5.5%. The president will be happy that inflation is lower, but disappointed that unemployment is higher. I tell him that in the short run there is a trade-off between the two. Just wait for expectations of inflation to adjust and we will return to 5.5% unemployment. (368-370)

   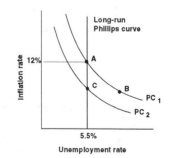

c. Now that expectations fully adjust, the short-run Phillips curve shifts to the left to PC_2 so that it intersects the long-run Phillips curve at inflation rate of below 12% at point C. The unemployment rate returns to 5.5% . The president is now pleased because inflation is lower and unemployment returned to 5.5%. But he wanted the unemployment rate to be below 5.5%. I tell him that 5.5% is the natural rate. If he were to follow an expansionary policy, unemployment would fall in the short run, but would return to 5.5% in the long run and inflation would be higher than it currently is. The higher inflation would undermine the economy's long-term growth. (368-370)

Multiple Choice Questions

1. b. Using the equation of exchange, $MV=PQ$, given these assumptions there is a close relationship between changes in M and changes in P. See page 359.

2. a. As the text discusses on page 359, in most cost/push inflation, price increases cause money supply increases, and therefore they lead them. The other answers are possible, but a is clearly the best.

3. a. See page 360.

4. c. The short-run Phillips curve holds expectations of inflation constant. Therefore, it shifts because changes in expectations of inflation cause everybody to build those expectations into their nominal price requests. See pages 362-363.

5. b. As discussed on pages 363-364, the long-run Phillips curve is vertical. Actually, there is some debate about whether it is downward sloping, but the text focuses on the vertical nature of the curve so that is the answer that should be given. Remember, one is choosing the best answer relative to what is presented in the text.

6. b. As discussed on page 367, that phrase is a mantra of Classical economists.

7. b. Classicals generally favor increasing the money supply at a rate of about 3% per year. That, they believe, would allow for real growth without inflation. See page 369.

8. b. The Classical view of the Phillips curve is that all forces push toward the natural rate of unemployment. See pages 368-369.

9. b. Since Point A is to the right of the long-run Phillips curve, actual unemployment exceeds the natural rate of unemployment. Therefore we would expect inflationary expectations to be decreasing, and hence inflation to be decreasing. See page 370, especially Exhibit 5.

10. a. Since Point A is to the left of the long-run Phillips curve, actual unemployment is below the natural rate of unemployment. Therefore we would expect inflationary expectations to be increasing, and hence inflation to be increasing. See pages 369-370, especially Exhibit 5.

11. d. See definition of stagflation on page 362.

12. a. As discussed on pages 369-370, Keynesian economists emphasize institutional and structural aspects of inflation.

13. a. As the text discusses on page 373, the just noticeable difference, which is the threshold below which our senses don't recognize that something has changed, provides a possible explanation of why, even when there is inflation, people will not change their behavior and, instead, blend that inflation into their price-setting decisions.

14. a. As discussed on page 374, an incomes policy is a Keynesian policy designed to offset structural causes of inflation.

15. c. As discussed on pages 375-376 price shocks are relative price changes which do not lead to price level changes. As long as the government does not raise the money supply, other prices will fall to offset the price shock.

Chapter 15: International Dimensions of Monetary and Fiscal Policies

Chapter at a glance

1a. There is significant debate about what U.S. international goals should be because exchange rates have conflicting effects and, depending on the state of the economy, there are arguments for high and low exchange rates. (381)

A high exchange rate (strong value of the $) helps hold down the prices of imports and therefore inflation. However, it creates a trade deficit and that has a depressing effect on aggregate demand and therefore the income level.

1b. Running a trade deficit is good in the short run but presents problems in the long run; thus there is debate about whether we should worry about a trade deficit or not. (382)

Trade deficit => imports > exports.

Short-run benefit: We are able to consume more than we would otherwise be able to do.

Long-run cost: We have to sell off U.S. assets because we are consuming more than we are producing. All the future interest and profits on those assets will thus go to foreigners, not U.S. citizens.

2. Domestic goals generally dominate international goals because (1) international goals are ambiguous, and (2) international goals affect a country's population indirectly and, in politics, indirect effects take a back seat. (382)

Often a country responds to an international goal only after the international community pressures it to do so.

3a. Monetary policy affects exchange rates through the interest rate path, the income path, and the price-level path, as shown in the diagram on pages 384 and 385. (384-385)

Expansionary monetary policy (increasing the money supply) lowers exchange rates. It decreases the relative value of a country's currency. Contractionary monetary policy has the opposite effect.

Be able to explain why!

3b. Monetary policy affects the trade balance through the income path, the price level path, and the exchange rate path, as shown in the diagram on page 386. (385-386)

Expansionary monetary policy makes a trade deficit larger.

Contractionary monetary policy makes a trade deficit smaller.

Be able to explain why!

4a. Fiscal policy affects exchange rates through the income path, the interest rate path, and the price-level path, as shown in the diagram on page 387. (386-387)

The net effect of fiscal policy on exchange rates is ambiguous.

Be able to explain why!

4b. Fiscal policy affects the trade deficit though the income path and the price-level path, as shown in the diagram on page 388. (387-388)

Expansionary fiscal policy increases a trade deficit.

Contractionary fiscal policy decreases a trade deficit.

Be able to explain why!

5. Governments try to coordinate their monetary and fiscal policies because their economies are interdependent. (389)

Each country will likely do what's best for the world economy as long as it is also best for itself.

6. While internationalizing a country's debt may help in the short run, in the long run it presents potential problems, since foreign ownership of a country's debts means the country must pay interest to those foreign countries and that debt may come due. (390)

We have been internationalizing our debt since the early 1980s which means that we must, at some point in the future, export more than we import (consume less than we produce) to pay for this.

Short-answer questions

1. What should U.S. international goals be? (LO1)

2. Which dominate for a country: domestic or international goals? Why? (LO2)

3. If a country runs expansionary monetary policy, what will likely happen to the exchange rate? (LO3)

4. If a country runs contractionary monetary policy, what will likely happen to the trade balance? (LO4)

5. If a country runs expansionary fiscal policy, what will likely happen to the exchange rate? (LO4)

6.   If a country runs contractionary fiscal policy, what will likely happen to the trade balance? (LO4)

7.   Given the difficulty of doing so, why do countries try to coordinate their monetary and fiscal policies with other countries? (LO5)

8.   The United States in recent years has run a large capital account deficit and has become the world's largest debtor nation. What are some of the potential problems that this presents? (LO6)

Word Scramble

1. _____ _____   2._____ _____ _____

    a d e r t   n l e c b a a   x l l i f e e b   x n h g e e c a   a e r t

3._____ _____ _____

   d e x f i   a c e e g h n x   e t r a

Match the Terms and Concepts to Their Definitions

___ 1. exchange rate

___ 2. fixed exchange rate

___ 3. flexible exchange rate

___ 4. partially flexible exchange rate

___ 5. trade balance

a. Exchange rate that is set by a country's government, with the commitment to buying and selling that currency at the set rate.

b. The difference between a country's exports and its imports.

c. Exchange rate set by market forces (supply and demand for a country's currency).

d. Exchange rate where the government sometimes buys and sells currencies to influence the price directly and at other times simply accepts the exchange rate determined by supply and demand forces.

e. The rate at which one country's currency can be traded for another country's currency.

Problems and Exercises

1. You observe that over the past decade, a country's competitiveness has improved, reducing its trade deficit.

    a. What monetary or fiscal policies might have led to such results? Why?

    b. You also observe that interest rates have steadily fallen along with a fall in the exchange rate. What monetary or fiscal policies might have led to such results?

2. You have been hired as an adviser to Fantasyland, a country with perfectly flexible exchange rates. State what monetary and fiscal policies you might suggest in each of the following situations. Explain your answers.

    a. You want to increase domestic income and to reduce the exchange rate.

    b. You want to reduce interest rates, reduce inflation, and reduce the trade deficit.

    c. You want lower unemployment, lower interest rates, a lower exchange rate, and a lower trade deficit.

Multiple Choice Questions

1. An exchange rate is
    a. the rate the Fed charges commercial banks for loans.
    b. the rate the Fed charges individuals for loans.
    c. the rate at which one country's currency can be exchanged for another country's currency.
    d. the speed at which exchange occurs.

2. If a country has fixed exchange rates
    a. the government need not worry about the exchange rate.
    b. governments are committed to buying and selling currencies at a fixed rate.
    c. the exchange rate is set by law.
    d. the exchange rate has a fixed component and a flexible component.

3. If a country has a flexible exchange rate, the exchange rate
    a. is determined by flexible government policy.
    b. is determined by market forces.
    c. fluctuates continuously and will always change by at least 1 percent per year.
    d. fluctuates continuously and will always change by at least 10 percent per year.

4. Countries prefer
    a. a high exchange rate.
    b. a low exchange rate.
    c. sometimes a low and sometimes a high exchange rate.
    d. a fixed exchange rate.

5. Countries prefer
    a. a trade deficit.
    b. a trade surplus.
    c. sometimes a trade deficit and sometimes a trade surplus.
    d. a trade equilibrium.

6. Expansionary monetary policy has a tendency to
    a. push interest rates up and exchange rates down.
    b. push interest rates down and exchange rates down.
    c. push income down and exchange rates down.
    d. push imports down and exchange rates down.

7. Contractionary monetary policy has a tendency to
    a. push interest rates up and exchange rates down.
    b. push interest rates down and exchange rates down.
    c. push income down and imports down.
    d. push imports down and exchange rates down.

8. If the exchange rate has gone up, it is most likely that the government ran
    a. an expansionary monetary policy.
    b. a contractionary monetary policy.
    c. an expansionary fiscal policy.
    d. a contractionary fiscal policy.

9. If the trade deficit has gone up, it is most likely that the government ran
    a. an expansionary monetary policy.
    b. a contractionary monetary policy.
    c. a contractionary fiscal policy.
    d. an expansionary monetary policy and a contractionary fiscal policy

10. Expansionary monetary policy tends to
    a. push prices up and the trade deficit down.
    b. push prices down and the trade deficit down.
    c. push income up and the trade deficit down.
    d. push income up and the trade deficit up.

11. Expansionary fiscal policy tends to push
    a. income up and exchange rates up.
    b. income up and exchange rates down.
    c. income up and imports up.
    d. income up and imports down.

12. If the exchange rate has gone up, it is most likely that the government ran
    a. an expansionary fiscal policy.
    b. a contractionary fiscal policy.
    c. Who knows?
    d. an expansionary monetary policy.

13. Contractionary fiscal policy tends to push
    a. income down and imports up.
    b. income down and the trade deficit up.
    c. prices down and the trade deficit down.
    d. prices down and imports up.

14. Assume the United States would like to raise its exchange rate and lower its trade deficit. It would pressure
    Japan to run
    a. contractionary monetary policy.
    b. contractionary fiscal policy.
    c. expansionary monetary policy
    d. expansionary fiscal policy.

15. According to the textbook, generally, when international goals and domestic goals conflict
    a. the international goals win out.
    b. the domestic goals win out.
    c. sometimes it's a toss-up which will win out.
    d. international monetary goals win out but international fiscal goals lose out.

16. When a country runs a large capital account surplus, the amount of crowding out that occurs because of fiscal
    policy is
    a. increased.
    b. decreased.
    c. unaffected.
    d. sometimes increased and sometimes decreased.

Answers

Short-answer questions

1. By "international goals" economists usually mean the exchange rate and the trade balance that policy makers should shoot for. There is significant debate in the United States about what our international goals should be, and there are arguments for both high and low exchange rates, and for both trade deficits and trade surpluses. The argument for a high exchange rate is that it lowers the cost of imports; the argument against it is that it raises the price of exports, making U.S. goods less competitive. The argument in favor of a trade deficit is that it allows a country to consume more than it produces; the argument against is that that trade deficit will have to be paid off at some point. (380-382)

2. Generally, domestic goals dominate for two reasons. (1) International goals are often ambiguous, as discussed in answer 1 above and page 382 of the textbook, and (2) international goals affect a country's population indirectly and, in politics, indirect effects take a back seat. (382)

3. Expansionary monetary policy tends to push income and prices up and interest rates down. All these phenomena tend to push the exchange rate down. Contractionary monetary policy has the opposite effect. (384-385)

4. Contractionary monetary policy tends to push income and prices down and interest rates up. The strongest effect of these phenomena on the trade balance in the short run is the effect on income, which causes a fall in imports and a fall in the trade deficit. (385-386)

5. Expansionary fiscal policy pushes interest rates, income, and prices up. The higher income and higher prices increase imports and put downward pressure on exchange rates. The higher interest rate pushes exchange rates in the opposite direction so the net effect of fiscal policy on exchange rates is unclear. (386-387)

6. Contractionary fiscal policy pushes income and prices down. This tends to decrease imports and increase competitiveness, decreasing a trade deficit. (387-388)

7. The policies of one country affect the economy of another. So it is only natural that they try to coordinate their policies. It is also only natural that since voters are concerned with their own countries, that coordination is difficult to achieve unless it is in the interest of both countries. (389)

8. While internationalizing a country's debt may help in the short run, in the long run it presents potential problems, since foreign ownership of a country's debts means the debtor country must pay interest to those foreign countries, and also, that debt may come due. (390-391)

Word Scramble   1. trade balance   2. flexible exchange rate   3. fixed exchange rate

Match the Terms and Concepts to Their Definitions

1-e; 2-a; 3-c; 4-d; 5-b.

Problems and Exercises

1. a. An increase in competitiveness and a decrease in the trade deficit are probably due to contractionary fiscal policy. Contractionary fiscal policy reduces inflation, improves competitiveness, and decreases income which reduces imports. Improved competitiveness and decreased income both work to reduce the trade deficit. Contractionary monetary policy would also reduce the trade deficit, but its effect on competitiveness is ambiguous. (382-388)

    b. If interest rates have also fallen, it is likely that fiscal policy has been very contractionary because contractionary monetary policy would have led to higher interest rates and a higher exchange rate value of the dollar. (382-388)

2. a. Expansionary monetary policy will reduce the exchange rate through its effect on interest rates and will increase domestic income. Expansionary fiscal policy will increase domestic income. The increase in income will increase imports which will tend to decrease the exchange rate, but higher interest rates will tend to lead to a higher exchange rate. The effect of expansionary fiscal policy on exchange rates is ambiguous. (382-388)

    b. Contractionary fiscal policy will tend to reduce inflation and interest rates. The reduction in inflation will improve competitiveness and a reduction in income will reduce imports. Both work to reduce the trade deficit. (382-388)

    c. Expansionary monetary policy will reduce unemployment and reduce interest rates. Lower interest rates will tend to make exchange rates fall. Expansionary monetary policy, however, will make the trade deficit higher. Expansionary fiscal policy will also reduce unemployment. Interest rates, however, will rise and so will the trade deficit. This mix of goals is difficult to attain. (382-388)

Multiple Choice Questions

1. c. See page 381.

2. b. To keep the exchange rate at the stated amount governments must be willing to buy and sell currencies so that the quantity supplied and quantity demanded are always equal at the fixed rate. See page 381.

3. b. There are no predetermined levels of change with a flexible exchange rate. See page 381.

4. c. The answer is "sometimes a low and sometimes a high exchange rate" because, as discussed on page 381. there are rationales for both.

5. c. The domestic economy's needs change over time and as they do, so does the country's preferred trade situation. Both a deficit and a surplus have their advantages and disadvantages. See pages 381-382.

6. b. See the diagram on page 384.

7. c. See the diagram on page 385.

8. b. As discussed on page 385 the b answer is definitely correct. As discussed on page 387, fiscal policy has an ambiguous effect on exchange rates.

9. a. Both expansionary monetary policy and expansionary fiscal policy increase the trade deficit. Thus only a fits. See the discussion and charts on pages 385-388.

10. d. See the discussion on pages 385-386 and the diagram on page 386.

11. c. The effect of expansionary fiscal policy on exchange rates is ambiguous, which eliminates a and b. Increased income increases imports, not decreases them. (386-387)

12. c. The effect of expansionary fiscal policy on the exchange rate is ambiguous, as shown on the diagram on page 387, eliminating a and b. As discussed on pages 382-384, an expansionary monetary policy pushes the exchange rate down, eliminating d, leaving only c.

13. c. See diagram on page 388 and the discussion on pages 386-388.

14. c. The effect of fiscal policy on the exchange rate is ambiguous, so the only sure option is c. See Exhibit 1 on page 389.

15. b. As discussed in the text on page 389, usually, because of political considerations, domestic goals win out.

16. b. Since there is a capital account surplus, capital must be flowing into the country. That capital usually ends up buying some government debt, which reduces crowding out, as discussed on page 390.

Chapter 16: Open Economy Macro: Exchange Rate and Trade Policy

Chapter at a glance

1a. The balance of payments is a country's record of all transactions between its residents and the residents of all foreign countries. (395)

Is broken down into the:
1. *current account*
2. *capital account*
3. *official transactions account.*

✔ *Remember: If it is a minus (plus) sign, money is going out (coming in). Moreover, if foreigners are buying our goods, services, or assets, that represents a demand for the dollar (an inflow) in international exchange rate markets. If we buy foreign goods, services, or assets, that represents a supply of dollars (an outflow).*

1b. The balance on goods and services is the difference between the value of goods and services a nation exports and the value of goods and services it imports. (396)

The balance of trade is often discussed in the popular press as a summary of how the U.S. is doing in international markets. However, it only includes goods exported and imported—not services. Trade in services is just as important as trade in merchandise, so economists pay more attention to the combined balance on goods and services.

1c. Since the balance of payments consists of both the capital account and the trade account, if the capital account is in surplus and the trade account is in deficit, there can still be a balance of payments surplus. (397)

The capital account measures the flows of payments between countries for assets such as stocks, bonds, and real estate. The current (or trade) account measures the flows of payments for goods and services.

1d. A deficit in the balance of payments means that the private quantity supplied of a currency exceeds the private quantity demanded. A surplus in the balance of payments means the opposite. (399)

Whenever the exchange rate is above equilibrium (below equilibrium) then the country will experience a balance of payments deficit (surplus).

2. Three important fundamental determinants of exchange rates are prices, interest rates, and income. (399)

A decrease in the value of a currency can be caused by:

1. *An increase in the nation's inflation rate (because this causes the relative price of the nation's goods to rise, domestic consumers will import more, increasing the supply of the nation's currency, while at the same time they export less, decreasing the demand for the currency—an increase in supply and a decrease in demand decreases the relative price of the nation's currency).*

2. *A decrease in the nation's interest rates (because this will decrease foreign demand for domestic assets, decreasing the demand for domestic currency, while at the same time domestic citizens will look abroad for higher rates of return, thereby increasing the supply of the currency—a decrease in demand and an increase in supply will decrease the relative price of the nation's currency).*

3. *An increase in the nation's income (because this will increase the demand for imports, increasing the supply of the nation's currency to buy those imports—an increase in supply decreases the relative price of the currency).*

3. A country fixes the exchange rate by standing ready to buy and sell its currency anytime the exchange rate is not at the fixed exchange rate. (401)

It is easier for a country to maintain a fixed exchange rate below equilibrium. All it has to do is to print and sell enough domestic currency to hold the value down.

However, if a country wants to maintain a fixed exchange rate above long-run equilibrium then it can do so only as long as it has the foreign currency (official) reserves to buy up its currency. Once it runs out of official reserves, it will be unable to intervene, and must either borrow, use indirect methods (domestic fiscal and monetary policies), ask other countries to buy its currency (to sell their currency), or devalue its currency.

In reality, because a country has a limited amount of official reserves, it only uses strategic currency stabilization (not a fixed exchange rate policy).

4. Purchasing power parity is a method of calculating exchange rates such that various currencies will each buy an equal basket of goods and services. Those exchange rates may or may not be appropriate long-run exchange rates. (403)

Long-run equilibrium exchange rates can only be estimated. The PPP (Purchasing Power Parity) is one method of doing so. However, for many economists, it has serious problems. They contend that the current exchange rate is the best estimate of the long-run equilibrium rate.

5a. Three exchange rate régimes are:
1. Fixed exchange rate: The government chooses an exchange rate and offers to buy and sell currencies at that rate.
2. Flexible exchange rate: Determination of exchange rates is left totally up to the market.
3. Partially flexible exchange rate: The government sometimes affects the exchange rate and sometimes leaves it to the market. (404)

Which is best is debatable.

5b. Fixed exchange rates provide international monetary stability and force governments to make adjustments to meet their international problems. (This is *also* a disadvantage.) If they become unfixed, they create monetary instability. (405)

✔ *Know these advantages and disadvantages!*

5c. Flexible exchange rate régimes provide for orderly incremental adjustment of exchange rates rather than large sudden jumps, and allow governments to be flexible in conducting domestic monetary and fiscal policy. (This is *also* a disadvantage.) They are, however, susceptible to private speculation. (406)

✔ *Know these advantages and disadvantages!*

5d. Partially flexible exchange rate régimes combine the advantages and disadvantages of fixed and flexible exchange rates. (406)

Most countries have opted for this policy. However, if the market exchange rate is below the rate the government desires, and the government does not have sufficient official reserves (to buy and increase the demand for its currency), then it must undertake policies that will either increase the private demand for its currency or decrease the private supply. Doing so either involves using traditional macro policy—fiscal and monetary policy—to influence the economy, or using trade policy to affect the level of exports and imports.

6. Some important international trade restrictions include tariffs, quotas, voluntary restraint agreements, and regulatory trade restrictions. (409)

Know the difference between these different trade restrictions as well as embargoes and nationalistic appeals!

7. Economists generally support free trade because trade restrictions lower aggregate output, reduce international competition, and often result in harmful trade wars that hurt everyone. (412)

The costs of trade restrictions (which include, among other things, higher prices domestic consumers must pay) almost always outweigh the benefits (which include protection from foreign competition that provides higher short-run profits and greater short-run job security to the protected domestic industries).

However, strategic trade policies (threats to implement trade restrictions on another country if it doesn't reduce its trade barriers) can be used to promote free trade (if these threats are credible and the other country reduces its trade restrictions).

See also,
Appendix A: "The J-Curve"
Appendix B: "Why Exchange Rate Determination Is More Complicated than the Model Would Suggest"
Appendix C: "History of Exchange Rate Systems"

Short-answer questions

1. Distinguish between the balance of payments and the balance of trade. (LO1)

2. How can a country simultaneously have a balance of payments deficit and a balance of trade surplus? (LO1)

3. How does each part of the balance of payments relate to the supply and demand for currencies? (LO1)

4. What are the three fundamental determinants of exchange rates? (LO2)

5. If the demand and supply for a country's currency depends upon demand for imports and exports, and demand for foreign and domestic assets, how can a country fix its exchange rate? (LO3)

6. How do market exchange rates differ from exchange rates using the purchasing power parity concept? (LO4)

7. Define fixed exchange rates. (LO5)

8. Define flexible exchange rates. (LO5)

9. Define partially flexible exchange rates. (LO5)

10. Which are preferable, fixed or flexible exchange rates? (LO5)

11. What are a few of the most important international trade restrictions? (LO6)

12. Why do economists generally support free trade? (LO7)

Word Scramble

1. _____ _____ _____ 2. _____ _____ 3._____

 n l e c b a a   f o   a d e r t   c e n r r t u   u t o n c c a   f a r f i s t

Match the Terms and Concepts to Their Definitions

___ 1. balance of payments

___ 2. balance of trade

___ 3. capital account

___ 4. current account

___ 5. exchange rate intervention

___ 6. fixed exchange rate

___ 7. flexible exchange rate

___ 8. free trade

___ 9. official transactions account

___ 10. partially flexible exchange rate

___ 11. purchasing power parity

___ 12. strategic trade policies.

___ 13. tariffs

___ 14. voluntary restraint aggreement

a. A method of calculating exchange rates that attempts to value currencies at a rate so that each will buy an equal basket of goods.

b. Agreements in which countries voluntarily restrict their exports.

c. A country's record of all transactions between its residents and the residents of all foreign countries.

d. Taxes governments place on internationally traded goods, generally imports.

e. An exchange rate established by a government that sometimes affects the exchange rate and sometimes leaves it to the market.

f. An exchange rate established by a government that chooses an exchange rate and offers to buy and sell currencies at that rate.

g. An exchange rate the determination of which is left up to the market.

h. Threatening to implement tariffs to bring about a reduction in tariffs or some other concession from the other country.

i. Policy of allowing unrestricted trade among countries.

j. Government policy of buying and selling a currency to affect its price.

k. The difference between the value of goods a nation exports and the value of goods it imports.

l. The part of the balance of payments account that records the amount of a currency or other international reserves a nation buys or sells.

m. The part of the balance of payments account that lists all long-term flows of payments.

n. The part of the balance of payments account that lists all short-term flows of payments.

Problems and Exercises

1. State for each whether the transaction shows up on the balance of payments current account or the balance of payments capital account or neither.

    a. An American buys 100 stocks of Mercedes Benz, a German company.

    b. A Japanese businessperson buys Ameritec, an American bank.

    c. An American auto manufacturer buys $20 million in auto parts from a Japanese company.

    d. An American buys 100 shares of IBM stock.

   e.   Saturn exports 10,000 cars to Germany.

   f.   Toyota Motor Corporation, a Japanese firm, makes a $1 million profit from its plant in Kentucky, USA.

2.   For each of the following, state who is demanding and who is supplying what currency:

   a.   A French person buys a set of china from a U.S. firm.

   b.   A U.S. tourist in Japan buys a Japanese kimono from a department store.

   c.   An Italian exchange rate trader believes that the exchange rate value of the dollar will rise.

   d.   A Swiss investor in Germany.

3.   Draw supply and demand curves for British pounds, showing equilibrium quantity and price. Price is shown by price of pounds in dollars.

   a.   What is the demand for dollars in this case?

   b.   Explain a movement up along the supply curve.

   c.   Explain a movement down along the demand curve.

d. What would be the effect on the price of pounds of an increase in demand for pounds by the British? Show this graphically.

e. What would be the effect on the price of pounds of an increase in demand for dollars by the British? Show this graphically.

4. For each of the following, show graphically what would happen to the market for British pounds. Assume there are only two countries, the United States and Britain.

a. Income in the Britain rises.

b. Income in the United States rises.

c. The prices of goods in the United States increases.

d. Interest rates rise in Britain.

e. The value of the pound is expected to fall.

A1. At an exchange rate of Can$0.6 to US$1, Canada is exporting 20 million pounds of wheat to the United States at US$2 a pound. It is importing 8,000 cars from the United States at US$10,000 apiece. Now say that the value of the Canadian dollar falls to Can$0.80 to US$1. Canada's exports of wheat rise to 22 million pounds of wheat while car imports fall to 7,800 cars.

    a.   What is the original trade balance in Canadian dollars?

    b.   What has happened to the trade deficit?

    c.   What will likely happen in the long run?

B1. What buy or sell recommendations for U.S. dollars would you make in response to the following news?

    a.   U.S. monetary policy is expected to contract.

    b.   Inflation in Japan is expected to accelerate.

    c.   Growth in the United States is expected to be higher.

    d.   German interest rates rise.

    e.   The German central bank reduces its discount rate.

Multiple Choice Questions

1. If a country has perfectly flexible exchange rates and is running a current account deficit, it is running
   a. a capital account surplus.
   b. a capital account deficit.
   c. an official transactions surplus.
   d. an official transactions deficit.

2. In the balance of payments accounts, net investment income shows up in
   a. the current account.
   b. the capital account.
   c. the official transactions account.
   d. It is not an entry in the balance of payments.

3. If the official transactions account is significantly in surplus, the country is
   a. trying to hold up its exchange rate.
   b. trying to push down its exchange rate.
   c. trying to have no effect on its exchange rate.
   d. sometimes trying to increase and sometimes trying to decrease its exchange rate.

4. In recent years, the United States has generally
   a. run a balance of trade surplus.
   b. run a balance of trade deficit.
   c. had sometimes a balance of trade surplus and sometimes a balance of trade deficit.
   d. had a balance of trade equality.

5. In recent years, the United States generally
   a. has run a capital account surplus.
   b. has run a capital account deficit.
   c. has sometimes run a capital account surplus and sometimes run a capital account deficit.
   d. has run a capital account equality.

6. If there is a black market for a currency, the country probably has
   a. nonconvertible currency.
   b. a fixed exchange rate currency.
   c. a flexible exchange rate currency.
   d. a partially flexible exchange rate currency.

7. The graph on the right is of the supply and demand for French francs. If the French demand for U.S. imports increases
   a. the supply curve will shift to the right.
   b. the supply curve will shift to the left.
   c. the demand curve will shift to the right.
   d. the demand curve will shift to the left.

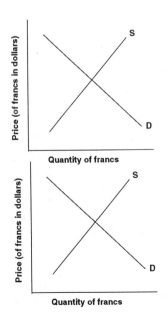

8. The graph on the right is of the supply and demand for French francs. If the U.S. demand for French imports increases
   a. the supply curve will shift to the right.
   b. the supply curve will shift to the left.
   c. the demand curve will shift to the right.
   d. the demand curve will shift to the left.

9. The graph on the right is of the supply and demand for French francs. If U.S. income increases
    a. the supply curve will shift to the right.
    b. the supply curve will shift to the left.
    c. the demand curve will shift to the right.
    d. the demand curve will shift to the left.

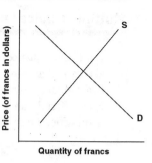

10. If there is a rise in the U.S. interest rate, one would expect the price of French francs in terms of dollars to
    a. rise.
    b. fall.
    c. remain unchanged.
    d. sometimes rise and sometimes fall.

11. If there is a rise in the U.S. price level, one would expect the price of French francs in terms of dollars to
    a. rise.
    b. fall.
    c. remain unchanged.
    d. sometimes rise and sometimes fall.

12. If a country runs expansionary monetary policy, in the short run one would expect the value of its exchange rate to
    a. rise.
    b. fall.
    c. be unaffected.
    d. sometimes rise and sometimes fall.

13. Say the Bangladeshi taka is valued at 42 taka to $1. Also say that you can buy the same basket of goods for 10 taka that you can buy for $1. In terms of dollars the purchasing power parity of the taka is
    a. overvalued.
    b. undervalued.
    c. not distorted.
    d. non convertible.

14. Compared to a fixed exchange rate system, a flexible exchange rate system
    a. allows countries more flexibility in their monetary policies.
    b. allows countries less flexibility in their monetary policies.
    c. has no effect on monetary policies.
    d. allows countries more flexibility in their industrial policies.

15. Tariffs are
    a. quantity limits placed on imports.
    b. agreements in which countries voluntarily restrict their exports.
    c. taxes governments place on internationally traded goods—generally imports.
    d. an all-out restriction on the import or export of a good.

16. Which of the following is *not* generally a reason for economists' opposition to trade restrictions?
    a. they lower aggregate output.
    b. they reduce international competition.
    c. they often result in harmful trade wars that hurt everyone.
    d. they increase output of foreign countries relative to the domestic country.

A1. According to the empirical phenomenon of the J-curve, when a country's exchange rate falls its
   a. trade deficit usually become larger initially, then decreases.
   b. trade deficit usually becomes smaller initially, then increases.
   c. capital account usually becomes larger initially, then decreases
   d. capital account usually becomes smaller initially, then increases.

B1. A currency trader will make a larger total profit from trading
   a. if the spread is larger.
   b. if the spread is smaller.
   c. The spread could be either larger or smaller.
   d. The spread will have no relationship to profits.

C1. The gold standard is a type of
   a. fixed exchange rate.
   b. partially flexible exchange rate.
   c. flexible exchange rate.
   d. nonconvertible exchange rate.

C2. The gold specie flow mechanism works primarily by flows of
   a. money from one country to another.
   b. services from one country to another.
   c. merchandise from one country to another.
   d. exchange rates from one country to another.

C3. Under the gold standard, if a country has a balance of payments deficit
   a. gold would flow out of the country.
   b. gold would flow into the country.
   c. the country's exchange rate would rise.
   d. the country's exchange rate would fall.

C4. SDRs refers to
   a. Specie Draft Rights.
   b. Specie Drawing Rights.
   c. Special Drawing Rights.
   d. Special Draft Rights.

Answers

Short-answer questions

1.   The balance of payments is a country's record of all transactions between its residents and the residents of all foreign nations. It is divided into the current account, the capital account, and the official transactions account. The balance of trade is one part of the balance of payments—specifically that part dealing with goods. It is not all that satisfactory a measure of the country's position in international markets since it does not include services. Generally, economists pay more attention to the combined balance on goods and services account. (395-398)

2.   As discussed in question 1, the balance of trade is one part of the balance of payments. Thus, if other parts of the international payments —for example, the capital account—are in deficit, the balance of trade could be in surplus. (395-396)

3.   The balance of payments records the flow of a currency in and out of a country (1) in order to buy and sell goods and services in the current account, (2) in order to buy and sell assets along with payments resulting from previous purchases of assets in the capital account, (3) in order to affect the value of a country's currency in the official transactions account. To buy foreign goods and assets one must supply domestic currency and demand foreign currency. Therefore, the balance of payments records the demand and supply of a country's currency during a given period of time. (395-398)

4.   Three fundamental determinants of the value of a country's exchange rate are (1) domestic income, (2) domestic price level and (3) domestic interest rates. (399)

5.   The current account and capital account reflect private demand and supply of a country's currency. If the official transactions account were zero, then the currency's value is market determined. If a country wants to fix the value of its currency to maintain its value at the fixed value, the government must buy and sell its currency using official reserves. Buying (selling) one's own currency shows up as a positive (negative) in the official transactions account.   (395-398, 400-401)

6.   Market exchange rates are determined by the demand and supply of a country's currency. Since not all goods, services and assets produced in a country can be traded internationally, the value of an exchange rate may not reflect the relative prices in each country. The purchasing power parity concept adjusts the value of a country's currency by determining that rate at which equivalent baskets of goods can be purchased in each country. (403-404)

7.   A fixed exchange rate is an exchange rate that the government chooses and then holds at the chosen rate, by standing ready to buy and sell at that rate. (404)

8.   Flexible exchange rates are exchange rates that are determined by the market without government intervention. (404)

9.   Partially flexible exchange rates are exchange rates that are determined by the market but are affected by government intervention. (404)

10. It depends. Each has its advantages and disadvantages. Flexible exchange rates give a country more control over domestic policy, but it can experience large fluctuations, hurting trade. (404-405)

11. The most important international trade restrictions include tariffs, quotas, voluntary restraint agreements, and regulatory trade restrictions. (409-410)

12. Economists generally support free trade because restrictions in trade lower output, reduce international competition (raising prices to consumers), and often result in harmful trade wars that hurt everyone. (411-412)

Word Scramble   1. balance of trade   2. current account   3. tariffs

Match the Terms and Concepts to Their Definitions
1-c; 2-k; 3-m; 4-n; 5-j; 6-f; 7-g; 8-i; 9-l; 10-e; 11-a; 12-h; 13-d; 14-b.

Problems and Exercises

1. a. Capital account. This is a long-term outflow. (395)
    b. Capital account. This is a long-term inflow. (395)
    c. Current account. This is merchandise imports, a short-term flow. (395)
    d. Neither. It is a domestic transaction. (395)
    e. Current account. This is merchandise exports, a short-term flow. (395)
    f. Current account. This is net investment income. (395)

2. a. The French person supplies francs and demands dollars because the French person sells francs to get U.S. dollars to purchase the china. (398-399)
    b. The U.S. tourist supplies dollars and demands Japanese yen because the tourist has to sell dollars to get yen. (398-399)
    c. The Italian trader will supply Italian lire and demand U.S. dollars because the trader wants to purchase that exchange that is believed to rise, the dollar. The trader must sell lire to get the dollars. (398-399)
    d. The Swiss investor will supply Swiss francs and demand German marks because the Swiss investor needs German marks to invest in Germany. (398-399)

3. A market for British pounds is shown to the right. Price of pounds in U.S. dollars is on the vertical axis and quantity of pounds is on the horizontal axis. Equilibrium price and quantity is determined by where they intersect. (398-401)

    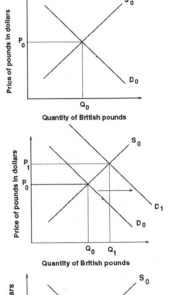

    a. If only two countries exist, the United States and Britain, the demand for dollars is the supply of pounds. (398-401)
    b. As the dollar value of the pound rises, individuals will supply more pounds. (398-401)
    c. As the dollar value of the pound declines, individuals will demand more pounds. (398-401)
    d. An increase in the demand for pounds by the British would shift the demand for pounds as shown on the graph to the right. The price of pounds in dollars would rise. (398-401)

    e. An increase in the demand for dollars by the British is equivalent to an increase in the supply of pounds. The supply curve for pounds would shift to the right as shown on the graph below. The price of pounds in dollars would fall. (398-401)

    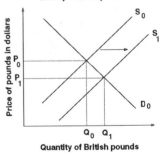

4. a. Demand for imports by the British rises; hence demand for dollars (supply of pounds) rises. This is shown in graph (a) below. (398-401)
    b. Demand for imports by Americans rises; hence demand for pounds rises. This is shown in the graph (b) below. (398-401)
    c. Demand for imports by the British falls; hence demand for dollars (supply of pounds) falls. This is shown in graph (c) below. (398-401)
    d. Demand for British assets will rise; hence the demand for the pound rises. This is shown in graph (d) below. (398-401)
    e. The demand for the pound falls. This is shown in graph (e) below. (398-401)

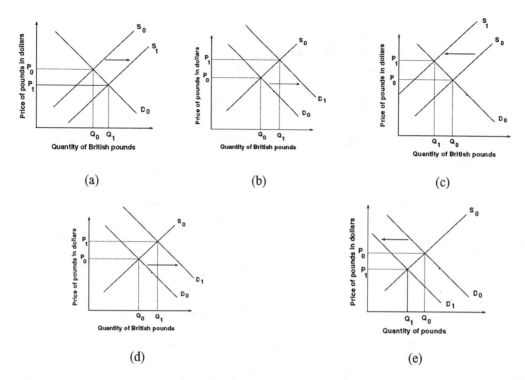

(a)   (b)   (c)

(d)   (e)

A1.a. Can$24 million trade deficit. Exports were Can$24 million (20 million × $US2 × exchange rate). Imports were Can$48 million (8,000 × $US10,000 × exchange rate). The trade balance is imports minus exports. (416-417)

b. The deficit has risen to Can$27.2 million. Exports are Can$35.2 million (22 million × $US2 x exchange rate). Imports are Can$62.4 million (7,800 × $US10,000 × exchange rate). The trade balance is imports minus exports. (416-417)

c. In the long run the quantity effects tend to dominate over the price effects and the trade deficit will be smaller than Can$24 million. (416-417)

B1.a. A contractionary U.S. monetary policy would tend to increase interest rates there. This will tend to increase the value of the dollar. We would recommend buying U.S. dollars. (417-420)

b. As goods in Japan become more expensive, the demand for the Japanese yen will fall. This will tend to reduce the value of the yen. We would recommend selling Japanese yen (buying U.S. dollars). (417-420)

c. Higher growth in the U.S. will increase the demand for imports. This means the supply of dollars will increase. The value of the dollar will fall. We would recommend selling U.S. dollars. (417-420)

d. Higher interest rates in Germany will tend to increase the demand for German marks. The exchange rate value of the German mark will rise. We would recommend buying German marks (selling U.S. dollars), other things equal. (417-420)

e. Lower interest rates in Germany will tend to decrease the demand for German marks. The exchange rate value of the German mark will fall. We would recommend selling German marks (buying U.S. dollars). (417-420)

Multiple Choice Questions

1. a. With perfectly flexible exchange rates the balance of payments must sum to zero; thus the capital account must be in surplus if the current account is in deficit. The official transactions account could not be negative because if there are perfectly flexible exchange rates, there are no official transactions. See pages 397-404.

2. a. Although net investment income might seem to many people as if it goes in the capital account, it is a return for a service and is considered part of the current account, as is discussed on page 396.

3. a. A surplus in the official transactions account means the balance of payments would otherwise be in deficit. The country is buying up its own currency. This means it is trying to hold up its exchange rate. See page 397-398.

4. b. See pages 395-396.

5. a. Running a capital account surplus is the other side of the balance sheet from the trade deficit. See pages 395-396.

6. a. All the others allow free exchange of currency and hence would not generate a black market. See page 401.

7. a. The French demand for U.S. imports is the supply of francs since paying for the imports requires supplying francs to buy dollars. See pages 398-399.

8. c. The U.S. demand for French imports is the demand for francs since paying for the imports requires buying francs. See pages 398-399.

9. c. If U.S. income increases, the U.S. demand for French imports will increase, shifting the demand for francs out. See page 399.

10. b. A rise in U.S. interest rates increases the demand for dollars, causing the price of francs in terms of dollars to fall. See page 399.

11. a. A rise in the U.S. price level would decrease the demand for U.S. imports, and hence decrease the supply of francs, causing the price of francs to rise. See page 399.

12. b. This is a review question from the previous chapter. Expansionary monetary policy decreases interest rates and thereby tends to decrease the exchange rate in the short run. See page 399 (this chapter) and page 384 (from the previous chapter).

13. b. Since the purchasing power parity exchange rate is lower than the actual exchange rate, the taka is undervalued. See page 403.

14. a. Under a fixed exchange rate system countries must use their monetary policies to meet international commitments. Thus flexible exchange rate policies allow them more flexibility in their monetary policies. Flexible exchange rates *may* allow them more flexibility in their industrial policies, but flexible exchange rates *definitely* do allow them more flexibility in their monetary policy, so a is the preferred answer. See pages 405-406.

15. c. See page 409 of textbook.

16. d. Trade restrictions hurt all countries. See pages 411-412.

A1. a. The J-curve refers to the trade deficit or surplus, so c and d can be eliminated. Because the price effects often predominate, the trade deficit usually becomes larger initially. See page 416.

B1. c. The larger the spread, the larger the profit per trade, but the smaller the number of trades, so the effect of the spread is impossible to determine in a general sense, although its effect could be determined with respect to a specific trade. See page 418.

C1. a. See page 421.

C2. a. When there is an imbalance of trade in the gold system, gold—which is money—flows from the deficit country to the surplus country, pushing the price level down in the deficit country and up in the surplus country. This process brings about a trade balance equilibrium, eventually. See page 421.

C3. a. See page 421 about the flow of gold. The last two answers could be eliminated since the gold standard involves fixed exchange rates.

C4. c. As discussed on page 422, SDRs refers to Special Drawing Rights.

Chapter 17:
The Art of Traditional Macro Policy

Learning Objectives

1. Conflicting goals of traditional macro policy are low inflation versus low unemployment and high growth and international trade and exchange rate goals versus domestic goals. Too contractionary a policy will cause unemployment and recession. Too expansionary a policy will accelerate inflation and expand trade deficits. (425)

Government has to walk a tightrope and use monetary and fiscal policy as a balance bar.

2. Economic relationships are not certain, which makes macroeconomic policy an art rather than a science. (425)

The macroeconomy is extremely complex–especially when we consider the effects of expectations about policy. However, policy makers don't want complexity. They want answers. Unfortunately, those answers often don't exist.

3. Theoretical models are abstract; they try to capture certain aspects of economic behavior that transcend institutions. Policy models combine individuals' actions that transcend institutions and individual actions that depend on institutions; they try to capture empirical regularities. (428)

Policy models are more dependent upon the <u>current</u> nature of institutions. If insitutions change, then the policy must change.

4. Modern macro policy economists focus on credibility because they see macro policy operating through expectations as much as through the real channels emphasized in the traditional models. (429)

Credible systematic policies are those that people believe will be implemented regardless of consequences.

5. Both Keynesians and Classicals generally agree that:
   1. Expansionary monetary and fiscal policies have short-run stimulative effects on income.
   2. Expansionary monetary and fiscal policies have potential long-run inflation effects.
   3. Monetary policy is politically easier to implement than fiscal policy.
   4. Expansionary monetary and fiscal policies tend to increase a trade deficit.
   5. Expansionary monetary policy places downward pressure on the exchange rate.
   6. Expansionary fiscal policy has an ambiguous effect on the exchange rate. (433)

However, their normative value judgements regarding the benefits and costs of government involvement are very different. There's no objective way to determine who's right.

See also,
    Appendix A: "Nonmainstream Approaches to Macro."
    Appendix B: "Earlier History of Macroeconomic Policy."

Short-answer questions

1. The president of Happyland has appointed you Chairman of her Council of Economic Advisers. She tells you she wants unemployment to be 2% and inflation to be zero. How do you respond? (LO1)

2. Why is macroeconomic policy considered an art rather than a science? (LO2)

3. What is the difference between a policy model and a theoretical model? (LO3)

4. In 1995, the U.S. government gave in to the Unabomber and asked newspapers to meet his demand to publish his manifesto about technological society. Does that "giving in" better represent a Keynesian or a Classical approach to problem? Which is the correct approach? (LO4)

5. List six points of agreement between Classicals and Keynesians. (LO5)

Word Scramble

1. _____ _____ _____ _____
   rat   of   carmo   yoilpc

2. _____ _____
   accehiimnst   yssnnmKiieea

3. _____ _____
   lraitnao   xetepacinots

Match the Terms and Concepts to Their Definitions

____ 1. art of macro policy

____ 2. credible systematic policies

____ 3. mechanistic Keynesianism

____ 4. rational expectations

a. Policies that people believe will be implemented regardless of consequences.

b. Expectations about the future based on the best current information, used in theoretical economic work that focuses on building dynamic feedback effects into macro models.

c. An art practiced by economists who advise governments about real-world macro policy. In the practice of that art, economists recognize that economic relationships are not certain and conducting macroeconomic policy is not a science.

d. The belief that the simple multiplier models actually describe the aggregate adjustment process and lead to a deterministic solution that policy makers can exploit in a mechanistic way.

Problems and Exercises

1. Keynesian and Classical economists differ in their vision and approach to issues. These approaches likely carry over to other elements of their lives.
    a. State which of the following statements was likely made by a Classical and which by a Keynesian.
       1. Life is tough; that's the way it is.

       2. Let them have an ice cream cone just this once.

       3. Dieting is simply a matter of reducing the intake of calories.

       4. Traditions should be followed in almost all cases.

    b. Explain the general approach for Keynesians and Classicals that underlay the answers you gave above.

Multiple Choice Questions

1. You have been appointed adviser to the president. He comes in and says he wants very low unemployment, zero inflation, and very high growth. You should
   a. advise him to use expansionary monetary policy.
   b. advise him to use contractionary monetary policy.
   c. tell him it is likely impossible using traditional tools.
   d. advise him to use a combination of expansionary monetary policy and contractionary fiscal policy.

2. You've been appointed adviser to the president. She wants interest rates to fall and wants to decrease unemployment. You would suggest
   a. expansionary monetary policy.
   b. contractionary monetary policy.
   c. expansionary fiscal policy.
   d. contractionary fiscal policy.

3. You've been appointed adviser to the president. She wants interest rates to rise and wants to decrease unemployment. You would suggest
    a. expansionary monetary policy.
    b. contractionary monetary policy.
    c. expansionary fiscal policy.
    d. contractionary fiscal policy.

4. You've been appointed adviser to the president. She wants interest rates and inflationary pressure fall. You would suggest
    a. expansionary monetary policy.
    b. contractionary monetary policy.
    c. expansionary fiscal policy.
    d. contractionary fiscal policy.

5. Modern Keynesians
    a. tend to be mechanistic Keynesians.
    b. tend to be interpretive Keynesians.
    c. do not exist because no modern economist would be a Keynesian.
    d. tend to be academic cowonomists.

6. An economist is calling for the implementation of credible, systematic policies, but argues that there should still be significant discretionary policy. This economist
    a. is likely a Classical economist.
    b. is likely a Keynesian economist.
    c. would equally likely be a Classical or Keynesian economist.
    d. does not exist because no economist would call for credible, systematic policies.

7. According to the text
    a. Keynesians are generally correct on policy.
    b. Classicals are generally correct on policy.
    c. Both Keynesians and Classicals are correct on policy sometimes.
    d. Both Keynesians and Classicals are incorrect on policy.

8. Keynesians and Classicals are least likely to agree that
    a. expansionary monetary and fiscal policies have significant long-run stimulative effects on real income.
    b. expansionary monetary and fiscal policies have potentially long-run stimulative effects on inflation.
    c. monetary is politically easier to use than fiscal policy.
    d. expansionary monetary and fiscal policy tend to increase the trade deficit.

9. In what range of the graph to the right will expansionary macro policy be most likely to increase real output the most?
    a. A.
    b. B.
    c. C.
    d. It is equally likely in all ranges.

10. In what range of the graph to the right will contractionary aggregate demand policy be most likely to slow inflation?
    a. A.
    b. B.
    c. C.
    d. It is equally likely in all ranges.

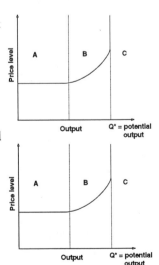

11. The Ricardian equivalence theorem states that
    a. it makes no difference whether one increases the money supply through M_1 or through M_2.
    b. it makes no difference whether government spending is financed by taxes or by a deficit.
    c. it makes no difference whether you use monetary policy or fiscal policy.
    d. it makes no difference whether one is a Keynesian or a Classical.

A1. Economists most likely to support a tax-based incomes policy are
    a. Austrian economists.
    b. Post Keynesian economists.
    c. radical economists.
    d. Classical economists.

A2. Economists most likely to support indicative planning would be
    a. Classical economists.
    b. Austrian economists.
    c. Institutionalist economists.
    d. No economists in their right minds would support indicative planning.

B1. The New Deal
    a. was a program in the 1970s that introduced public works.
    b. was a program in the 1930s that introduced public works.
    c. was an agreement between the Fed and the government on how to finance wartime spending.
    d. involved the introduction of wage and price controls.

B2. October 1979 is an important date in a history of the U.S. economy in that
    a. Keynesian policies were then first adopted.
    b. the Fed suddenly decreased the money supply targets enormously.
    c. the Fed suddenly increased the money supply targets enormously.
    d. rational expectations started to occur in the U.S. economy.

Answers

Short-answer questions

1. Life is tough, and you can't always get what you want. There are trade-offs that must be considered and achieving 2% unemployment and zero inflation is the equivalent to wanting to have kids who do what you tell them without questioning you. And here's my resignation. (425)

2. The study of economic models may be a science but when one translates those models into real-world settings there are ambiguities and judgments must be made that are more artistic than scientific. (425)

3. Theoretical models are deductive models based on first principles; they try to capture aspects of economic behavior that transcend institutions. Policy models are working models; they combine individuals' actions that transcend institutions with individual actions that depend on institutions, and try to capture empirical regularities, whatever the cause. (427-428)

4. Classicals are more likely to stick to rules despite negative short-term consequences, so this was probably a Keynesian response. Which is the correct response? It depends. (428-429)

5. Six points of agreement between Keynesians and Classicals are:

   1. Expansionary monetary and fiscal policies have short-run simulative effects on income.
   2. Expansionary monetary and fiscal policies have potential long-run inflation effects.
   3. Monetary policy is politically easier to use than fiscal policy.
   4. Expansionary monetary and fiscal policies tend to increase a trade deficit.
   5. Expansionary monetary policy places downward pressure on the exchange rate.
   6. Expansionary fiscal policy has an ambiguous effect on the exchange rate. (433)

Word Scramble   1. art of macro policy.   2. mechanistic Keynesianism   3. rational expectations

Match the Terms and Concepts to Their Definitions
1-c; 2-a; 3-d; 4-b.

Problems and Exercises

1. a. (1) Classical; (2) Keynesian, (3) Classical, (4) Keynesian.
   b. Classicals have a stronger focus on rules and are less likely to consider extenuating circumstances than are Keynesians. (426-433)

Multiple Choice Questions

1. c. As the text makes clear on pages 425-426, there are trade-offs, and good economists are continually pointing out the limits. This combination of goals is, for the most part, unattainable, given current policy options.

2. a. Since you want to decrease unemployment, it will have to be expansionary monetary policy or expansionary fiscal policy, but only expansionary monetary policy will work since the president also wants interest rates to fall. See page 426.

3. c. Since you want to decrease unemployment, it will have to be expansionary monetary policy or expansionary fiscal policy, but only expansionary fiscal policy will work since the president also wants interest rates to rise. See page 426.

4. d. Since you want to decrease inflationary pressure, it will have to be contractionary monetary policy or contractionary fiscal policy, but only contractionary fiscal policy will work since the president also wants interest rates to fall. See page 426.

5. b. As discussed on page 427, most Keynesian economists now believe the Keynesian model is simply a guide, not specific, and hence are interpretive Keynesians. The others are throwaway answers.

6. b. Both Classicals and Keynesians agree that credible, systematic policies are needed. However, the second part, stating that there should still be significant discretionary policy, is a strong sign that this economist is a Keynesian. See page 429.

7. c. In this text everyone is right some of the time; after all, the author wants to sell the book to all groups. See page 430.

8. a. Classicals see minimal long-run effects of policy on real income. See pages 426 and 433.

9. a. When the price-level flexibility curve is flat, expansionary aggregate demand policy will most likely increase real output the most. This range is called the Keynesian range. See Exhibit 4, page 433.

10. c. When the price-level flexibility curve is vertical, contractionary aggregate demand policy will most likely slow inflation. This range is called the Classical range. See Exhibit 4, page 433.

11. b. See page 432.

A1. b. See page 437-439.

A2. c. See pages 438-439.

B1. b. See page 440.

B2. b. The actual event is more complicated than this question allows, but the only answer that is close is b. Actually, the Fed stated that it switched from interest rate targeting to money supply targeting, but most observers believe the desire was simply to provide political cover for reducing money supply growth and squeezing the inflationary expectations out of the economy. See page 444.

Chapter 18:
Structural Supply-Side Macro Policies

Chapter at a glance

1. Structural supply-side macro policies are policies that increase the potential output the economy can achieve, thereby allowing a reduction in unemployment, by changing the structure of the economy and the incentives inherent in that structure. (446)

   Structural supply-side policies offer the hope of having it all—growth, prosperity, low fiscal deficits, and low unemployment.

   They are designed to shift the AS path out (not the AED curve), thereby increasing the target level of potential output, and allowing an expansion in output without an increase in inflation.

   Two types of structural policies are activist structural policies that involve <u>more</u> government activity than currently exists (generally favored by Keynesians), and laissez-faire structural policies that involve <u>less</u> government activity than currently exists (generally favored by Classicals).

2. Three general Classical laissez-faire structural supply-side policies are: (1) lowering tax rates; (2) reducing government social welfare spending; and (3) reducing government regulation. (448)

   Lower tax rates, it is argued, create a greater incentive to work, to save, and to invest. Moreover, if the economy is on the downward sloping portion of the Laffer curve, a tax rate cut will decrease a fiscal deficit.

   Reducing need-based social welfare programs, according to Classicals, will increase people's incentive to work, and thereby increase the economy's potential output (income).

   Streamlining, modifying, or eliminating many regulations will reduce the cost of doing busines and encourage new businesses; there will be more competition, and potential output will increase.

3. Much of the discussion of the Laffer Curve has been unfruitful because it does not make clear what time dimension or specific tax opponents and supporters are talking about. (450)

   The effect of a tax cut upon tax revenues depends upon where the economy is along the Laffer curve. Moreover, to make a judgment about whether a tax cut makes sense or not requires a much broader range of judgments than simply what happens to tax revenues. For example, would a tax cut cause government to reduce "wasteful spending"?

4a. Social welfare programs can reduce people's incentive to work, thereby decreasing potential output. (450)

   Many need-based programs involve an incentive to appear needy and to avoid accepting a job. However, eliminating these programs may cause some individuals who were genuinely and unavoidably in need to get less help.

4b. Social welfare programs can increase people's nutrition, and increase society's social cohesion, thereby increasing potential output. (456)

   Ironically, Keynesians see as supply-enhancing some of the same social spending programs that Classicals see as supply-decreasing government programs.

5. Classicals see a much bigger excess burden of taxation than Keynesians do because they see the revenue from taxation as being wasted. Keynesians see it as being transferred to more productive uses. (453)

   Classical economists favor cutting taxes and simultaneously cutting government spending—because they believe the economy can win in both ways.

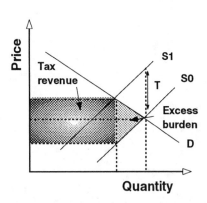

All economists argue that a tax creates excess burden equal to the shaded triangle. Classicals see the revenue to the government as additional excess burden. Keynesians see the revenue to the government as a transfer and thus, not an excess burden.

6. Three Keynesian structural supply-side policies are: (1) productivity-enhancing regulatory reforms; (2) activist industrial policies; and (3) incomes policies. (455)

    Productivity-enhancing regulatory reforms focus, not on cutting social programs and regulations as do the Classical proposals, but on modifying them, improving the positive aspects of the programs while eliminating the negative aspects.

7. An activist industrial policy is a policy under which the government works directly with businesses, providing funds, background research, and encouragement to specific industries It has serious potential political problems. (456)

    Examples include government partnerships with business to encourage exports (like Japan's MITI), strategic trade policy, government-led economic missions, and a targeted employment subsidy policy. A majority of economists argue that the costs outweigh the benefits of a general activist industrial policy. They favor a more informal arrangement.

8. An incomes policy is a policy that is supposed to work by directly holding down nominal wages and price increases, thereby possibly shifting the AS path out. It has serious potential political problems (459-460)

    Ideally, an incomes policy is designed to reduce wages and prices in monopolistic sectors. The politics of an incomes policy renders it extremely unlikely in the near future.

Short-answer questions

1. Once again, you are called to prep freshman Congresspeople. One asks, "The Fed doesn't seem to want to use expansionary monetary policy, and my constituents back home want a balanced budget. That eliminates the two ways you've told us government can get our economy rolling. What other suggestions do you have?" Since you are prepared for this question you tell them about structural supply-side policies and explain how structural macro supply-side policy differs from traditional macro policy. (LO1)

2. The Classical policymakers in the room are wary of your explanation in #1. You tell them three general Classical laissez-faire structural supply-side polices. (LO2)

3. One person in the group remembers that in the 1980s the supply-side policies to reduce taxes based upon the Laffer curve resulted in huge budget deficits. He asks, "What happened to the Laffer curve and why has much of the discussion of the Laffer curve been unfruitful?" (LO3)

4. The laissez-faire Congresspeople want to be armed for a debate about welfare. They ask, "How can reducing government spending on social welfare programs increase potential output?" You tell them. (LO4)

5.   How do the Keynesian and the Classical view of the excess burden of taxes differ? (LO5)

6.   The Congresspeople who are activist policymakers, listening to your answer to #4, begin to worry. They want to be able to argue in support of welfare. They ask, "How can increasing government spending on social welfare programs increase potential output?" You tell them. (LO6)

7.   What are the advantages of an activist industrial policy? (LO7)

8.   What sort of practical problems does an incomes policy run into? (LO8)

Word Scramble

1. _____ _____   2._____ _____   3._____ _____
   s x c e e s   u r b n d e   e c o m i n s   o i l c p y   e r a f L f   r c v u e

Match the Terms and Concepts to Their Definitions

___1.   activist industrial policy

___2.   activist structural supply-side policies

___3.   excess burden

___4.   incomes policy

___5.   industrial policy

___6.   Laffer curve

___7.   laissez-faire structural policies

___8.   military-industrial complex

___9.   MITI

___10. need-based social welfare programs

___11. productivity-enhancing social welfare programs

___12. strategic trade policy

___13. structural macro policies

___14. target level of potential output

___15. targeted employment subsidy policy

a.   Policies that increase the potential output the economy can achieve, thereby reducing unemployment, by changing the structure of the economy and the incentives inherent in that structure rather than by changing aggregate demand.

b.   The highest achievable output level without accelerating inflation.

c.   Policies that involve more government activity than currently exists.

d.   Policies that involve less government activity than currently exists.

e.   A curve that shows the relationship between tax rates and tax revenues.

f.   Social welfare programs in which eligibility is determined by need.

g.   A loss to producers and consumers that is not gained by anyone else.

h.   Social welfare programs that increase productivity and the economy's potential income.

i.   The formal policy that government takes toward business.

j.   A policy under which government works directly with businesses.

k.   Policy under which one country threatens to retaliate unless other countries reduce their explicit or implicit trade barriers.

l.   A policy in which government pays business to hire specific groups of workers.

m.   A close connection among the armed forces, the industries that manufacture weapons, and members of Congress from states and districts that depend heavily on the defense industry.

n.   A policy directly designed to hold down nominal wage and price increases.

o.   Japan's Ministry of international Trade and Industry, which guides Japan's activist industrial policy.

Problems and Exercises

1.   Suppose you get a need-based payment of $800 a month if you have no income, but you get a need-based payment of $200 if you earn $800 a month. You are deciding whether to take a job at Taco Cabana that pays $5 an hour for 40 hours a week, or $800 a month.

   a. What is your monthly incremental income (the net after you take away the reduction in your need-based payment) after taking the job?

   b. What is the implicit tax rate on your income?

c.   What will likely happen to your decision to work because of this implicit tax? Will you work for Taco Cabana or will you decide not to work?

d.   Would your answers to a, b, and c affect your supply-side policy proposals? How?

2.   The supply and demand curves for bananas are given below. Suppose the government imposes a tax, T, on banana sellers.

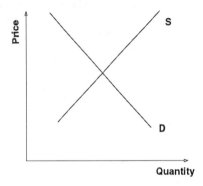

a.   What do the Classicals believe to be the excess burden on the graph?

b.   What do the Keynesians think the excess burden is on the graph?

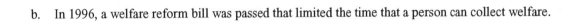

3. For each of the following, state whether it is a structural policy or a traditional macro policy, or both. Explain the policy's effect using the macro policy model assuming the economy is in the perfectly flexible price range of the aggregate supply path.

    a. From 1993 to early 1995, the Federal Reserve raised the Fed Funds target from 3% to 6%.

    b. In 1996, a welfare reform bill was passed that limited the time that a person can collect welfare.

    c. In 1982, top marginal tax rates were lowered from 70% to 36%.

    d. In 1997, the Prime Minister of Japan pushed to reduce regulation of business in Japan that will reduce the cost to businesses and consumers an estimated $250 billion a year.

Multiple Choice Questions

1. Structural supply-side policies
   a. shift the AED curve out and increase potential output.
   b. shift the AS path out and increase potential output.
   c. shift both the AED and the AS path out and increase potential output.
   d. shift neither the AED nor the AS path but increase potential output in other ways.

2. Classical methods to create supply-side incentives to increase output include
   a. lowering tax rates, reducing government social welfare spending, and reducing government regulation.
   b. lowering tax rates, reducing government social welfare spending, and increasing government regulation.
   c. lowering tax rates, increasing government social welfare spending, and increasing government regulation.
   d. increasing tax rates, increasing government social welfare spending, and increasing government regulation.

3. The difference between supply-side and Keynesian "tax cutting" policies is that
   a. while the supply-side view holds that tax cuts spur economic growth through the multiplier effect, the Keynesian view does not.
   b. the supply-side view is that "tax cutting" stimulates the economy while the Keynesian view is that it doesn't.
   c. the supply-side view focuses on tax rates and microeconomic incentives while the Keynesian view focuses on tax revenues and aggregate demand.
   d. the supply-side focuses on the effect of tax cuts on aggregate demand while the Keynesian view focuses on the effect of tax cuts on potential income.

4. Which of the following about the Laffer curve to the right is *false*?
   a. As you increase the tax rate from 40% to 60%, tax revenues will rise.
   b. As you increase the tax rate from 60% to 80%, tax revenues will fall.
   c. As you decrease the tax rate from 80% to 60%, tax revenues will fall.
   d. As you decrease the tax rate from 80% to 60%, tax revenues will rise.

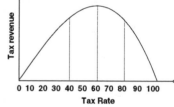

5. The Laffer curve is an inadequate tool to predict the effects of a tax cut because
   a. though it has a time dimension, it does not distinguish between short-run and long-run effects.
   b. though it has a time dimension, it does not talk about any specific tax, which makes it very ambiguous.
   c. it has no time dimension and it does not talk about any specific tax, making it very ambiguous.
   d. it leads to the conclusions that most of the time tax cuts are good but one can't know when to cut taxes because the time dimension is absent from the curve.

6. With which of the following would a Classical economist most likely to agree?
   a. Social welfare programs reduce people's incentives to work and reduce an economy's potential output.
   b. Social welfare programs reduce people's needs and people then have an incentive to appear less needy.
   c. Social welfare programs help maintain social order and cohesion, and thus increase potential income.
   d. Social welfare programs are wasteful in the short-run but are investments in the future.

7. Which of the following is a policy a Classical supply-sider is likely to advocate?
   a. a decrease in the payroll tax.
   b. raise the minimum wage.
   c. institute a targeted employment subsidy policy.
   d. institute an incomes policy.

8. Excess burden is
   a. A loss to consumers that producers gain.
   b. A loss to producers that consumers gain.
   c. A loss to consumers and producers that the government gains.
   d. A loss to consumers and producers that nobody gains.

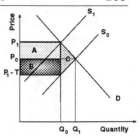

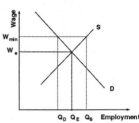

9. According to the Classicals, which of the following areas represent excess burden due to a tax?
    a. A.
    b. A+B.
    c. A+B+C.
    d. C.

10. If the minimum wage is set at W_{min} the employment level in the economy will be at
    a. Q_D.
    b. Q_E.
    c. Q_S.
    d. zero.

11. The Keynesian view regarding productivity-enhancing social programs is that
    a. the negative incentive effects of these programs make such policies nonviable.
    b. these programs have no negative incentive effects, and have tremendous supply-enhancing effects.
    c. the supply-enhancing effects of these policies often outweigh the negative incentive effects.
    d. although these policies have no supply-enhancing effects, one should support them for moral reasons.

12. An incomes policy is a policy designed to
    a. hold down price increases only.
    b. hold down nominal wage increases only.
    c. hold down nominal wage and price increases.
    d. change relative prices and wages.

13. An incomes policy is supposed to
    a. shift the AED curve out.
    b. shift the AED curve in.
    c. shift the AS path up.
    d. flatten the AS path and shift it out.

Answers

Short-answer questions

1. A structural macro supply-side policy increases the potential output an economy can achieve, thereby reducing unemployment, by changing the structure of the economy and the incentives inherent in that structure, rather than by changing aggregate demand as traditional macro policy does.   See pages 446-447.

2. Three general Classical laissez-faire structural supply-side polices are (1) lowering tax rates, (2) reducing government social welfare spending, and (3) reducing government regulation. See pages 448-452.

3. Much of the discussion of the Laffer curve has been unfruitful because it does not make clear the time dimension under discussion, i.e., it does not make a distinction between short-run and long-run effects. Also, it does not make clear which specific tax is being talking about. Different tax cuts will have different effects on incentives, and talking about some ambiguous tax cut isn't very helpful. See pages 449-450.

4. Social welfare programs that are need-based can make people try to appear more needy than they are and can reduce people's incentive to work because the more they work the less assistance they will get from the government. This set of perverse incentives will decrease potential output. Decreasing such programs can increase the incentives to work, and thus increase potential income. See pages 450-451.

5. Keynesians believe that the excess burden of taxation is lower than what the Classicals believe it to be. Both agree that the red triangle in Exhibit 4 on page 453 represents excess burden. The Classicals see the revenues collected from taxation as wasteful, whereas Keynesians see them as a transfer from one sector to another. See pages 452-454, especially Exhibit 4.

6. Social welfare programs can increase people's nutrition, making them more productive workers, thereby increasing potential output. Also, by increasing social cohesion, they can increase potential output. See page 456.

7. By providing funds, background research and encouragement to specific high-growth industries, activist industrial policies can increase a country's international competitiveness, and so its potential output can be increased. See pages 456-457.

8. Incomes polices have potential political problems. They make distributional issues explicit and by doing so often create more dissension among social groups than existed before. Also, relative prices in a market economy change over time. An incomes policy is not good at determining which relative prices should change and which should not. So incomes policies often work against the market. See pages 459-460.

Word Scramble   1. excess burden   2. incomes policy   3. Laffer curve.

Match the Terms and Concepts to Their Definitions
   1-j; 2-c; 3-g; 4-n; 5-i; 6-e; 7-d; 8-m; 9-o; 10-f; 11-h; 12-k; 13-a; 14-b; 15-l.

Problems and Exercises

1. a.   You would be now earning a total of $1000 ($800 from Taco Cabana plus $200 as need-based payment). This is only $200 more than what you would make if you weren't working at all. So, your incremental income is only $200. See page 450.
   b.   The implicit tax rate on your wage is 75%, (600/800), since your need-based payment has dropped by $600 from $800 a month to $200 a month. See pages 450-451.

c. Because of the implicit tax rate your after-tax hourly wage rate will be only $1.25 ($200/160hrs). You would probably find it less attractive to work for Taco Cabana than to receive the $800 payment without working at all. At the same time, you might look for under-the-table work to make some additional income. (450-451)

d. Such calculations suggest that policy makers should recommend policies that take into account the incentive effects of social programs. I would support programs whereby welfare is offered with a time limit and allow people, for a time, to collect both welfare and a salary during that time. Another way to reduce the implicit tax is to offer free childcare if welfare recipients found a job. New state legislation that requires that welfare recipients be actively looking for work has reduced the welfare rolls by eliminating those with under-the-table jobs who don't have time to look for other legitimate jobs. (450-451)

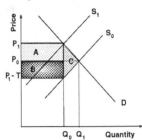

2. a. All economists agree that the area represented by the triangle C is excess burden. Classicals, however, in addition see rectangles A and B (total tax revenue collected by the government) as excess burden since they see the tax revenues as being wasted by the government. (453-454)

b. Keynesians believe that only triangle C is excess burden generated by taxation. They think that government revenues are being used for productive purposes, and hence don't see rectangles A and B as being excess burden. (453)

3. a. Monetary policy is a traditional macro policy that changes output by shifting the AED curve. The contractionary monetary policy will shift the AED curve to the left and output will not change, prices will rise. See Chapter 13 for a further discussion.

b. A time limit on welfare is both a structural policy and a traditional macro policy. As a structural policy it will increase the number of people who are looking for work. This increases resources available for production, shifting the AS path to the right, leading to higher output and lower price level. As a traditional macro policy it will reduce expenditures, shifting the AED curve to the left leading to a drop in output and a fall in the price level. It depends upon the relative effect of each whether output will rise or fall. (450-451)

c. This is both a structural and a traditional macro policy. To the extent that lower marginal tax rates increase people's willingness to undertake market activity, this is a structural policy that shifts the AS path to the right leading to higher output and a lower price level. To the extent that it results in lower tax payments, it shifts the AED curve to the right leading to even higher output and possibly higher prices. (450-451)

d. Reducing government regulation is a structural policy and a traditional macro policy. To the extent that unfettered businesses will be able to devote more resources to production instead of complying with government regulation, it shifts the AS path to the right leading to greater output and a lower price level. To the extent that government regulation employed government workers who needed supplies to carry out their regulation, this shifts the AED curve to the left lowering output and even lower prices. Whether output rises or falls depends upon the relative effect of each. (450-451)

Multiple Choice Questions

1. b. Structural supply-side policies shift out the AS path, thereby increasing the target level of potential output without an increase in inflation. See pages 446-447.

2. a. See page 448.

3. c. The supply-side view is that lower tax rates work through supply incentives; Keynesians see lower taxes working through aggregate demand. See page 448.

4. c. If you decrease the tax rate from 80% to 60%, tax revenues will rise, not fall. See pages 448-449.

5. c. See pages 449-450.

6. a. Because individuals are guaranteed a certain income, they will have a tendency to shirk work. Thus, potential income will decrease. See page 450.

7. a.   Classicals believe that decreasing the payroll tax will encourage businesses to create more jobs and thus increase potential income. The rest are policies that Keynesians would tend to agree with. See pages 452-453.

8. d.   See page 453.

9. c.   All economists agree that triangle C represents excess burden. Classicals, however, in addition see rectangles A and B (total tax revenue collected by the government) as excess burden since they see tax revenues as being wasted by the government. See page 453-454.

10. a.   If the minimum wage is set above the market equilibrium wage rate, there will be unemployment in the economy, and the employment level will be at Q_D. See page 455.

11. c.   While Keynesians agree that there are negative incentive effects of social programs, they believe that the supply-enhancing effects make them desirable. See page 456.

12. c.   See page 459.

13. d.   Incomes polices attempt to flatten out Range B and push the level of full employment out. See page 459.

Chapter 19: Deficits and Debt

Chapter at a glance

1. A deficit is a shortfall of incoming revenue under outgoing payments. A debt is accumulated deficits minus accumulated payments. (463)

   The deficit is a flow concept, whereas the debt is a stock concept.

   ✔ *Debt is a result of accumulated deficits.*

2. The deficit is simply a summary measure of the financial health of the economy. To understand that summary you must understand the methods that were used to calculate it. (467-468)

   Different accounting procedures yield different figures for both the deficit and the debt.

   When considering debt one should view debt in relation to assets (or GDP). Moreover, government debt is different than an individual's debt. Government is ongoing; government can pay off the debt by printing money; and much of the government debt is internal—owed to its citizens.

3. Since in a growing economy a continual deficit is consistent with a constant ratio of debt to GDP, and GDP serves as a measure of the government's ability to pay off the debt, a country can run a continual deficit. (470)

   GDP serves the same function for government as income does for an individual. The greater the GDP (income); the greater the ability to handle debt.

4. Real deficit = Nominal deficit − (Inflation X Total debt). (471)

   Inflation wipes out debt. Inflation also causes the real deficit to be less than the nominal deficit. However, inflation means a higher percentage of the deficit (or spending) will be devoted to debt service (paying interest on the debt). Moreover, the cost of eliminating the debt through inflation is paid by creditors who do not anticipate the inflation.

5. Even though the real deficit is lower than the nominal deficit, there is still cause for concern because the U.S. budget fails to include many obligations and the government uses many accounting tricks. (475)

   The U.S. government has often used gimmicks to make the deficit look smaller than it is.

6. Because the deficit has many dimensions and each is widely debated, there are many alternative reasonable views about the deficit. (478)

   Economists' views range from:
   1. *The wolf-at-the-door group who believe the deficit will bring about imminent doom.*

   2. *The domesticated-pussycat group who believe the deficit doesn't matter.*

   3. *The termites-in-the-basement group who believe the deficit will cause serious problems in the long run.*

Short-answer questions

1. Distinguish between the terms *deficit* and *debt*. (LO1)

2. How much importance do most economists give to the budget deficit? (LO2)

3. In an expanding economy a government should run a continual deficit. True or false? Why? (LO3)

4. If the nominal interest rate is 6%, the inflation rate is 4%, the nominal deficit is $100 billion, and the debt of the country is $2 trillion, what is the real deficit? (LO4)

5. If the nominal interest rate is 5%, the inflation rate is 5%, the real deficit is $100 billion, and the debt of the country is $1 trillion, what is the nominal deficit? (LO4)

6. If a politician presents you with a plan that will reduce the nominal budget deficit by $40 billion, but will not hurt anyone, how would you in your capacity as an economist likely respond? (LO5)

7. The text presented three general views that economists hold about the deficit. What are those three views, and which one of them is right? (LO6)

Word Scramble

1. _____
   t b d e

2. _____
   t i i d c f e

3. _____ _____
   l r e a   t i i f e d c

Match the Terms and Concepts to Their Definitions

____ 1. Budget Enforcement Act of 1990

____ 2. cash flow accounting system

____ 3. debt

____ 4. debt service

____ 5. deficit

____ 6. external government debt

____ 7. funded pension system

____ 8. Gramm-Rudman Hollings Act

____ 9. internal government debt

____ 10. nominal deficit

____ 11. off-budget expenditure

____ 12. policy régime

____ 13. real deficit

____ 14. structural deficit

____ 15. unfunded pension system

a. A federal law establishing mandatory deficit targets for the United States.

b. A federal law establishing a pay-as-you-go test for new spending and tax cuts, along with additional spending limits for government.

c. Accumulated deficits minus accumulated surpluses.

d. An accounting system entering expenses and revenues only when cash is received or paid out.

e. An expenditure that is not counted in the budget as an expenditure.

f. Government debt owed to individuals in foreign countries.

g. Government debt owed to its own citizens.

h. Pension system in which pensions are paid from current revenues.

i. Pension system in which money is collected and invested in a special fund from which payments are made.

j. The nominal deficit adjusted for inflation's effect on the debt.

k. The interest rate on debt times the total debt.

l. The deficit determined by looking at the difference between expenditures and receipts.

m. The deficit that would remain when the cyclical elements have been netted out.

n. The general set of rules, whether explicit or implicit, governing the monetary and fiscal policies a country follows.

o. A shortfall per year of incoming revenue under outgoing payments.

Problems and Exercises

1. Calculate the debt and deficit in each of the following:

   a. Your income has been $30,000 per year for the last five years. Your expenditures, including interest payments, have been $35,000 per year for the last five years.

   b. Your income is $50,000 per year; $15,000 of your $65,000 expenditures are for the purchase of the rights to an invention.

   c. Your wage income is $20,000 per year. You have a bond valued at $100,000 which pays $10,000 per year. The market value of that bond rises to $110,000. Expenses are $35,000 per year. Use the opportunity cost approach in your calculations.

2. For each of the following calculate the real deficit:

   a. Inflation is 5%. Debt is $2 trillion. Nominal deficit is $100 billion.

   b. Inflation is -3%. Debt is $500 billion. Nominal deficit is $20 billion.

   c. Inflation is 10%. Debt is $3 trillion. Nominal deficit is $100 billion.

   d. Inflation is 8%. Debt is $20 billion. Nominal deficit is $5 billion.

3. Assume a country's nominal GDP is $7 trillion, government expenditures less debt service are $1.5 trillion, and revenue is $1.3 trillion. The nominal debt is $4.9 trillion. Inflation is 2% and real interest rates are 5%. Expected inflation is fully adjusted.

   a. Calculate debt service payments.

   b. Calculate the nominal deficit.

   c. Calculate the real deficit.

   d. Suppose inflation rose to 4%. Again, expected inflation is fully adjusted. Recalculate (a) - (c).

4.   Assume a country's nominal GDP is $200 billion, government expenditures less debt service are $16 billion, and revenue is $20 billion. The nominal debt is $160 billion. Inflation is falling at a rate of 1% per year and real interest rates are 3%. Expected inflation is fully adjusted.

  a.   Calculate debt service payments.

  b.   Calculate the nominal deficit.

  c.   Calculate the real deficit.

  d.   Suppose inflation rose to 2% per year. Inflation expectations do not adjust. How do your answers to (a) - (c) change?

Multiple Choice Questions

1.   A deficit is
     a. the total amount of money that a country owes.
     b. the shortfall of payments under revenues in a particular time period.
     c. the shortfall of revenues under payments in a particular time period.
     d. accumulated debt.

2.   Since World War II, nominal U.S. government debt has usually been
     a. rising.
     b. falling.
     c. sometimes rising and sometimes falling.
     d. non-existent because the U.S. government has no debt.

3.   Country A has a debt of $10 trillion. Country B has a debt of $5 trillion.
     a. Country A is in a better position than Country B.
     b. Country B is in a better position than Country A.
     c. One cannot say what relative position the countries are in.
     d. Countries A and B are in equal positions.

4.   As a percentage of GDP, since World War II
     a. debt in the United States has been rising.
     b. debt in the United States has been falling.
     c. debt in the United States has been sometimes rising, sometimes falling.
     d. the U.S. government has had no debt.

5.   If there is growth and the country has decided it wants to keep its ratio of debt to GDP constant
     a. it should run a deficit.
     b. it should run a surplus.
     c. it should run a balanced budget deficit.
     d. the deficit has no effect on debt.

6. The nominal deficit is $100 billion; inflation is 4 percent; total debt is $2 trillion. The real deficit is
   a. zero.
   b. $20 billion.
   c. $80 billion.
   d. $100 billion.

7. The nominal deficit is $200 billion; inflation is 20 percent; total debt is $1 trillion. The real deficit is
   a. zero.
   b. $20 billion.
   c. $80 billion.
   d. $100 billion.

8. The real deficit is $100 billion; inflation is 4 percent; total debt is $2 trillion. The nominal deficit is
   a. zero.
   b. $120 billion.
   c. $180 billion.
   d. $200 billion.

9. Creditors
   a. always lose in an inflation.
   b. always gain in an inflation.
   c. sometimes lose and sometimes gain in an inflation, depending on what happens to real interest rates.
   d. sometimes gain and sometimes lose in an inflation, depending on what happens to the deficit.

10. According to most economists, the deficit
    a. is very important.
    b. is not important at all.
    c. is important primarily as one indicator of the financial health of the economy.
    d. should always be matched by surpluses.

11. Which of the following statements is true?
    a. A funded pension system is preferable to an unfunded pension system.
    b. An unfunded pension system is preferable to a funded pension system.
    c. Whether an unfunded pension system is preferable to an unfunded pension system depends.
    d. An unfunded pension system and a funded pension system are essentially identical.

12. If there is an unfunded pension system with fixed retirement ages and there is a baby boom, when the members of that baby boom retire
    a. the pension system will be in great shape.
    b. the pension system will be in horrendous shape.
    c. the baby boom will have no effect on the pension system.
    d. the pension system will be abandoned.

13. If the U.S. government raised the retirement age to 72 starting in 2010, the current budget deficit would be
    a. reduced.
    b. increased.
    c. unaffected.
    d. eliminated.

14. According to the textbook, most economists
    a. have a wolf-at-the-door view of the deficit.
    b. have a domesticated-pussycat view of the deficit.
    c. have a termites-in-the-basement view of the deficit.
    d. do not even consider the deficit.

Answers

Short-answer questions

1. A deficit is a shortfall of revenues under payments. It is a flow concept that has a time period dimension. A debt is accumulated deficits minus accumulated surpluses. It exists at a moment of time, not over a period of time. (463)

2. While there are differences of opinion, most economists are hesitant to attach too much importance to a deficit. The reason why is that the deficit depends on the accounting procedures used, and these can vary widely. Sometimes a deficit may be of serious concern; at other times it might be of no concern. Thus, only with much more additional information will an economist attribute importance to a deficit. It is financial health—by which is meant the ability to cover costs over the long term—of the economy that most economists are concerned with. (467, 473)

3. It depends. In an expanding economy with no deficits the ratio of debt to GDP will be falling; if the government wants to hold the debt-to-GDP constant it will need to run a continual deficit. If it wants to reduce that ratio, then it need not run a continual deficit. (470)

4. To calculate the real deficit you multiply inflation times the total debt (4% × $2 trillion), giving $80 billion; then subtract that from the nominal deficit of $100 billion. So in this example the real deficit equals $20 billion. The interest rate does not enter into the calculations. (470-471)

5. To calculate the nominal deficit you multiply inflation times the total debt (5% × $1 trillion), giving $50 billion, and add that to the real deficit of $100 billion. So in this example the nominal deficit equals $150 billion. There interest rate does not enter into the calculation. (471)

6. TANSTAAFL. I would check to see what accounting gimmick the politician was proposing and what the plan would do to the long-run financial health of the country. (474-477)

7. The three views were the wolf-at-the-door view, the domesticated pussycat view, and the termites-in-the-basement view. Of these, the majority of economists hold the termites-in-the-basement view. The textbook author seems to think the termites-in-the-basement view is the correct view, but since there is disagreement, and I have not studied the issue, I withhold judgment, following the text's line that "It depends." (478-481)

Word Scramble   1. debt   2. deficit   3. real deficit

Match the Terms and Concepts to Their Definitions

1-b; 2-d; 3-c; 4-k; 5-o; 6-f; 7-i; 8-a; 9-g; 10-l; 11-e; 12-n; 13-j; 14-m; 15-h.

Problems and Exercises

1. a. Deficit is $5,000 per year; Debt is $25,000. On page 463, deficit is defined as income less expenditures and debt is defined as accumulated deficits. For each of the past 5 years, you have incurred an annual deficit of $5,000. Total debt is $5,000 times five years, or $25,000. (463)
    b. Deficit is $15,000; Debt is $15,000. Page 465 tells you that what is included as expenses is ambiguous. If you count the purchase of the rights to the invention as a current expenditure, the deficit is $15,000. If you had no previous debt, debt is also $15,000. If, however, you count the purchase of the invention as an investment and include it in your capital budget, then your expenses are only $50,000 and your current account will be in balance. (463, 466)
    c. Surplus of $5,000. Page 466 tells you that using an opportunity cost approach, a person holding bonds should count the rise in the bonds' market value as revenue. Here, wage income is $20,000 per year, interest income is $10,000 and the bond's value has increased by $10,000. Total income is $40,000. Income of $40,000 less expenses of $35,000 per year yields a budget surplus of $5,000. (463, 466)

2. As discussed on page 471, the real deficit is the nominal deficit adjusted for inflation's effect on the debt. The definition of real deficit states: Real deficit = Nominal deficit - (Inflation x Total debt).
   a. $0: $100 billion − .05 × $2 trillion. (471)
   b. $35 billion: $20 billion − (−.03) × $500. (471)
   c. Surplus of $200 billion: $100 billion − .10 × $3 trillion. (471)
   d. $3.4 billion: $5 billion − .08 × $20 billion. (471)

3. a. $343 billion: Debt service payment = nominal interest rate x nominal debt. The nominal interest rate when expected inflation is fully adjusted is the real interest rate plus inflation (5+2). Debt service payment = .07 × $4.9 trillion. (471-473)
   b. $543 billion deficit: The nominal deficit is revenues less government expenditures (including debt service), $1.3 trillion - ($1.5 trillion + $.343 trillion). (471-473)
   c. $445 billion deficit: The real deficit = Nominal deficit − (Inflation ×Total debt) = $.543 trillion − (.02 × $4.9 trillion). (471-473)
   d. Since bondholders must be compensated for the loss in the value of their bonds, they demand a nominal interest rate of 9% (5 + 4). Debt service payment is now $441 billion (.09 × $4.9 trillion). The nominal deficit is higher at $641 billion. ($1.3 trillion − ($1.5 trillion + $.441 trillion)). The real deficit has not changed. It is still $445 billion (The real deficit = Nominal deficit − (Inflation × Total debt) = $.641 trillion − (.04 × $4.9 trillion)). (471-473)

4. a. $3.2 billion: Debt service payment = nominal interest rate x nominal debt. The nominal interest rate when expected inflation is fully adjusted is the real interest rate plus inflation (3+(−1)). Debt service payment = .02 × $160 billion. (471-473)
   b. Surplus of $800 million: The nominal deficit is revenues less government expenditures (including debt service), $20 billion − ($16 billion + $3.2 billion). (471-473)
   c. Deficit of $800 million: The real deficit = Nominal deficit − (Inflation × Total debt) = −.8 billion − (−.01 x $160 billion). (471-473)
   d. The answers to (a) and (b) do not change but the answer to (c) does. Since bondholders do not expect the 2% inflation, they do not have to be compensated for the loss in the value of their bondholdings and the nominal interest rate does not change. Debt service payment is still $3.2 billion; the nominal deficit is still $800 million. The real deficit does, however, change to a real surplus of $4 billion. The real deficit = Nominal deficit − (Inflation × Total debt) = −.8 billion − (.02 × $160 billion). (471-473)

Multiple Choice Questions

1. c. See page 463.

2. a. See Exhibit 1, page 464.

3. c. Debt must be judged relative to assets and to total GDP. See page 467.

4. c. See Exhibit 2, page 469.

5. a. Real growth will reduce the ratio of existing debt to GDP so to hold the ratio constant a continual deficit is necessary. See page 470.

6. b. Real deficit = Nominal Deficit − (Inflation × Total Debt); $100−$80 = $20 billion. See page 471.

7. a. Real deficit = Nominal Deficit − (Inflation × Total Debt); $200−$200 = 0. See page 471.

8. c. Nominal deficit = Real Deficit + (Inflation × Total Debt); $100+$80 = $180 billion. See page 471.

9. c. If the interest rates adjust for the inflation, the creditors will not lose, and if they adjust more than the inflation, creditors will gain. See page 473.

10. c. While there is debate about the deficit, the text argues that the majority of economists take a middle-of-the-road view of the deficit, believing that one should not be concerned about the deficit itself but, rather, about the deficit *as an indicator of the financial health of the economy*, since it is that financial health that should be the real concern. See pages 467and 478.

11. c.   In this text just about everything depends. So when one is given a general question such as this, the "it depends" option is a good one. See pages 475-477 for what the choice depends upon.

12. b.   When members of the baby boom retire there will be few workers and many pensioners. The d option is unlikely because systems usually adapt when forced to do so. See page 476.

13. c.   The U.S. uses a cash flow accounting method, so changes affecting the future are not seen in the current budget. See page 474-476.

14. c.   See page 480.

Chapter 20:
Growth and the Macroeconomics of Developing and Transitional Economies

Chapter at a glance

1. Growth occurs because of an increase in inputs, given a production function; development occurs through a change in the production function. (485)

   Growth is a macro goal because it increases the average absolute standard of living.

2. There are differences in normative goals between developing and developed countries because their wealth differs. Developing countries face true economic needs whereas developed countries' economic needs are considered by most people to be normatively less pressing. (485)

   The main focus of macro policy in developing countries is on how to increase growth through development to fulfill people's basic needs.

3. Economies at different stages of development have different institutional needs because the problems they face are different. Institutions that can be assumed in developed countries cannot necessarily be assumed to exist in developing countries. (487)

   Developed nations have stable governments and market structures which are often lacking in developing countries.

4. "The dual economy" refers to the existence of the two sectors in most developing countries: a traditional sector and an internationally-oriented modern market sector. (488)

   Often, the largest percentage of the population participates in the traditional sector. Tradition often resists change.

5. A régime change is a change in the entire atmosphere within which the government and the economy interrelate; a policy change is a change in one aspect of government's actions. (489)

   A régime change and macro institutional policies designed to fit the cultural and social dimensions of developing and transitional economics are what developing economies need.

6. Central banks recognize that printing too much money causes inflation, but often feel compelled to do so for political reasons. Debate about inflation in developing and transitional countries generally concerns those political reasons, not the relationship between money and inflation. (492)

   Governments in developing and transitional economies risk being thrown out of office unless they run deficits and issue too much money.

7. Full convertibility means one can exchange one's currency for whatever legal purpose one wants. Convertibility on the current account limits those exchanges to buying goods and services. (494)

   Very few developing countries allow full convertibility.

8. The "borrowing circle" concept replaced traditional collateral with guarantees by friends of the borrower. It was successful because the invisible handshake in Bangladesh, where the borrowing circle originated, was very strong. (498)

   This is the creative type of macro institutional policy much needed in developing countries.

Short-answer questions

1.   What is the difference between growth and development? (LO1)

2.   Why is there often a difference in the normative goals of developed and developing countries? (LO2)

3.   Why do economies at different stages of development often have different institutional needs? Explain. (LO3)

4.   What is meant by the term "the dual economy"? (LO4)

5.   Distinguish between a régime change and a policy change. (LO5)

6. Inflation is simply a problem of central banks in developing countries issuing too much money. Is this true or false? Why? (LO6)

7. What are two types of convertibility? (LO7)

8. The three Cs of Western banking are capital, collateral, and character. If one were describing the Grameen bank's approach to banking how would the three Cs change? (LO8)

Word Scramble

1. _____ _____   2._____   3._____ _____
   eégimr   nhgeca   yttoonnliiidca   wrroonigb   rliecc

Match the Terms and Concepts to Their Definitions

____ 1. balance of payments constraint

____ 2. basic needs

____ 3. borrowing circle

____ 4. conditionality

____ 5. convertibility on the current account

____ 6. developing economy

____ 7. dual economy

____ 8. exchange rate policy

____ 9. full convertibility

____ 10. inflation tax

____ 11. macro institutional policies

____ 12. policy change

____ 13. restructuring

____ 14. soft budget constraint

____ 15. trade credits

a. A change in one aspect of government's actions, such as monetary policy or fiscal policy.

b. Adequate food, clothing, and shelter for the people in a society.

c. The existence in most developing countries of two sectors, a traditional sector and an internationally-oriented modern market sector.

d. An economy that has a low level of GDP per capita and a relatively undeveloped market structure, and has never had an alternative, developed economic system.

e. An implicit tax on the holders of cash and the holders of any obligations specified in nominal terms.

f. Buying and selling foreign currencies in order to help stabilize the exchange rate.

g. Changing the underlying economic institutions of an economy.

h. Limitation on expansionary domestic macro policy due to a shortage of international reserves.

i. Loan system in which collateral is not required. Instead, the borrower must find friends to guarantee the repayment.

j. Loose financial constraints on firms' decisions in centrally-planned economies.

k. Making loans that are subject to specific conditions.

l. Policies to change the underlying macro institutions and thereby increase output.

m. Short-term loans to facilitate inter-firm trade.

n. System that allows people to exchange currencies freely to buy goods and services, but not to buy assets in other countries.

o. System where individuals can change dollars into any currency they want for whatever legal purpose they want.

Multiple Choice Questions

1. The concept "dual economy" refers to
   a. the tendency of developed countries to have a traditional sector and an internationally-oriented sector.
   b. the tendency of both developed and developing countries to have a traditional sector and an internationally-oriented sector.
   c. the tendency of developing countries to have a traditional sector and an internationally-oriented sector.
   d. the fight, or dual, between developed and undeveloped countries.

2. If a country changes its entire approach to policy, that is called
   a. a major policy change.
   b. a policy change.
   c. a régime change.
   d. a constitutional change.

3. The soft budget constraint refers to
   a. the use of government moral suasion on firms.
   b. the use of moral suasion by central banks on firms.
   c. the ability of firms to get loans without significant difficulty.
   d. the use of moral suasion by international agencies on developing countries.

4. The inflation tax is
    a. a tax on those individuals who cause inflation.
    b. a tax on firms who cause inflation.
    c. a tax on both individuals and firms who cause inflation.
    d. a tax on holders of cash and any obligations specified in nominal terms.

5. The revenue of an inflation tax
    a. goes only to government.
    b. goes only to private individuals.
    c. goes to both private individuals and government.
    d. is a meaningless term because there is no revenue from an inflation tax.

6. If you hold a fixed interest rate debt denominated in domestic currency and there is a large inflation, you will
    a. likely lose.
    b. likely gain.
    c. likely experience no effect from the large inflation.
    d. find that the large inflation could cause you either to gain or to lose.

7. If you hold a fixed interest rate debt denominated in a foreign currency, and there is a large domestic inflation, you will
    a. likely lose some.
    b. likely gain some.
    c. likely lose all your debt.
    d. likely experience no direct effect from the large inflation.

8. Conditionality refers to
    a. the U.S. government's policy of only making loans to countries subject to specific conditions.
    b. the IMF's policy of making loans to countries subject to specific conditions.
    c. central banks' policies of making loans to firms only under certain conditions.
    d. the conditions under which inter-firm credit is allowed in transitional economies.

9. According to a World Bank report, the developmental success of the Asian Tigers is in part attributed to
    a. using Keynesian policies.
    b. closing their countries to foreign technology.
    c. opening their economies to foreign technology.
    d. borrowing large amounts of money from abroad.

10. The borrowing circle refers to
    a. a group of countries who borrow from one another.
    b. the tendency of loans to be repaid, thus completing the borrowing circle.
    c. the making of loans to an individual if other individuals agree to repay the loan for the borrower if necessary.
    d. the concept that savings and investment must be equal.

Answers

Short-answer questions

1. Growth occurs because of an increase in inputs, given a production function. Development occurs through a change in the production function. Development involves more fundamental changes in the institutional structure than does growth. (485)

2. Developing countries face true economic needs. Their concern is with basic needs such as adequate clothing, food, and shelter. Developed countries' needs are considered less pressing—for example, will everyone have access to a CD player?(485)

3. Economies at different stages of development have different institutional needs because the problems they face are different. Institutions that can be assumed in developed countries cannot necessarily be assumed to exist in developing countries. For example, developing countries often lack the institutional structure that markets require. (487)

4. Dual economy refers to the existence of the two distinct sectors in most developing countries: a traditional sector and an internationally-oriented modern market sector. (488)

5. A régime change is a change in the entire atmosphere within which the government and the economy interrelate; a policy change is a change in one aspect of government's actions. A régime change affects underlying expectations about what the government will do in the future; a policy change does not. (489)

6. Any simple statement is generally false, and this one is no exception. The reason why this one is false is that while it is true that inflation is closely tied to the developing country's central bank issuing too much money, the underlying problem behind the central bank's actions is often large government deficits that cannot be financed unless the central bank issues debt and then buys the bonds, which requires an increase in the money supply (printing money to pay for the bonds). (492-493)

7. Two types of convertibility are full convertibility and current account convertibility. Full convertibility means you can change your money into another currency with no restrictions. Current account convertibility allows exchange of currency to buy goods but not to invest outside the country. Many developing countries have current account convertibility, but not full convertibility. (494-495)

8. The Grameen Bank introduced the "borrowing circle" approach to banking. It offered to replace collateral with a guarantee by a group of four friends of the borrower. Thus, it reduced the role of two of the Cs (capital and collateral) and put more emphasis on the third C—character. Thus, the Grameen Bank's approach to banking might be described as the Big C (Character) approach. (497-498)

Word Scramble   1. régime change   2. conditionality   3. borrowing circle

Match the Terms and Concepts to Their Definitions
1-h; 2-b; 3-i; 4-k; 5-n; 6-d; 7-c; 8-f; 9-o; 10-e; 11-l; 12-a; 13-g; 14-j; 15-m.

Multiple Choice Questions

1. c.   As seen on page 488, c is definition of dual economy. Choice d was put in to throw you off—when the word means "a fight," it is, of course, spelled with an "e"—"duel."

2. c.   See page 489.

3. c.   See page 490.

4. d.   The answer has to be d, as discussed on page 493. The individuals and firms who cause the inflation are gaining from the inflation; they pay no inflation tax.

5. c.   The only answer that makes any sense is c. The "revenue" goes from holders of fixed nominal interest rate debt to those who owe that debt. Those who owe the debt include both private individuals and government. See pages 493-494.

6. a.   Inflation wipes out the value of fixed interest rate debt. See pages 493-494.

7. d.   Because the debt is denominated in a foreign currency, what happens to the domestic price level does not directly affect you. There could be indirect effects but d specifies direct effects. See pages 493-494.

8. b.   See page 495.

9. c.   As discussed on page 496, the World Bank report says the Asian Tigers got some fundamentals right, one of those fundamentals being opening up their economies to foreign technology.

10. c.   See pages 497-498.

Pretest III
Chapters 14 - 20

Take this test in test conditions, giving yourself a limited amount of time to complete the questions. Ideally, check with your professor to see how much time he or she allows for an average multiple choice question and multiply this by 33. This is the time limit you should set for yourself for this pretest. If you do not know how much time your teacher would allow, we suggest 1 minute per question, or about 35 minutes.

1. Assuming velocity is relatively constant and real income is relatively stable, an increase in the money supply of 40 percent will bring about an approximate change in the price level of
    a. 4 percent.
    b. 40 percent.
    c. 80 percent.
    d. zero percent.

2. The short-run Phillips curve shifts around because of
    a. changes in the money supply.
    b. changes in expectations of employment.
    c. changes in expectations of inflation.
    d. changes in expectations of real income.

3. An economist has just said, "Inflation is everywhere and always a monetary phenomenon." You would deduce this economist
    a. is likely to be a Keynesian economist.
    b. is likely to be a Classical economist.
    c. could be either a Keynesian economist or a Classical economist.
    d. must be neither a Keynesian economist nor a Classical economist, because neither of these groups would ever say that.

4. If the economy is at point A in the Phillips curve graph to the right, what prediction would you make for inflation?
    a. It will increase.
    b. It will decrease.
    c. It will remain constant.
    d. It will explode.

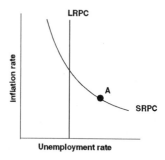

5. An economist has just made the statement that institutional and structural aspects of inflation are important. You would deduce that this economist
    a. is likely a Keynesian economist.
    b. is likely a Classical economist.
    c. could be either a Keynesian economist or a Classical economist.
    d. must not be an economist, since no economist would make such a statement.

6. Classicals generally see supply price shocks
    a. as a cost-push pressure.
    b. as a demand-pull pressure.
    c. as a relative price change.
    d. as an institutional change.

7. If a country has a flexible exchange rate, the exchange rate
   a. is determined by flexible government policy.
   b. is determined by market forces.
   c. fluctuates continuously and will always change by at least 1 percent per year.
   d. fluctuates continuously and will always change by at least 10 percent per year.

8. Expansionary monetary policy has a tendency to
   a. push interest rates up and exchange rates down.
   b. push interest rates down and exchange rates down.
   c. push income down and exchange rates down.
   d. push imports down and exchange rates down.

9. If the trade deficit has gone up, it is most likely that the government ran
   a. an expansionary monetary policy.
   b. a contractionary monetary policy.
   c. a contractionary fiscal policy.
   d. an expansionary monetary policy and a contractionary fiscal policy.

10. Contractionary fiscal policy tends to push
    a. income down and imports up.
    b. income down and the trade deficit up.
    c. prices down and the trade deficit down.
    d. prices down and imports up.

11. According to the textbook, generally, when international goals and domestic goals conflict
    a. the international goals win out.
    b. the domestic goals win out.
    c. sometimes it's a toss-up which will win out.
    d. international monetary goals win out but international fiscal goals lose out.

12. If a country has perfectly flexible exchange rates and is running a current account deficit, it is running
    a. a capital account surplus.
    b. a capital account deficit.
    c. an official transactions surplus.
    d. an official transactions deficit.

13. In the balance of payments accounts, net investment income shows up in
    a. the current account.
    b. the capital account.
    c. the official transactions account.
    d. It is not an entry in the balance of payments.

14. If there is a black market in a currency, the country probably has
    a. nonconvertible currency.
    b. a fixed exchange rate currency.
    c. a flexible exchange rate currency.
    d. a partially flexible exchange rate currency.

15. The graph on the right is of the supply and demand for French francs. If U.S. income increases
    a. the supply curve will shift to the right.
    b. the supply curve will shift to the left.
    c. the demand curve will shift to the right.
    d. the demand curve will shift to the left.

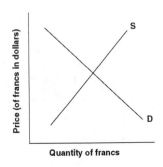

16. If a country runs expansionary monetary policy, in the short run one would expect the value of its exchange rate to
    a. rise.
    b. fall.
    c. be unaffected.
    d. sometimes rise and sometimes fall.

17. Compared to a fixed exchange rate system, a flexible exchange rate system
    a. allows countries more flexibility in their monetary policies.
    b. allows countries less flexibility in their monetary policies.
    c. has no effect on monetary policies.
    d. allows countries more flexibility in their industrial policies.

18. You have been appointed adviser to the president. He comes in and says he wants very low unemployment, zero inflation, and very high growth. You should
    a. advise him to use expansionary monetary policy.
    b. advise him to use contractionary monetary policy.
    c. tell him it is likely impossible using traditional tools.
    d. advise him to use a combination of expansionary monetary policy and contractionary fiscal policy.

19. You've been appointed adviser to the president. She wants interest rates to rise and wants to decrease unemployment. You would suggest
    a. expansionary monetary policy.
    b. contractionary monetary policy.
    c. expansionary fiscal policy.
    d. contractionary fiscal policy.

20. An economist is calling for the implementation of credible, systematic policies, but argues that there should still be significant discretionary policy. This economist
    a. is likely a Classical economist.
    b. is likely a Keynesian economist.
    c. would equally likely be a Classical or Keynesian economist.
    d. does not exist because no economist would call for credible, systematic policies.

21. Keynesians and Classicals are least likely to agree on
    a. expansionary monetary and fiscal policies have significant long-run stimulative effects on real income.
    b. expansionary monetary and fiscal policies have potentially long-run stimulative effects on inflation.
    c. monetary is politically easier to use than fiscal policy.
    d. expansionary monetary and fiscal policy tend to increase the trade deficit.

22. In what range of the graph to the right will expansionary macro policy be most likely to increase real output the most?
    a. A.
    b. B.
    c. C.
    d. It is equally likely in all ranges.

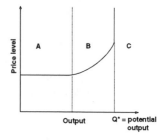

23. Structural supply-side policies
    a. shift the AED curve out and increase potential output.
    b. shift the AS path out and increase potential output.
    c. shift both the AED and the AS path out and increase potential output.
    d. shift neither the AED nor the AS path but increase potential output in other ways.

24. Classical methods to create supply-side incentives to increase output include
    a. lowering tax rates, reducing government social welfare spending, and reducing government regulation.
    b. lowering tax rates, reducing government social welfare spending, and increasing government regulation.
    c. lowering tax rates, increasing government social welfare spending, and increasing government regulation.
    d. increasing tax rates, increasing government social welfare spending, and increasing government regulation.

25. According to the Classicals, which of the following areas represent excess burden due to a tax?
    a. A.
    b. A+B.
    c. A+B+C.
    d. C.

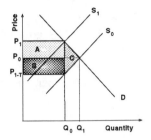

26. The Keynesian view regarding productivity-enhancing social programs is that
    a. the negative incentive effects of these programs make such policies nonviable.
    b. these programs have no negative incentive effects, and have tremendous supply-enhancing effects.
    c. the supply-enhancing effects of these policies often outweigh the negative incentive effects.
    d. although these policies have no supply-enhancing effects, one should support them for moral reasons.

27. Country A has a debt of $10 trillion. Country B has a debt of $5 trillion.
    a. Country A is in a better position than Country B.
    b. Country B is in a better position than Country A.
    c. One cannot say what relative position the countries are in.
    d. Countries A and B are in equal positions.

28. The nominal deficit is $100 billion; inflation is 4 percent; total debt is $2 trillion. The real deficit is
    a. zero.
    b. $20 billion.
    c. $80 billion.
    d. $100 billion.

29. According to most economists, the deficit
    a. is very important.
    b. is not important at all.
    c. is important primarily as one indicator of the financial health of the economy.
    d. should always be matched by surpluses.

30. If a country changes its entire approach to policy, that is called
    a. a major policy change.
    b. a policy change.
    c. a régime change.
    d. a constitutional change.

31. The inflation tax is
    a. a tax on those individuals who cause inflation.
    b. a tax on firms who cause inflation.
    c. a tax on both individuals and firms who cause inflation.
    d. a tax on holders of cash and any obligations specified in nominal terms.

32. If you hold a fixed interest rate debt denominated in domestic currency and there is a large inflation, you will
    a. likely lose.
    b. likely gain.
    c. likely experience no effect from the large inflation.
    d. find that the large inflation could cause you either to gain or to lose.

33. Conditionality refers to
    a. the U.S. government's policy of only making loans to countries subject to specific conditions.
    b. the IMF's policy of making loans to countries subject to specific conditions.
    c. central banks' policies of making loans to firms only under certain conditions.
    d. the conditions under which inter-firm credit is allowed in transitional economies.

Answers

1. b (14:1)	12. a (16:1)	23. b (18:1)
2. c (14:4)	13. a (16:2)	24. a (18:2)
3. b (14:6)	14. a (16:6)	25. c (18:9)
4. b (14:9)	15. c (16:9)	26. c (18:11)
5. a (14:12)	16. b (16:12)	27. c (19:3)
6. c (14:15)	17. a (16:14)	28. b (19:6)
7. b (15:3)	18. c (17:1)	29. c (19:10)
8. b (15:6)	19. c (17:3)	30. c (20:2)
9. a (15:9)	20. b (17:6)	31. d (20:4)
10. c (15:13)	21. a (17:8)	32. a (20:6)
11. b (15:15)	22. a (17:9)	33. b (20:8)

Key: The figures in parentheses refer to multiple choice question and chapter numbers. For example (1:4) is multiple choice question 1 from chapter 4.